John Baldessari

in collaboration with

Naomi Shohan

# Editorial

Cristina Bechtler

Art and film have had a long, close, sometimes passionate, sometimes critical relationship throughout the 20th Century. Think of Jean-Luc Godard's use and references to painting, of Douglas Gordon's adaptation of Hitchcock's classic in his video installation *24 Hour Psycho*, or Doug Aitken's (our artist for *PA* issue 2) embrace of the cinematic. In particular, art since the 1960s is unimaginable without its profound dialogue with cinema.

This issue of *PA* presents a unique combination: film stills from the outsider's view – the artist's take on Hollywood, and film stills from the insider's view – the set designer who has worked on many major film productions such as *American Beauty, Constantine, The Replacement Killers, The Sorcerer's Apprentice*.

I have been intrigued by the work of John Baldessari for many decades, from his pioneering use of photography within 1960s conceptualism right up to the present. His precision and wry, laconic humour is uniquely his but it has influenced a whole generation of artists. It is John who came up with the brilliant suggestion of working on this issue of *PA* with Naomi Shohan, a former student of his. Across the pages of the magazine John and Naomi play visual ping-pong with images and ideas. In a conversation with Amy Cappellazzo they further elaborate their different approaches and discuss the ideas they share about photography and narrative.

I would like to warmly thank them both for the wonderful work. John, for the fantastic exclusive Special Edition *Face and Whale* reproduced on our cover (you can order the print on the last page). Naomi, not only for her intriguing photographs but also her unflagging efforts and enthusiasm during the seemingly endless copyright issues we faced in making this issue possible. We hope the delay was worthwhile. Many thanks go to Jessica Morgan for her enlightening text, to Amy Cappellazzo as author and to David Campany, my co-editor.

Cristina Bechtler

# An Email Conversation Between John Baldessari, Amy Cappellazzo, and Naomi Shohan

Naomi, Aug 4, 2010

Dear Amy-

What I would love is to hear your thoughts. Maybe as a starting point we could do this talk as a triangulation, or *Rashomon-Rorschach*. At any rate, I would be very interested in hearing what you think - looking from the outside at this juxtaposition of John's work with my stills - before John and I each define our points of view.

What do you think?

Naomi

Amy, Aug 6

Excellent. I will try, though my instinct was to queue you two and let your genius unfold...

John - I have known your work for a long time and have always loved, in particular, perhaps two incidental things about it: 1) the work is often an intersection of humor and anxiety-truly a mixed marriage. 2) the „parts", i.e. the visual excerpts from which you make your work, usually expand the effect and meaning, rather contract it. You add so much by subtracting! Maybe the most recent works more than ever. Has this always been your way of working, or more so now in the cut and paste world of images?

Naomi - your images are like hyper-lush dreams. They are rich in imagery, texture and detail. You can almost smell the flowers in Annette Bening's garden. Your stills have the quality of capturing life in such detail and meaning, it makes me wonder if life is general is that vivid and I am missing it. You add layers and context in such a complete way.

John, Aug 10

Dear Amy,

If one removes a few drips from a Pollock I doubt whether it would alter its quality, but what can be removed from a Newman, for example?

To me, a work is perfect when nothing can be taken away. Incidental things? Yes, I aim to reverse hierarchies of vision. Someone's feet rather than their face.

Humor/ Anxiety? Life is absurd. Can a tragic image of a quadriplegic be funny as well? *Catch 22* made war tragic by being comedic. Parts? Yes, a part can indicate a whole, like a pottery shard, this strategy makes the mind work. Subtraction always has been my method of operation.

As Thoreau wrote, „Simplify, simplify, simplify!"

Yrs in art,

John

Amy, Aug 10

John's reply - any thoughts, Naomi? He is advocating the virtues of paring down, but what about augmentation as a way of arriving at a perfect work (or job, as you like to say?)

Amy, Aug 12

John - so if an ideal work of art is one where nothing more can be subtracted, what about work that benefits from augmentation? You must have been tempted to add, be a maximalist, at one point or another. You are more Newman than Pollock for sure. But more Warhol than Agnes Martin or Judd, most certainly.

Naomi - since your work is about constantly piling on references, connotations, images that stir the imagination, soul and loins, how do you respond to this concept of substracting? Would be different if you were making quaint French films 30 years ago?

John, Aug 17

Dear Amy,

I've done a few horror vacui pieces just to see what I would do. But essentially I'm like a chef who doesn't like too many ingredients.

Your comment has made me envision a bleached Warhol à la Agnes Martin and a black and white silk-screened Agnes Martin. Or a diamond encrusted Judd? A white on white Pollock?

Is there a Latin term for visual diarrhea? Imagorrhea?

John

Naomi, Aug 20

Dear Amy-

For me, perfection is when I've done exactly enough. When everything holds together and relates. My image of that is something like the meniscus on a glass of water. The style of the equilibrium (tone) I create might be raucous, or spare, baroque, goofy, but in any case aims to be inviolably correct for story, character and action (genre, target audience and budget).

French films made 30 years ago were generally a lot more sophisticated than the ones I work on today, and many involved a lot less set construction. However, someone had to choose where to film and to think about how the light and color (or lack of color) would work in that place, its details and its style. Semiotics was in full bloom, so...

xNaomi

Amy, Sep 1

So you both seem generally opposed to wild excess. John, you the chef who doesn't like too many ingredients and Naomi, you who aims to do exactly enough. Measure is key. In looking at your work side by side with this in mind I wonder, might this shared temperance stem from a similar focus? Yes, John you subtract while Naomi embellishes, but the elements you leave behind in your images are often the parts of a scene that you, Naomi, would be adding, i.e. the miscellaneous objects, the wardrobe, the scenery, the before or after rather than the climax. You both make context that coaxes viewers toward an idea. But in focusing on a background that is infinite in possibilities, how do you both select your pieces? How do you determine what needs to be seen, what cannot be subtracted or done without?

John, Sept 7

Dear Amy,

I believe in reversing hierarchies of vision. If one looks at a person, the face usually is prioritized. Why not invert our predilection and consider the person's feet the most important?

For example:

Feet seen with a portion of a hat and a hippopotamus (all else has been removed from the photograph) an alternative narrative could ensue.

An interesting experiment would be for Naomi to add imagery to my deracinated pages and for me to remove imagery from her production still pages.

I like constructing narratives out of unlikely stuff - a stair and a barrel for example. My aim is to obtain the most effect with the least means and to invigorate imagery that has become stagnant and exhausted.

Best,

John

Naomi, Sept 8

Dear Amy,

Oops. I didn't mean to give the impression that I don't like excess. I love excess! But you only get to use it when the project needs it, and then just the right kind. So you're right: Measure is key.

I wonder if we could do away with the word '"embellish?" It's more like figuring out what 'there should be there,' and putting it there, in front of the camera. Some of the finesse is in building out(in) the ways it -the there- will be shot and lit.

You're also right that god is in the details. And everything is god.

When you drink a cup of coffee at an airport in NYC, what is that? Or the airport in Rome? How about Kinshasa? Mumbai? A friend's house? At a job interview? Middle Earth? How does the place inform your story? Or the way you move? How do you look sitting there? "Picture yourself..." That's what I think about. And I think about who you are and what is going to happen here, and what already has.

Or can the story be told just by the way the sugar melts into your coffee, how much is spilled (leaving a small mark on the table), a sign somewhere outside saying something (is it crooked, official, misspelled...), the sagging sock on the man at the next table? John might think so, or take that a starting point for further... And I think so. (And would be happy to watch a film that was nothing but stuff like that.) But I will make sure the light coming in from that high window is filtered by years of badly smudged soot and there are traces of red dye everywhere because it is the Hindu holiday where sisters anoint brothers' foreheads. The air-conditioning vent must be the right vintage and make, and the ceiling tiles are put in on the diagonal so the low clearance is emphasized in perspective for the wide shot. Or not.

So you are right. By means of architecture, color, cultural, temporal, historical cues, I attempt to construct specific conditions so that the camera can deliver to you, the audience, in a series of thousands of stills, the visual metaphor that expresses the intended spirit of the particular film - which you may then deconstruct to your pleasure.

Amy, Sep 9

Love this!

Naomi, Sep 9

Oh, good. I have been struggling with how to talk about things so that I don't err on the side of either hubris or humility, and thus alienate future prospective employers!!

I've wasted a ton of time musing and typing away on the similarities and differences in what JB and I do: all the contextual, historical and mechanical art concerns. I kept finding myself tempted to use the same words to describe both of us and then hemming and hawing a lot about he does art and I do not and then what the difference is there. All of it was incredibly boring and un-illuminating.

After I wrote you yesterday, I realized that there is something we have in common that might be worth mentioning as it is not necessarily intrinsic to the process of everyone making any kind of art (or not-art). That thing is our mutual concern for narrative and the way we both have of approaching a visual project by way of narrative.

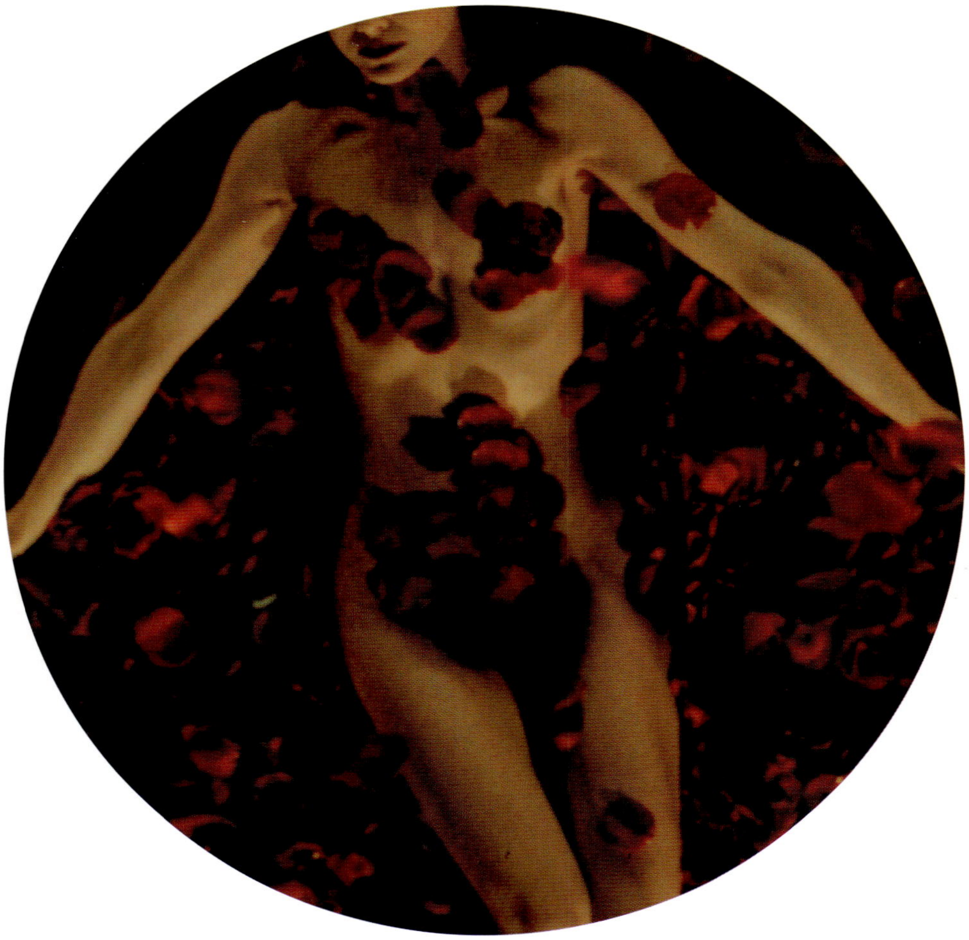

MENA SUVARI, “AMERICAN BEAUTY”, DREAMWORKS/PARAMOUNT, 1999

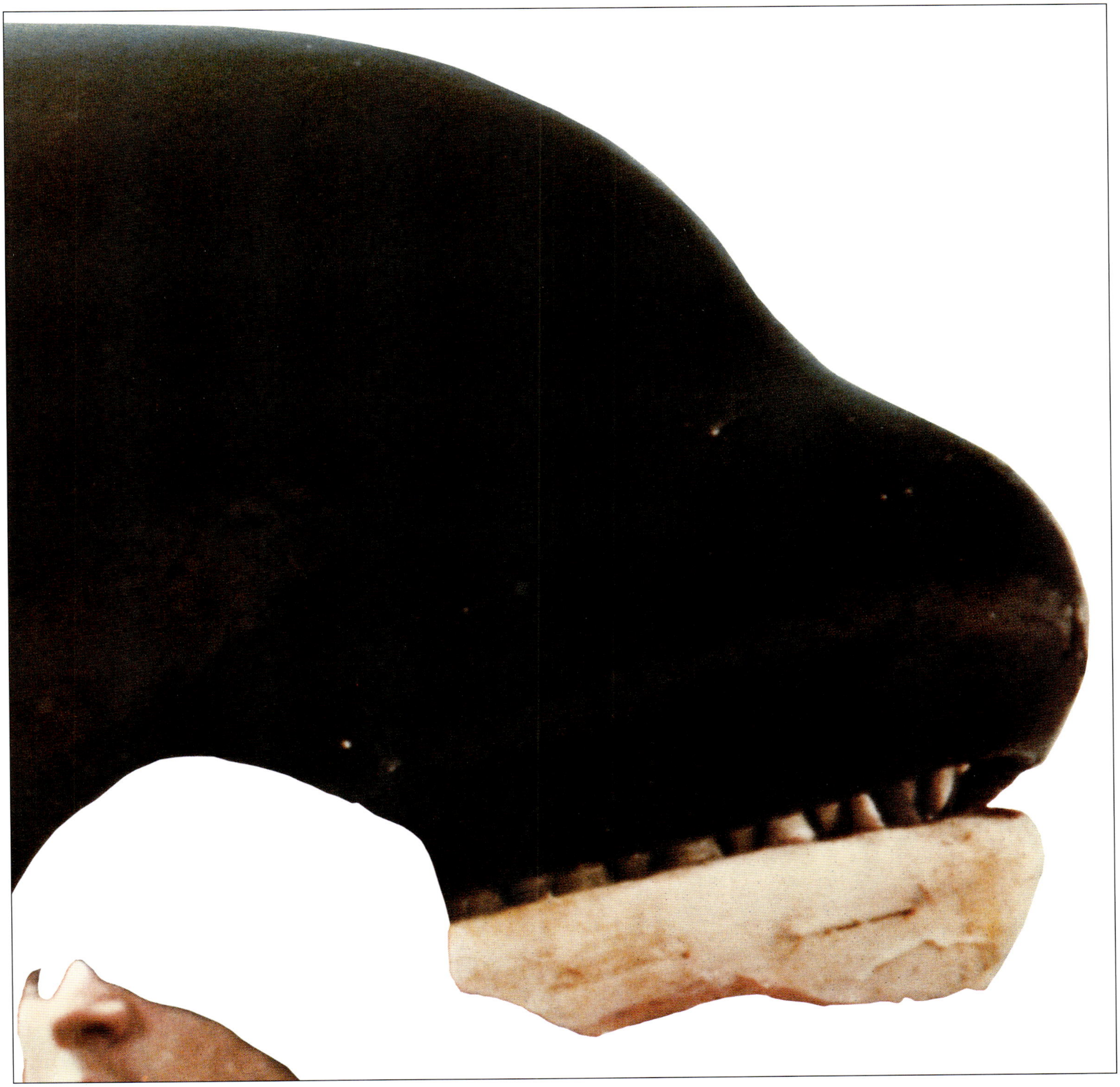

FACE AND WHALE

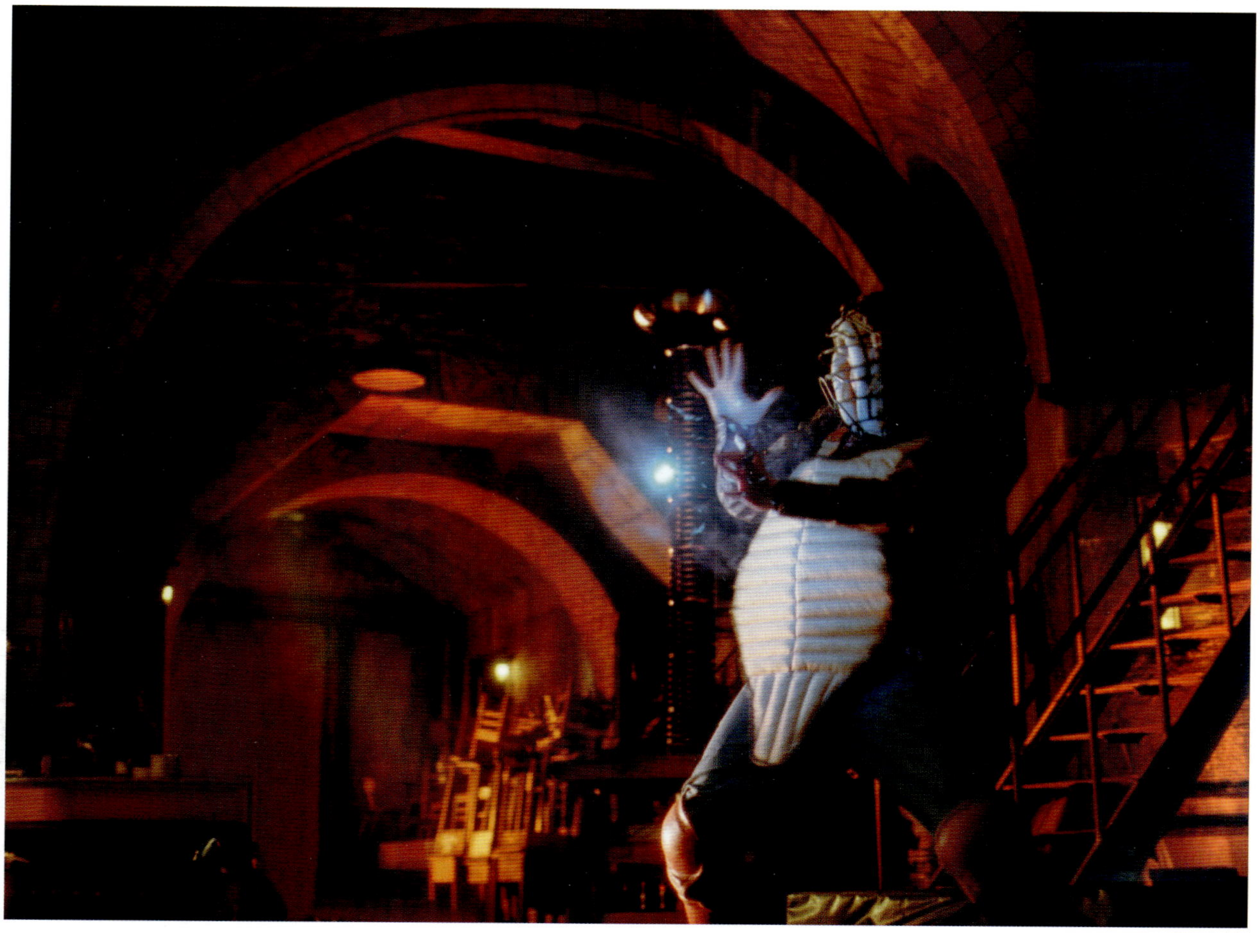

JAY BARUCHEL, “THE SORCERER’S APPRENTICE”, DISNEY ENTERPRISES, 2009

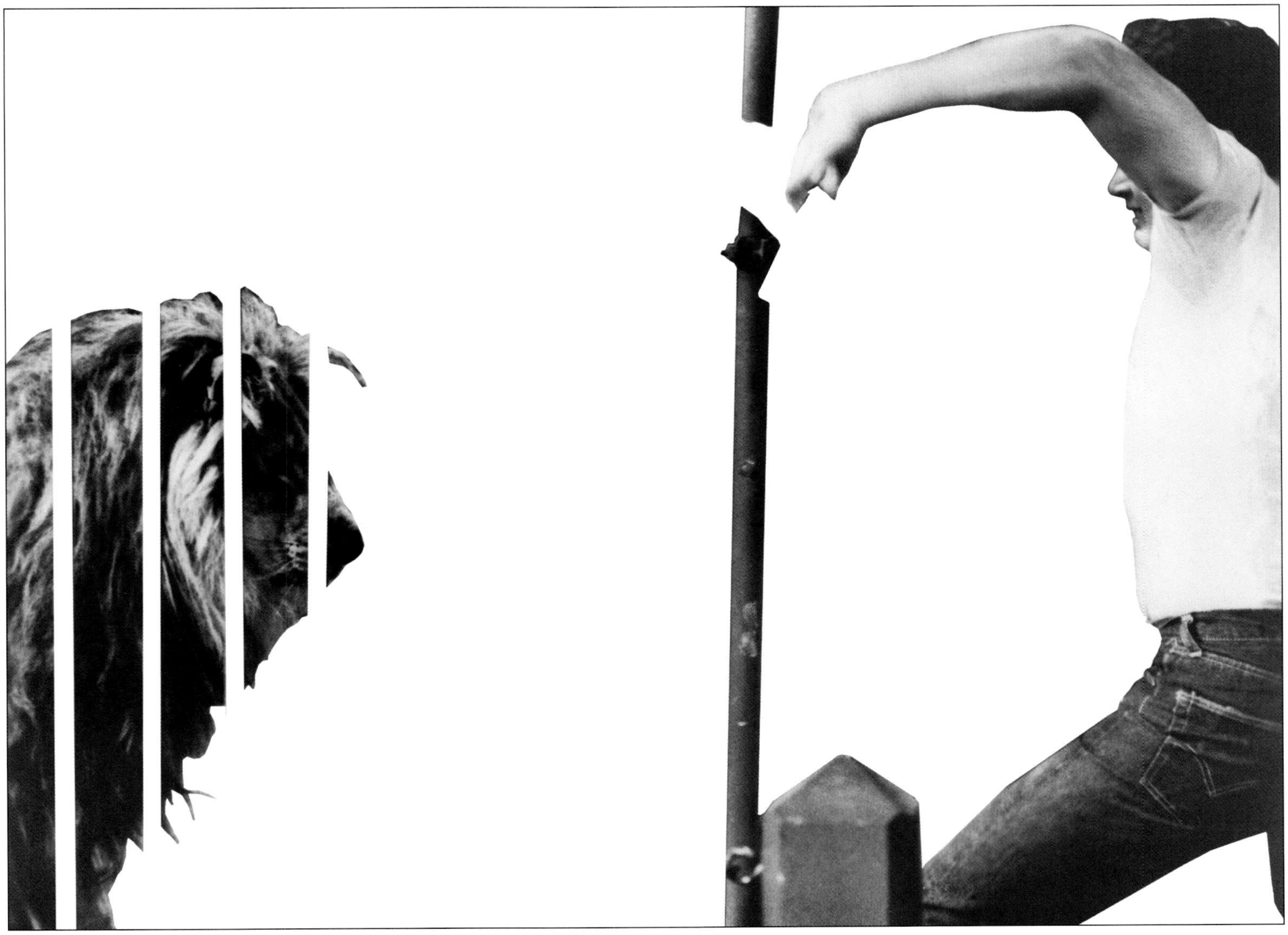

PERSON, POST, POLE AND LION

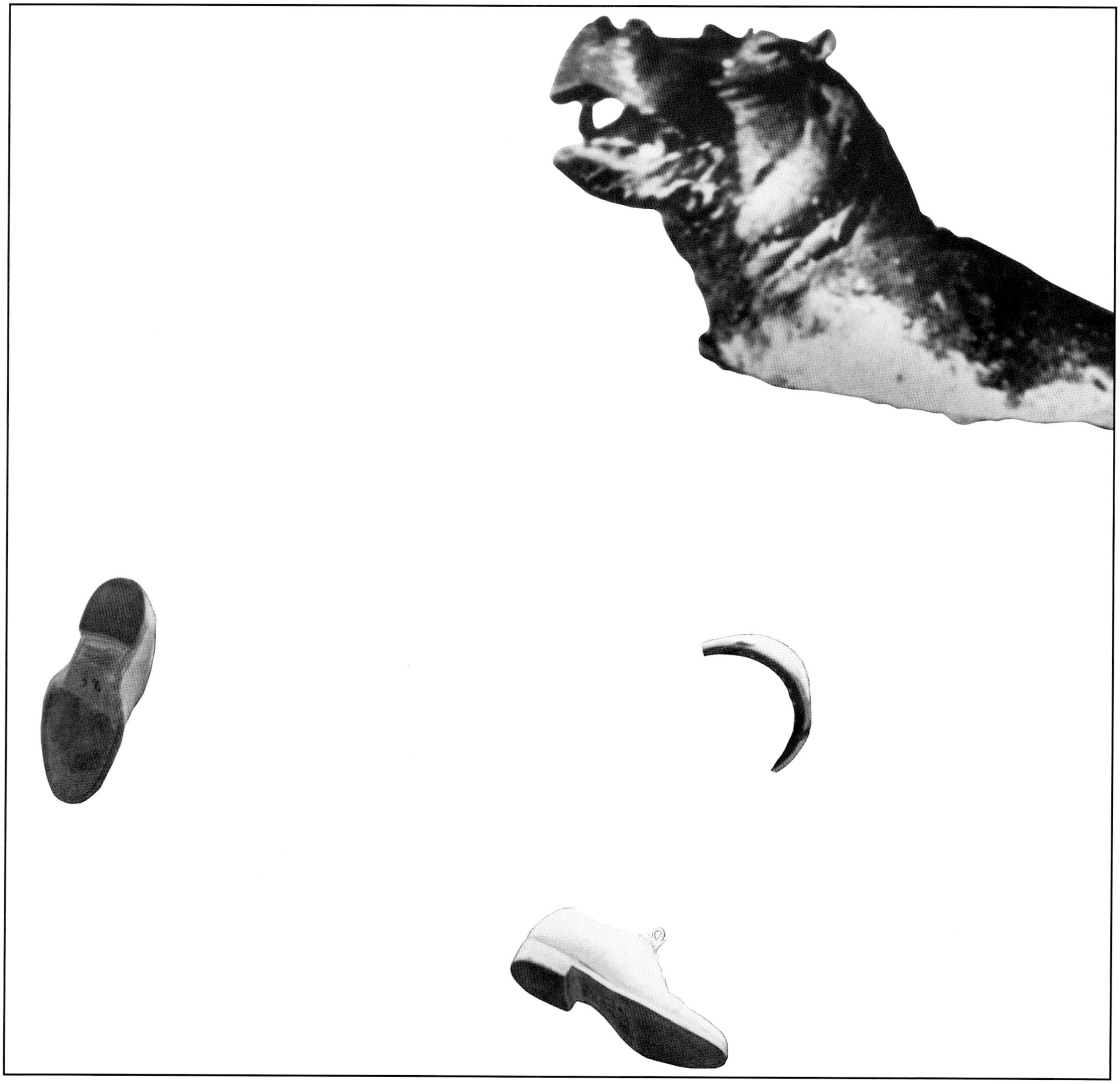

FEET, HIPPOPOTAMUS AND HAT

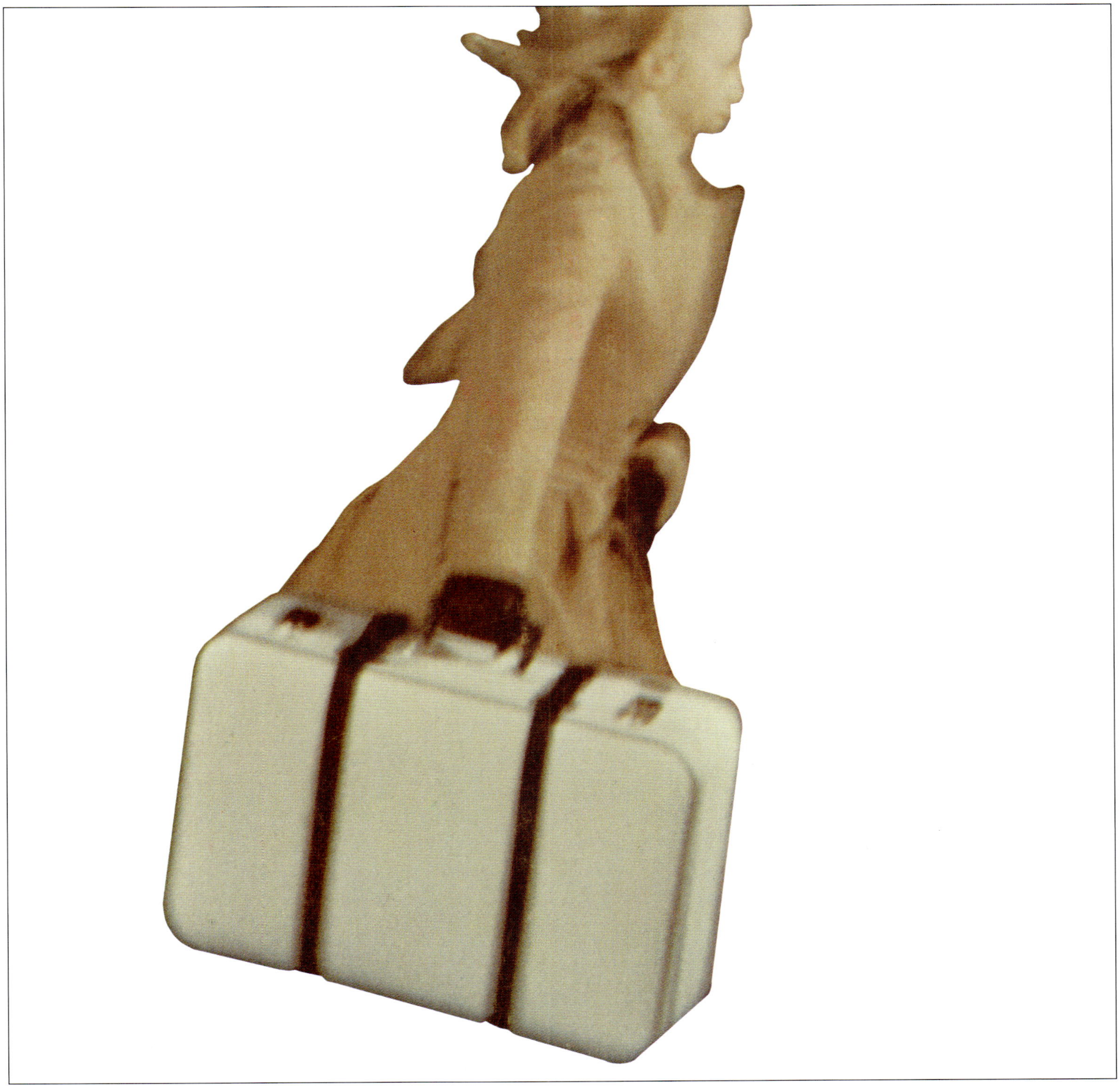

SUITCASE AND PERSON

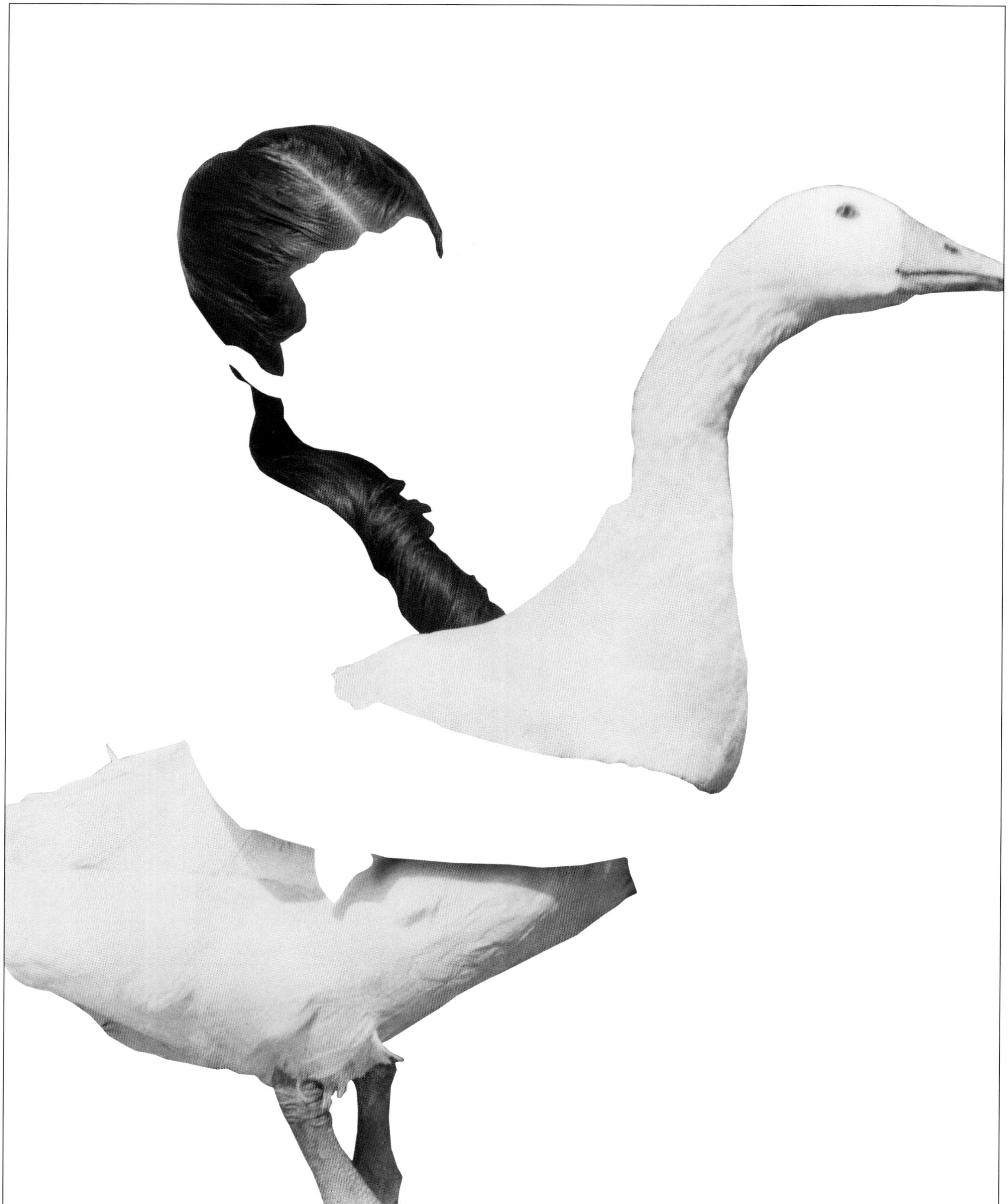

HAIR AND GOOSE

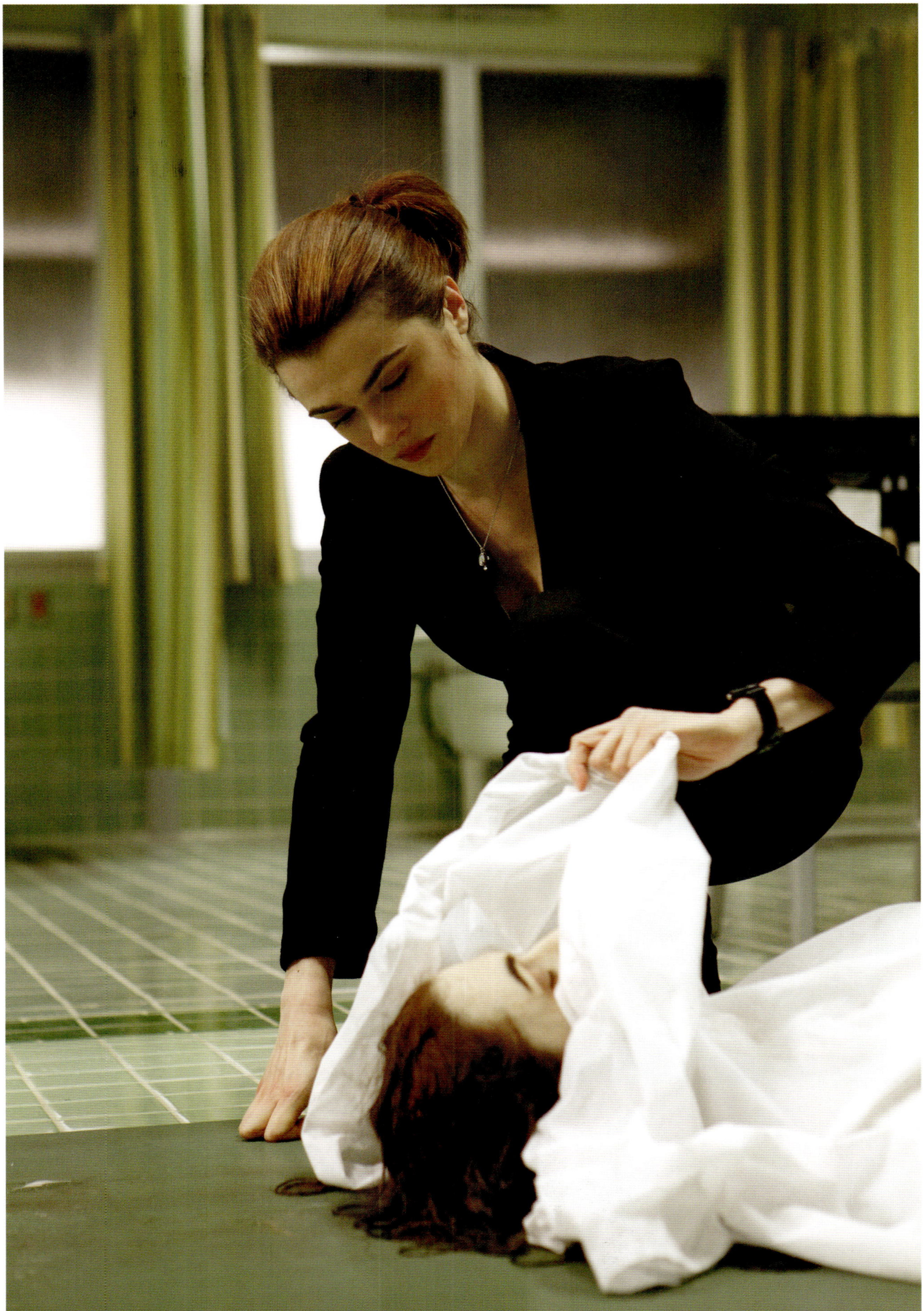

RACHEL WEISZ, “CONSTANTINE”, WARNER BROTHERS, 2005

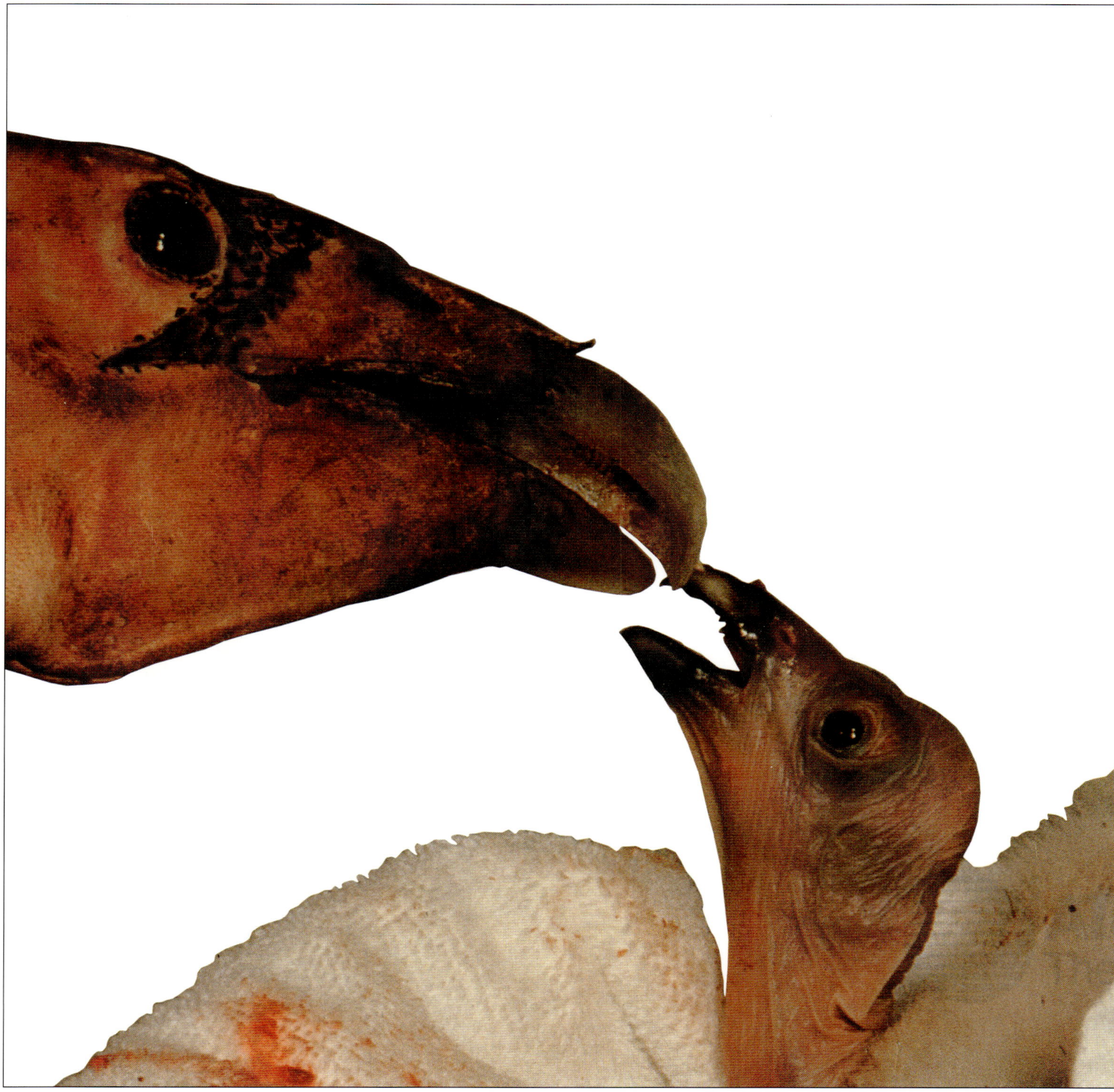

CONDORS AND TOWEL

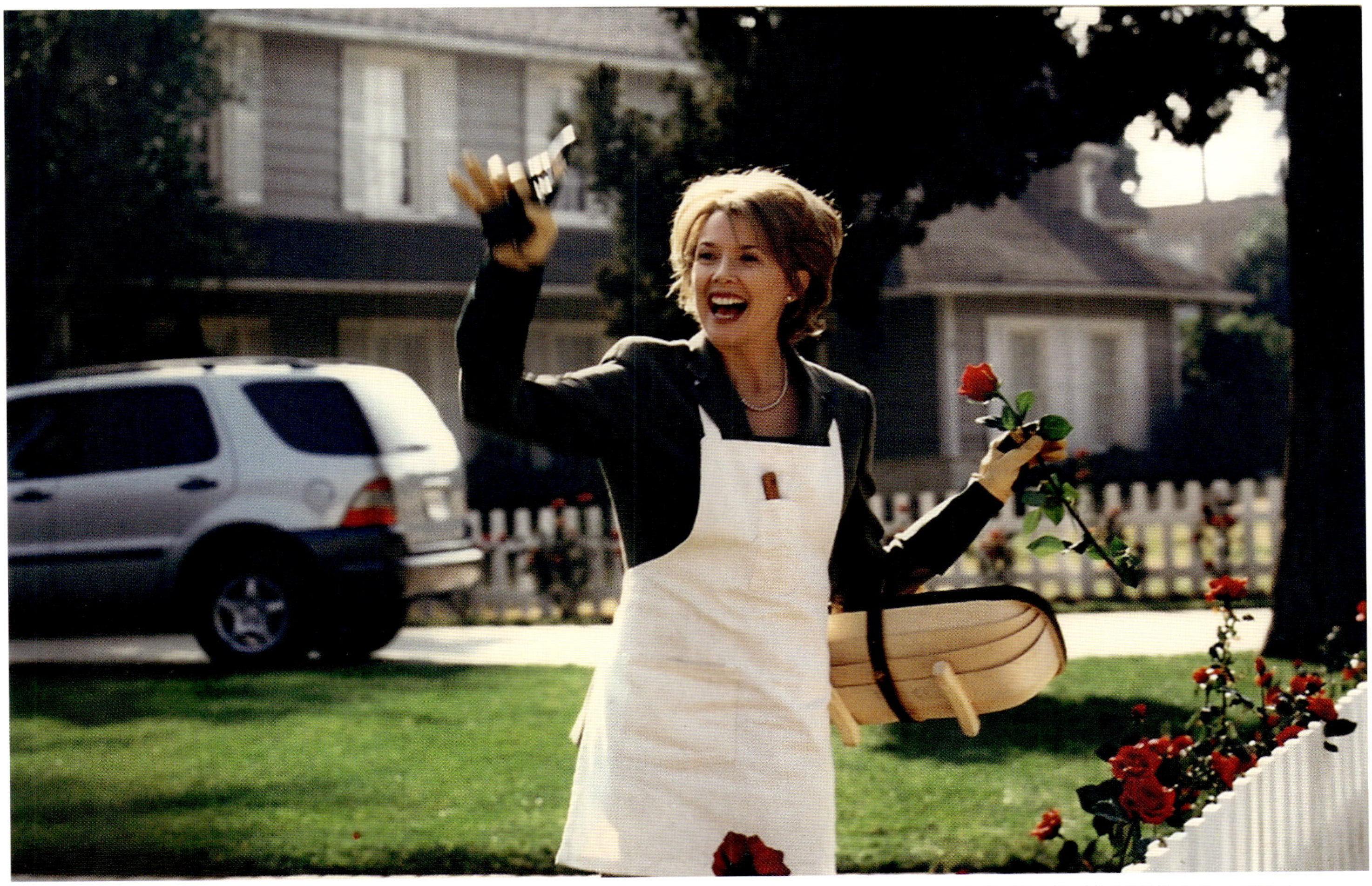

ANNETTE BENING, “AMERICAN BEAUTY”, DREAMWORKS/PARAMOUNT, 1999

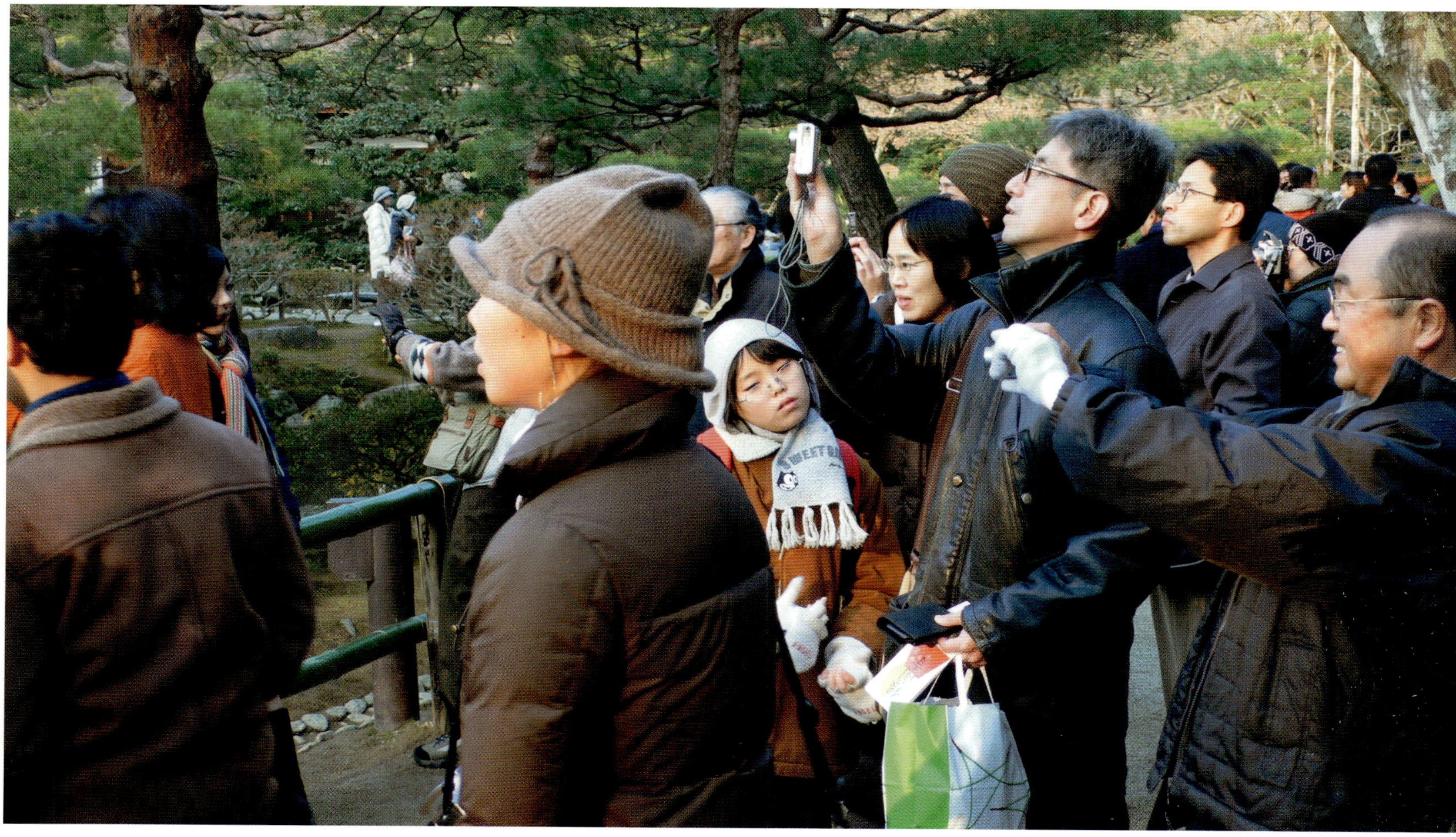

LOCATION REFERENCE, KYOTO

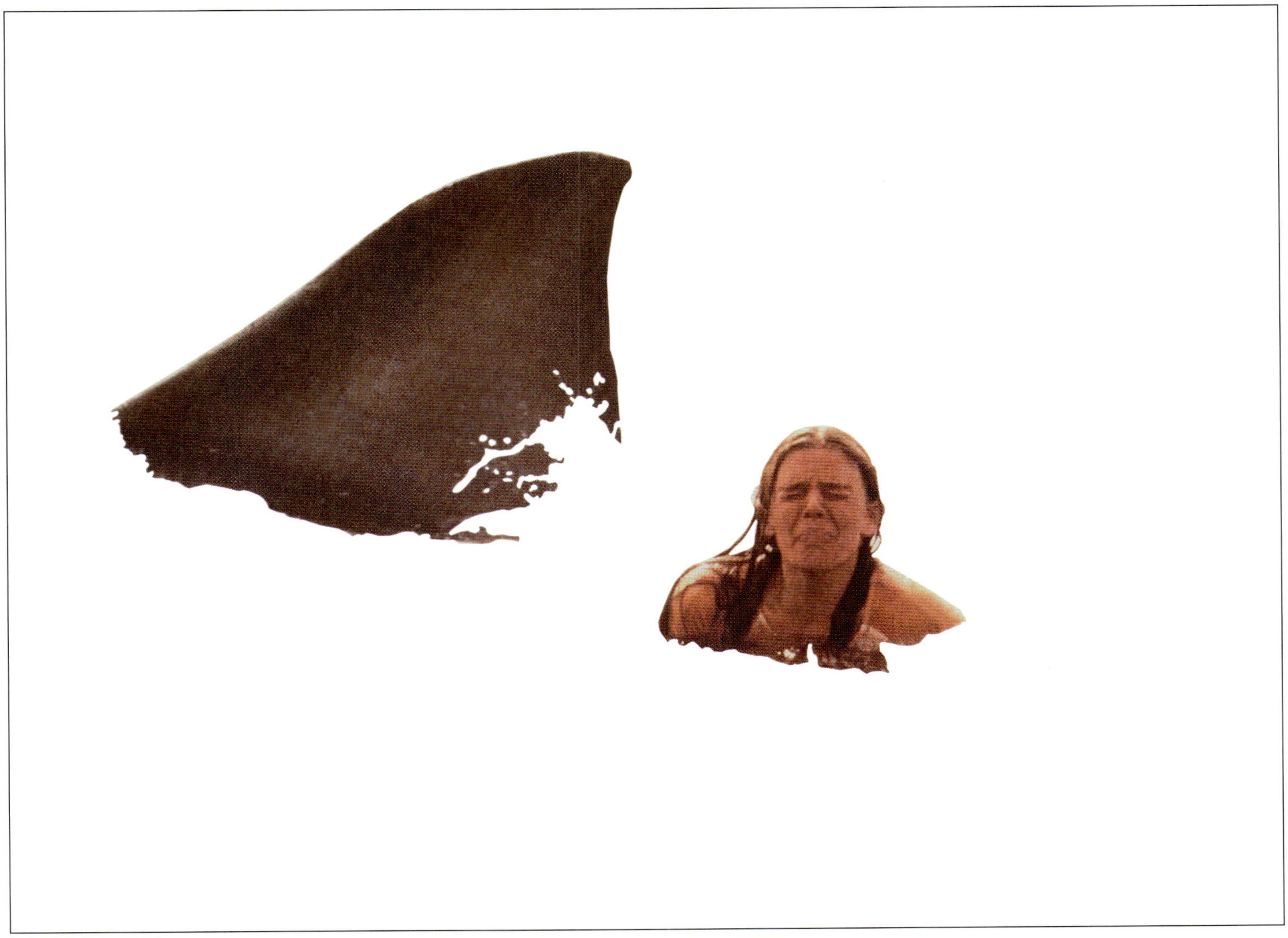

SHARK FIN AND PERSON

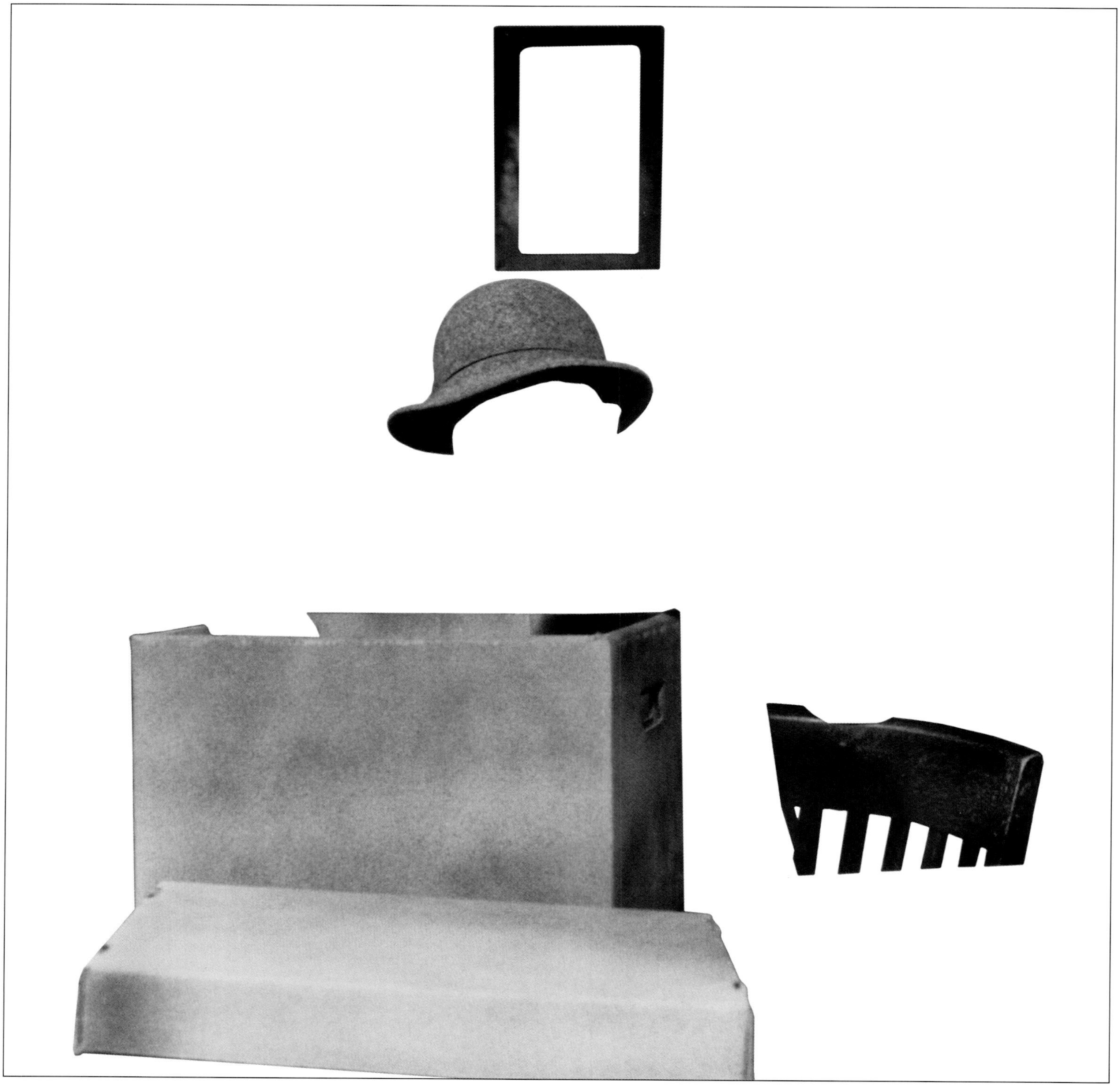

BOX, HAT, FRAME AND CHAIR

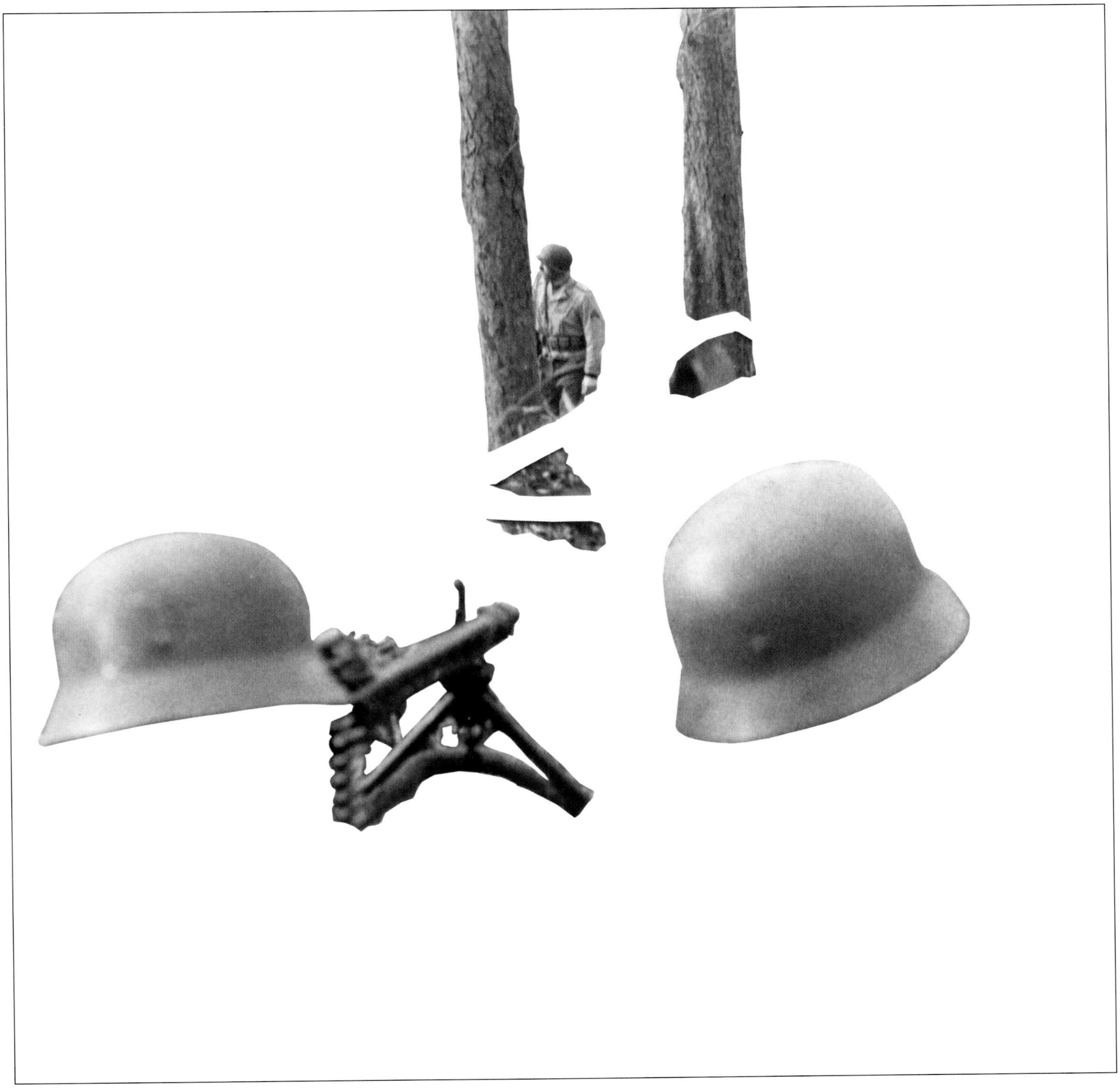

HELMETS, MACHINE GUN, TREES AND PERSON

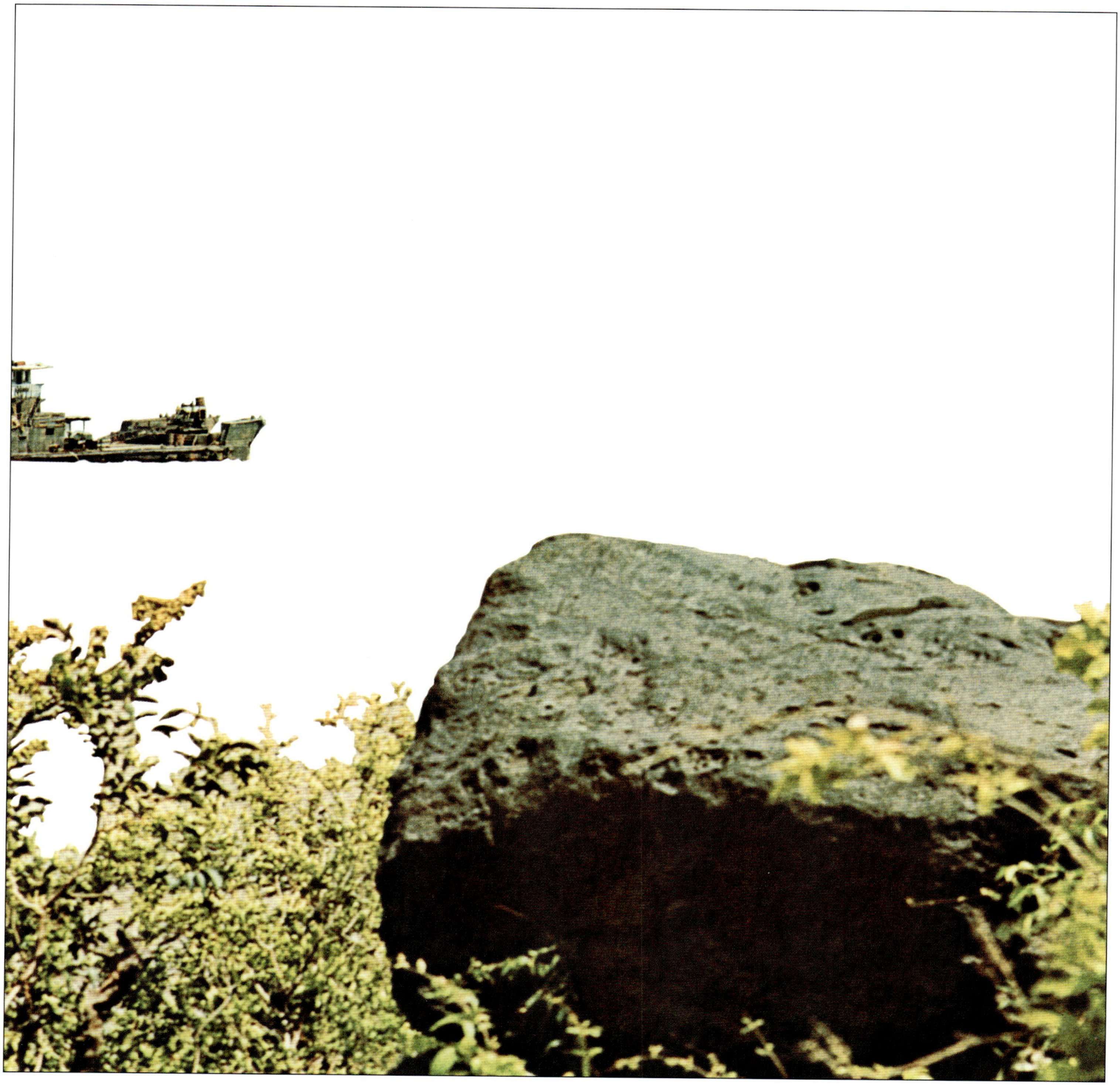

SHIP, SHRUB AND ROCK

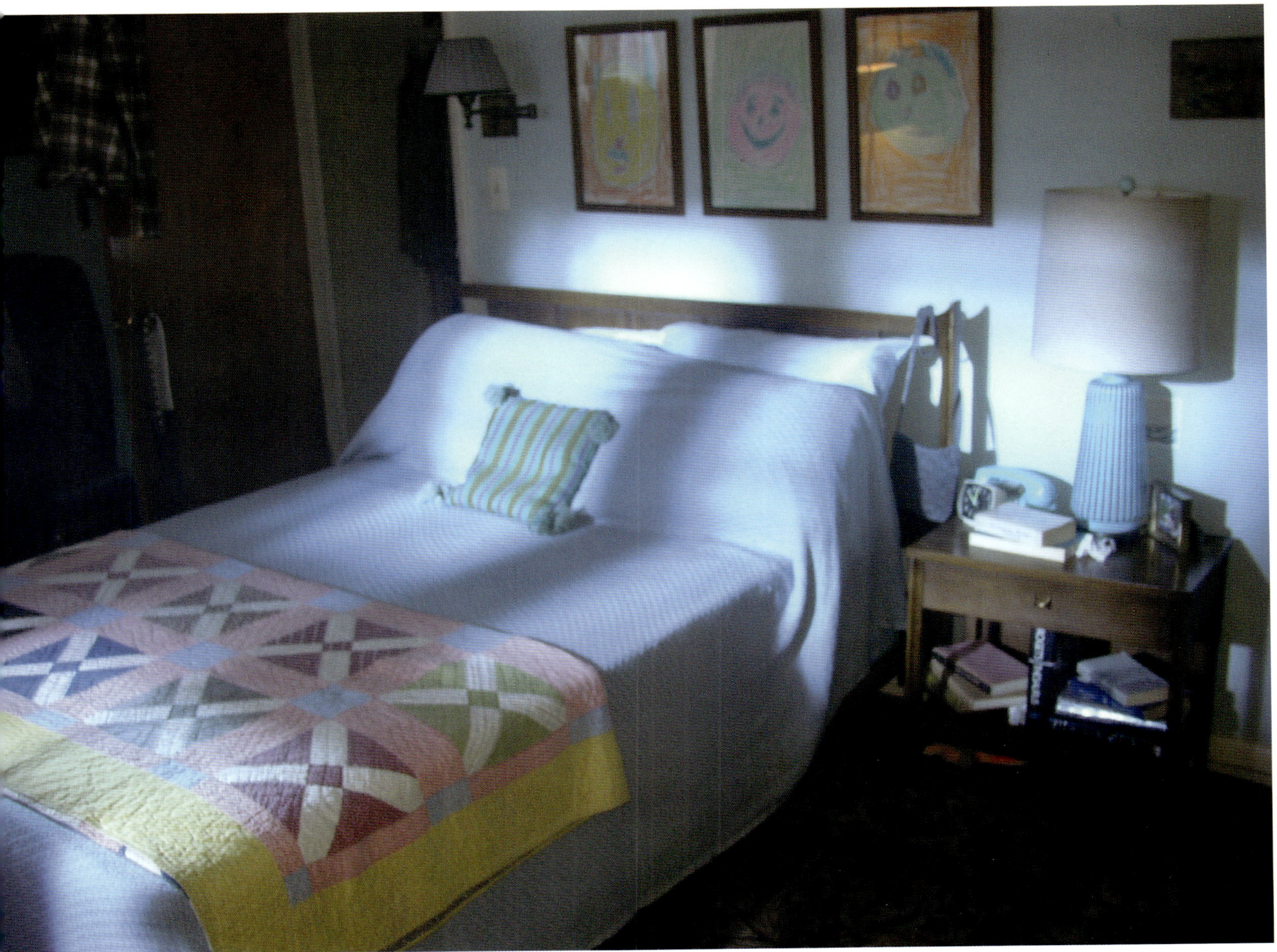

PARENTS' BEDROOM, "THE LOVELEY BONES", DREAMWORKS/PARAMOUNT, 1999

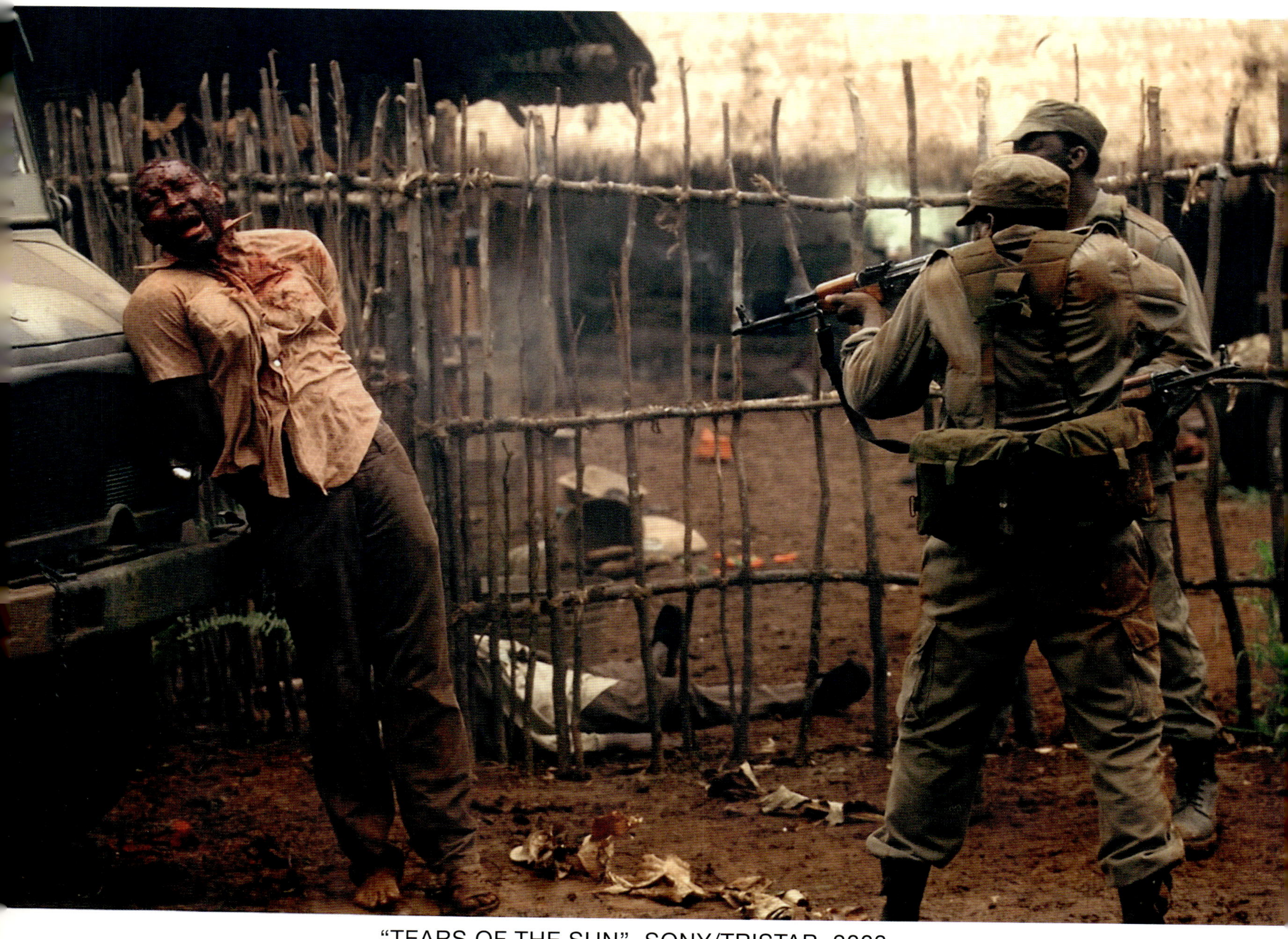

“TEARS OF THE SUN”, SONY/TRISTAR, 2003

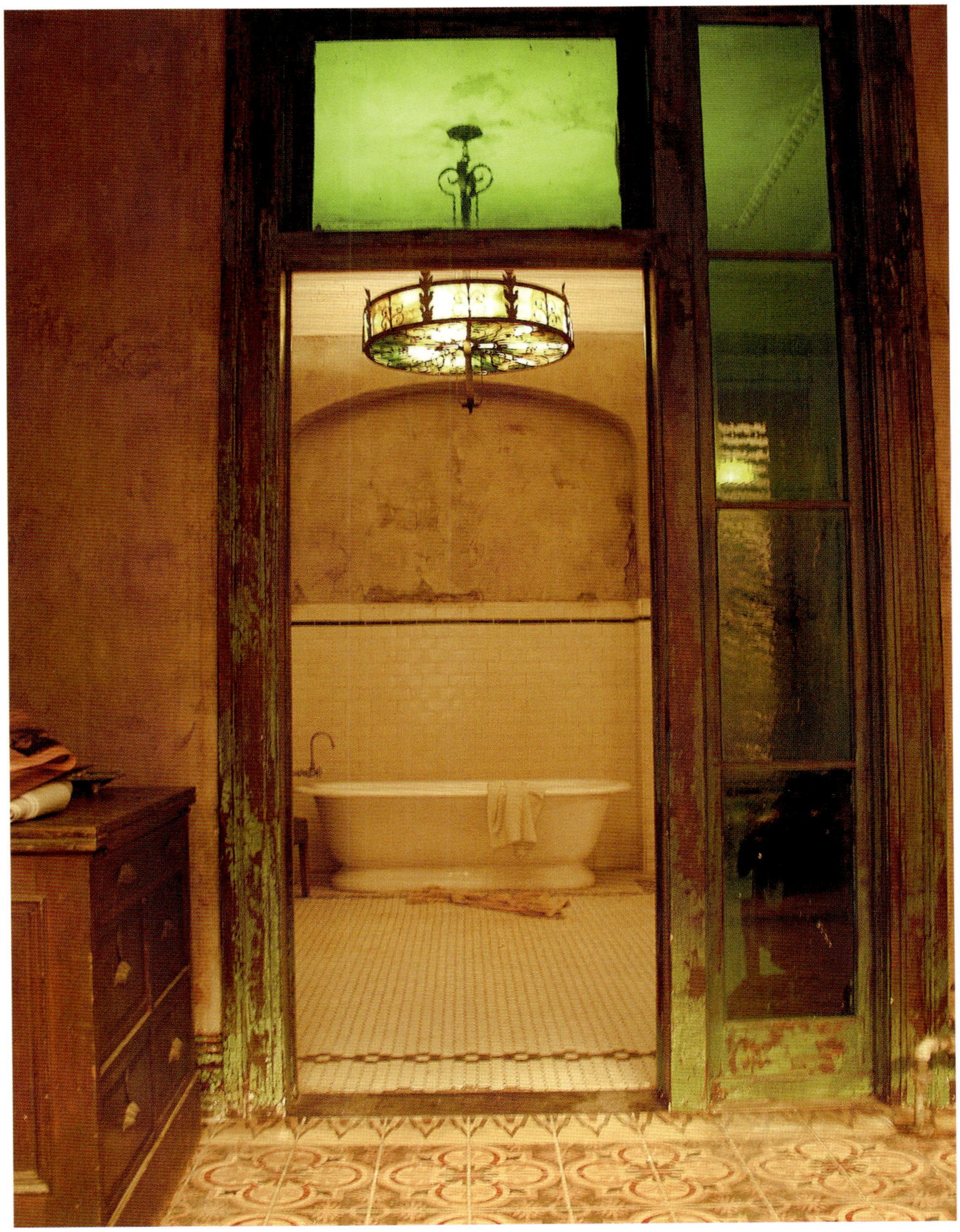

“CONSTANTINE”, WARNER BROTHERS, 2005

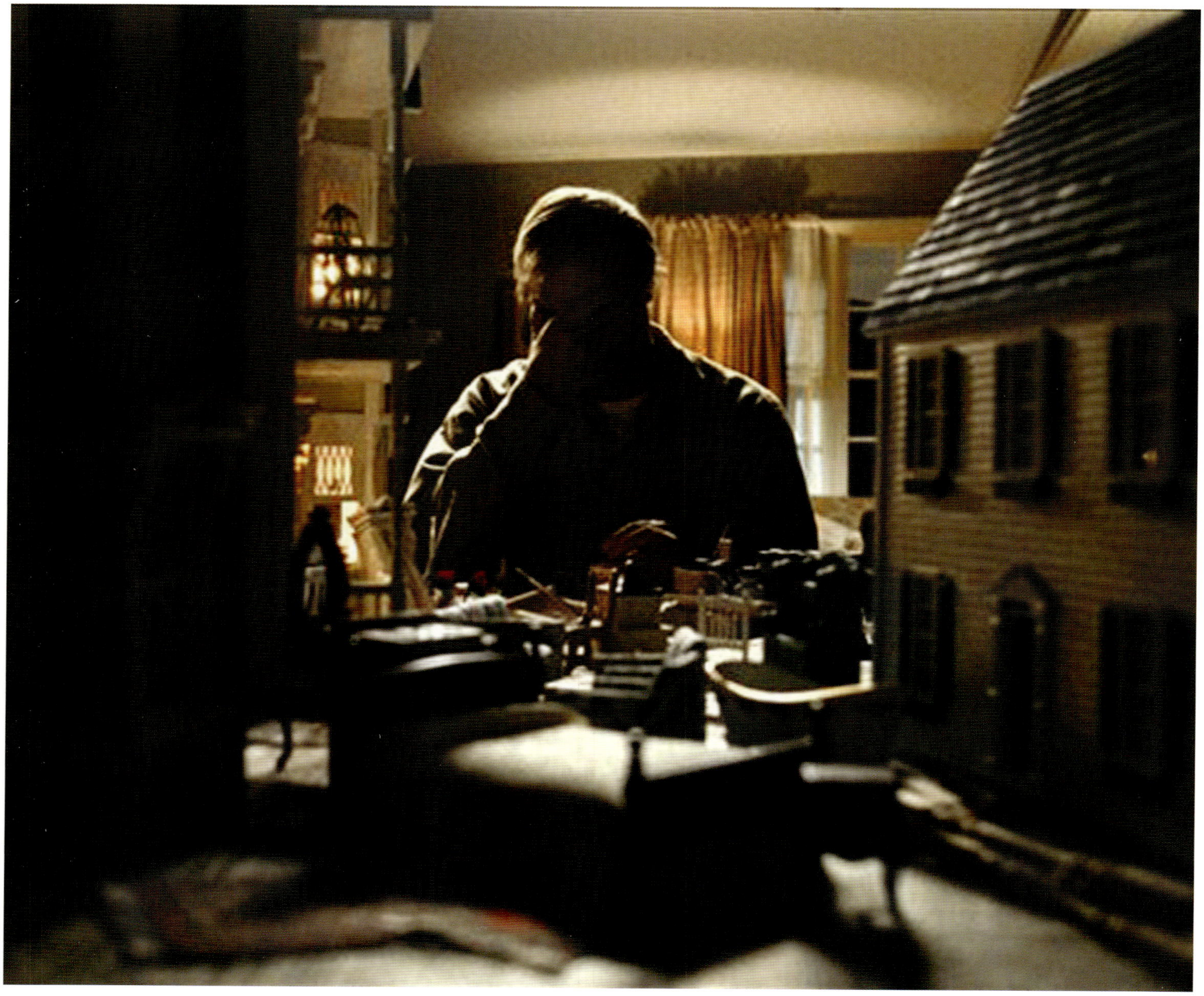

STANLEY TUCCI, “THE LOVELEY BONES”, DREAMWORKS/PARAMOUNT, 1999

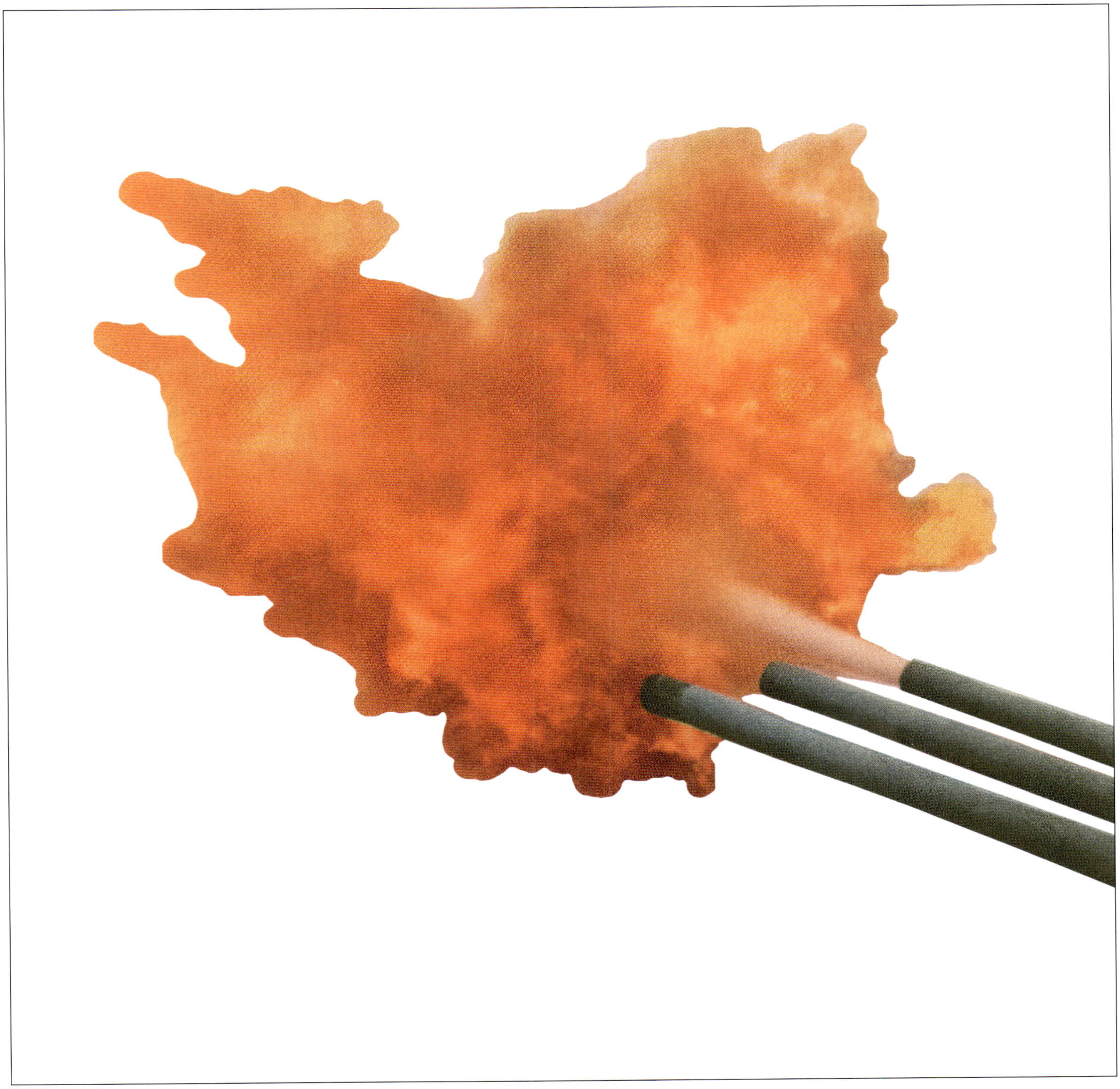

BLAST AND CANNONS

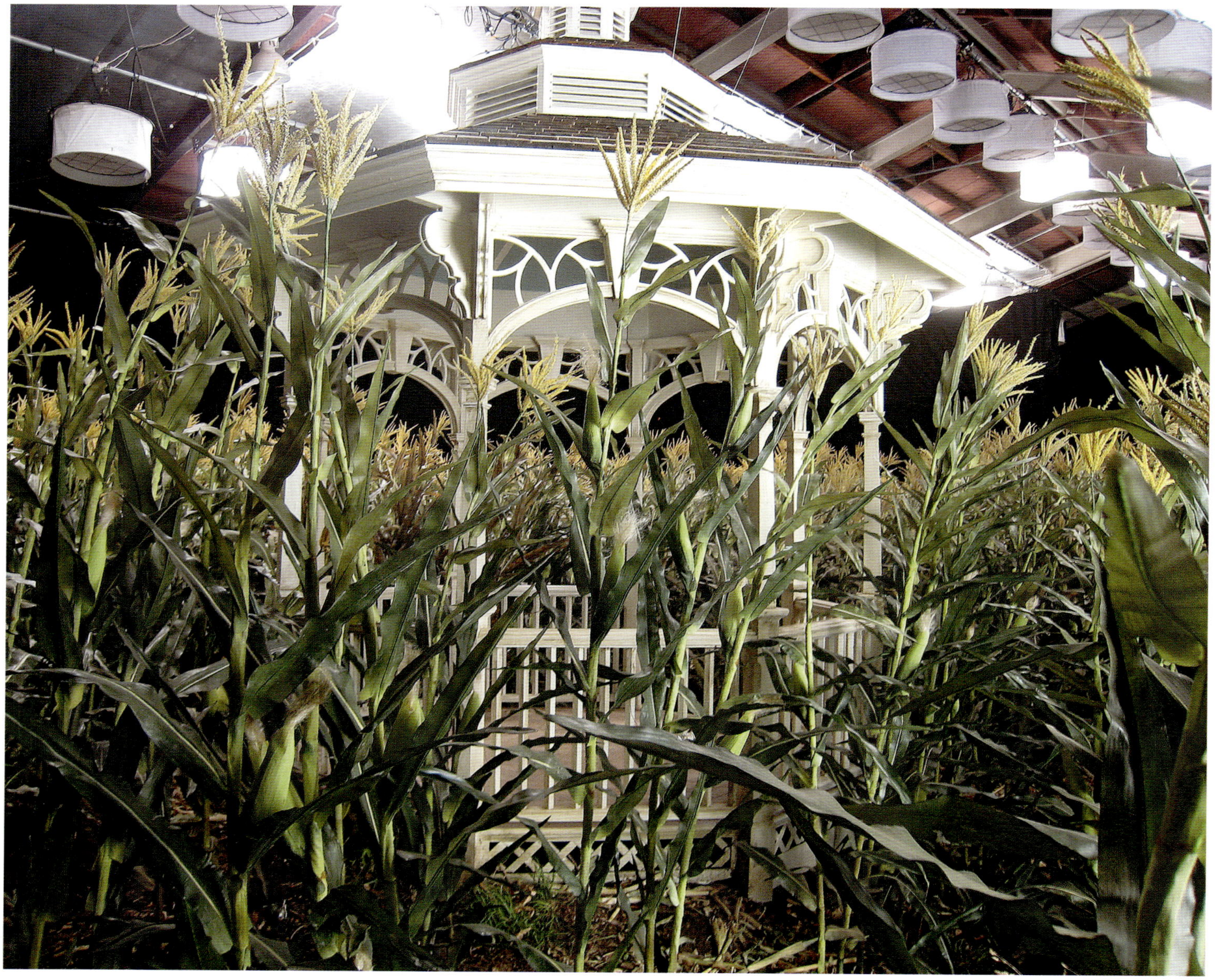

“THE LOVELEY BONES”, DREAMWORKS/PARAMOUNT, 2009

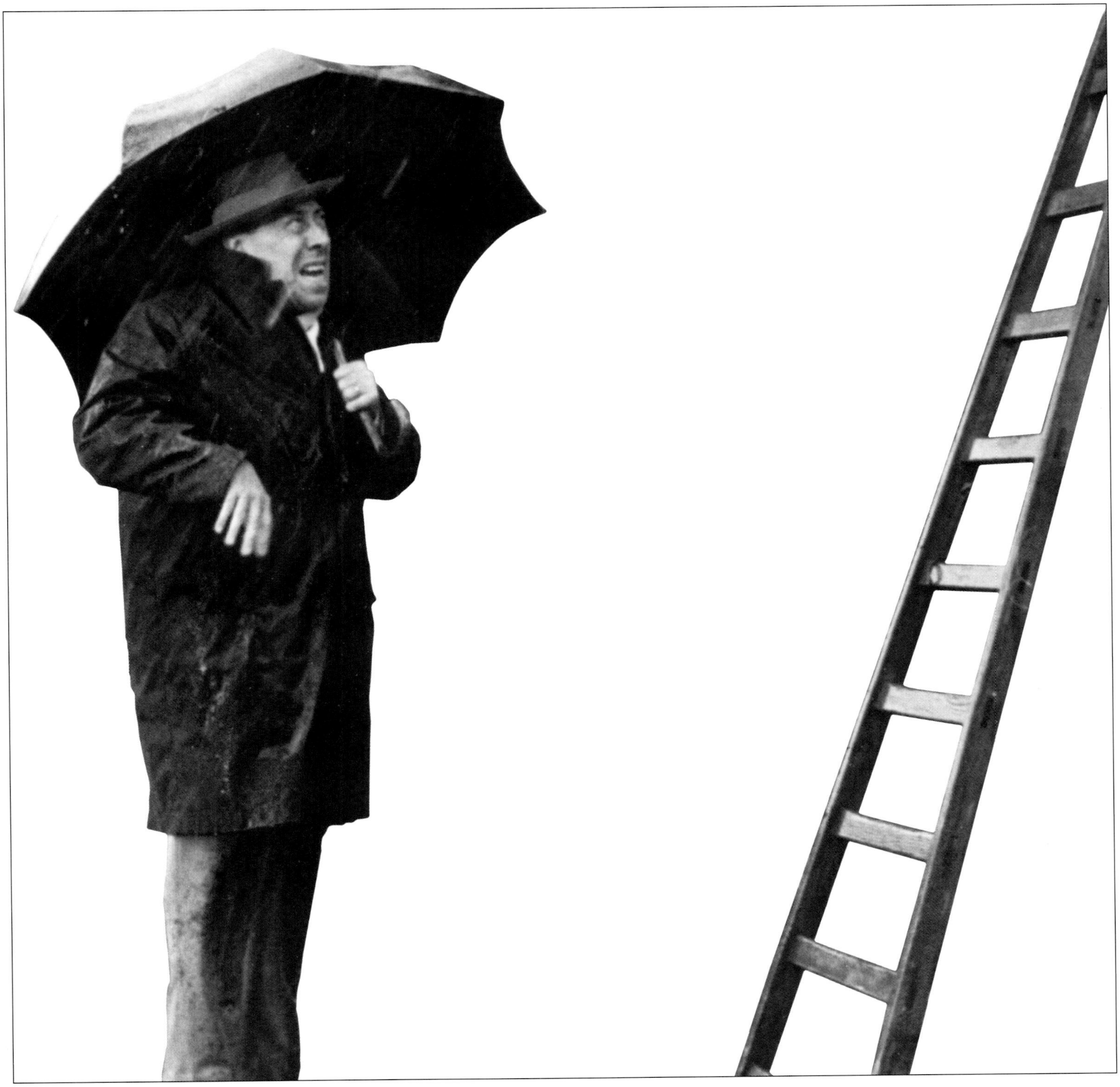

UMBRELLA, PERSON AND LADDER

"THE SORCERER'S APPRENTICE", DISNEY ENTERPRISES, 2009

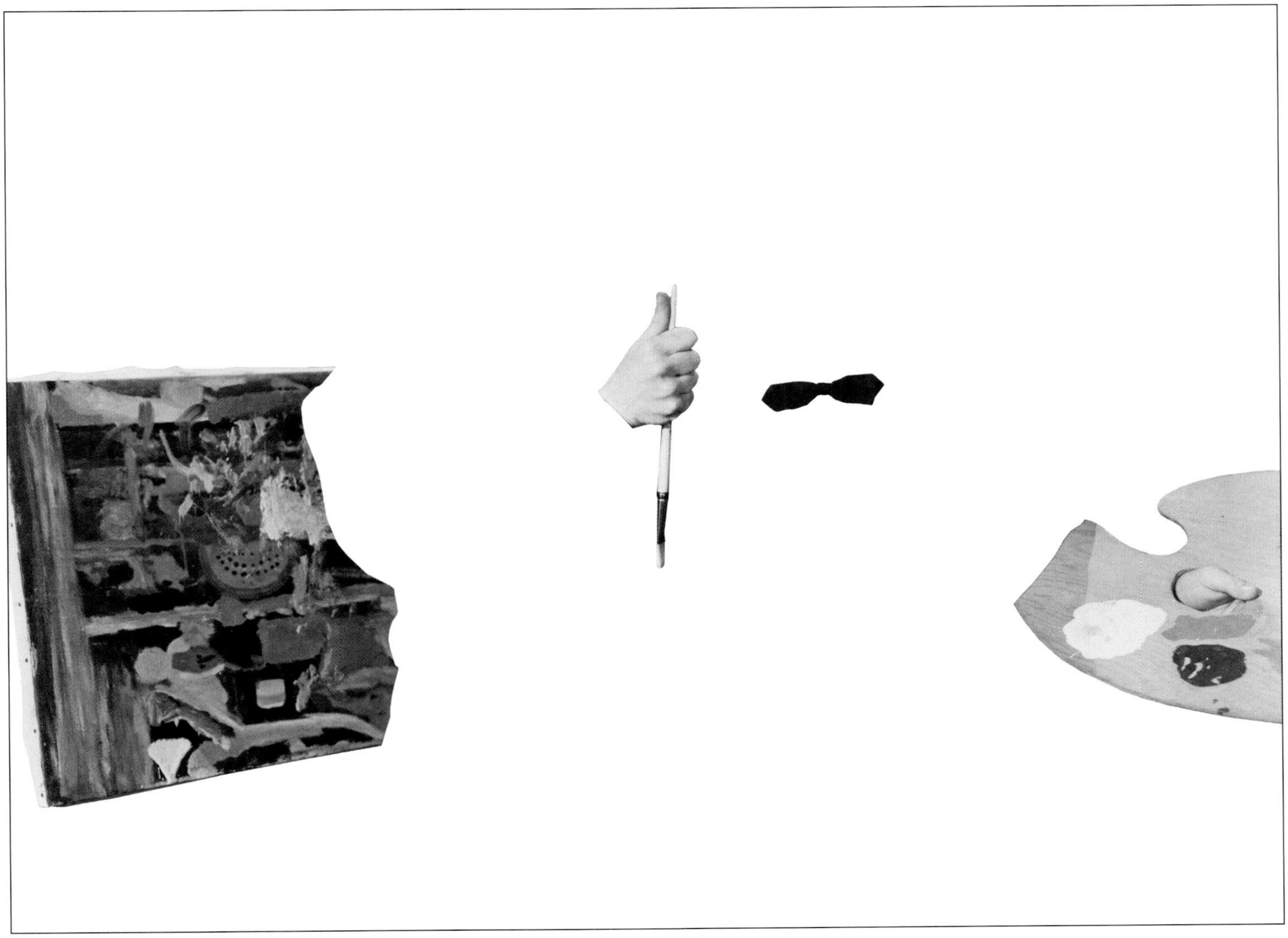

CANVAS, HAND, BRUSH, BOW TIE AND PALETTE

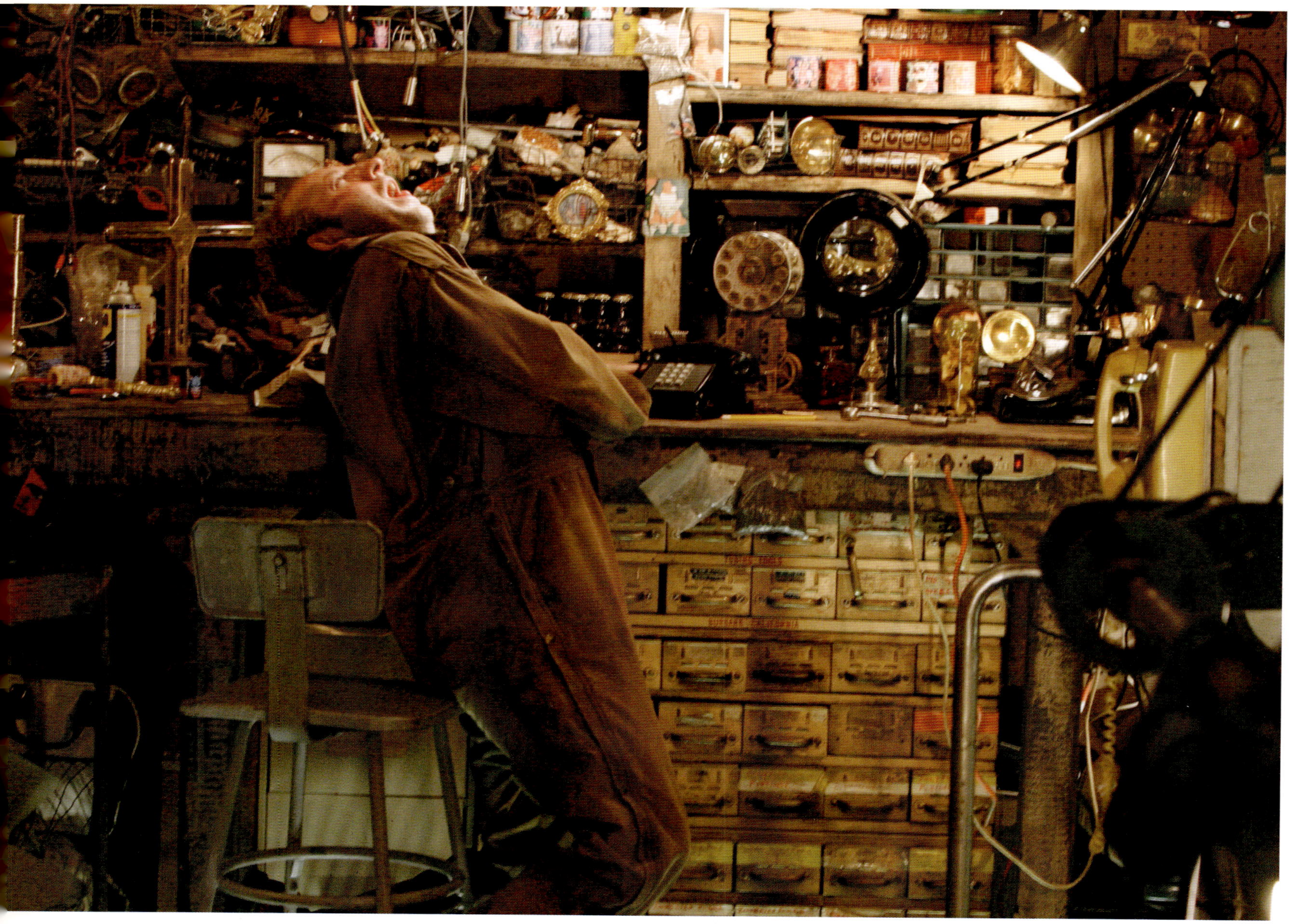

MAX BAKER, “CONSTANTINE”, WARNER BROTHERS, 2005

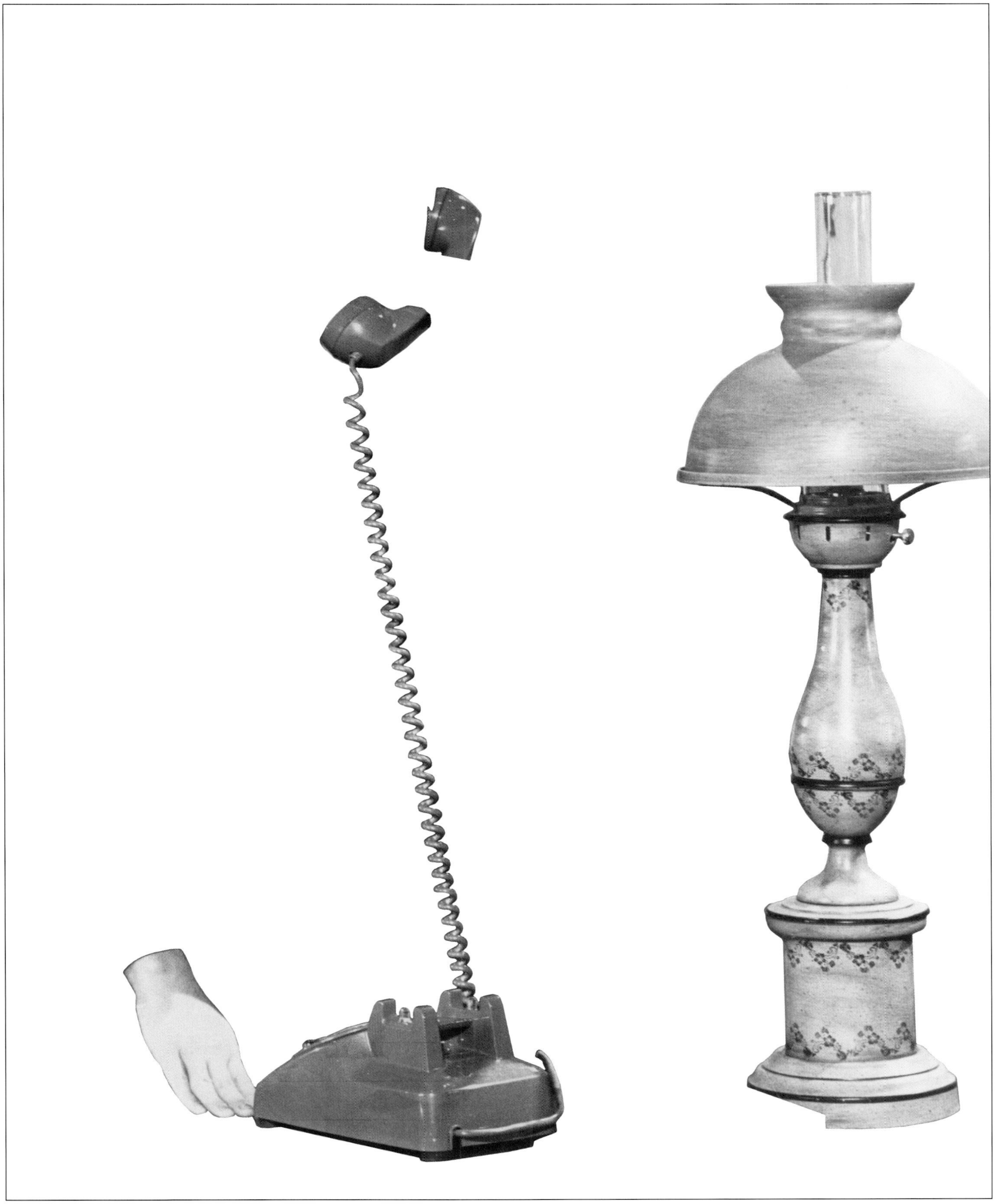

HAND, TELEPHONE AND LAMP

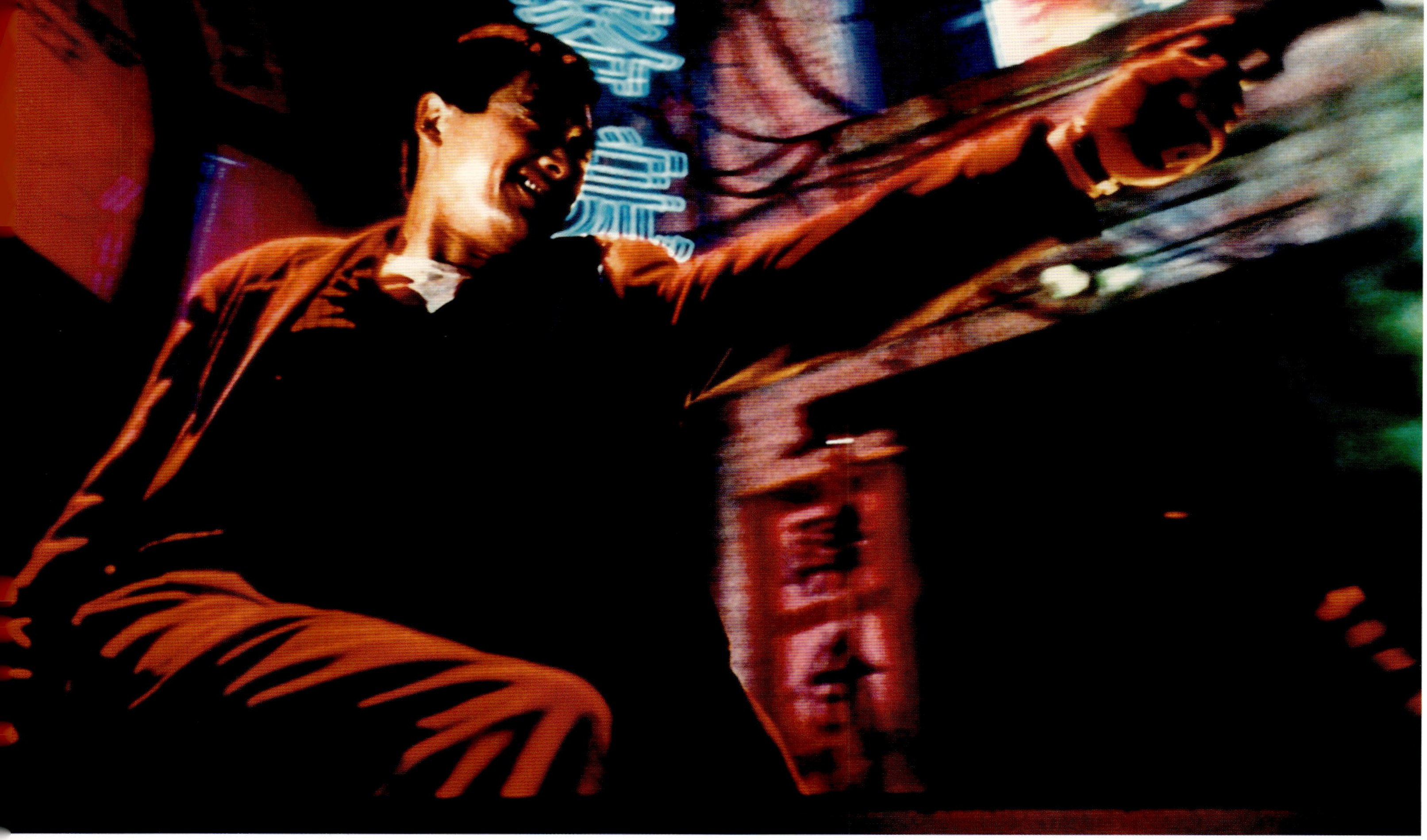

CHOW YUN-FAT, "THE REPLACEMENT KILLERS", SONY/TRISTAR, 1998

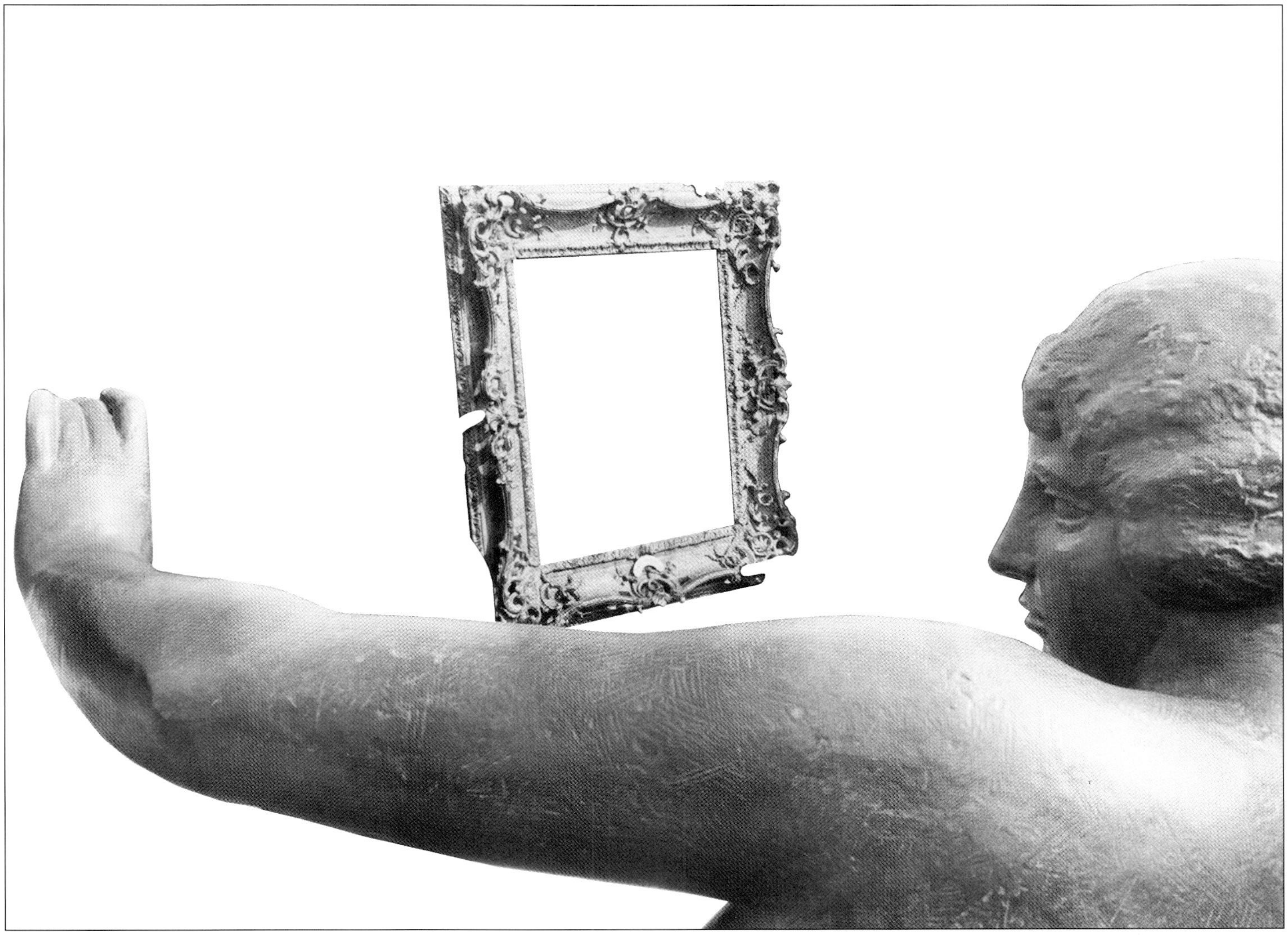

SCULPTURE AND FRAME

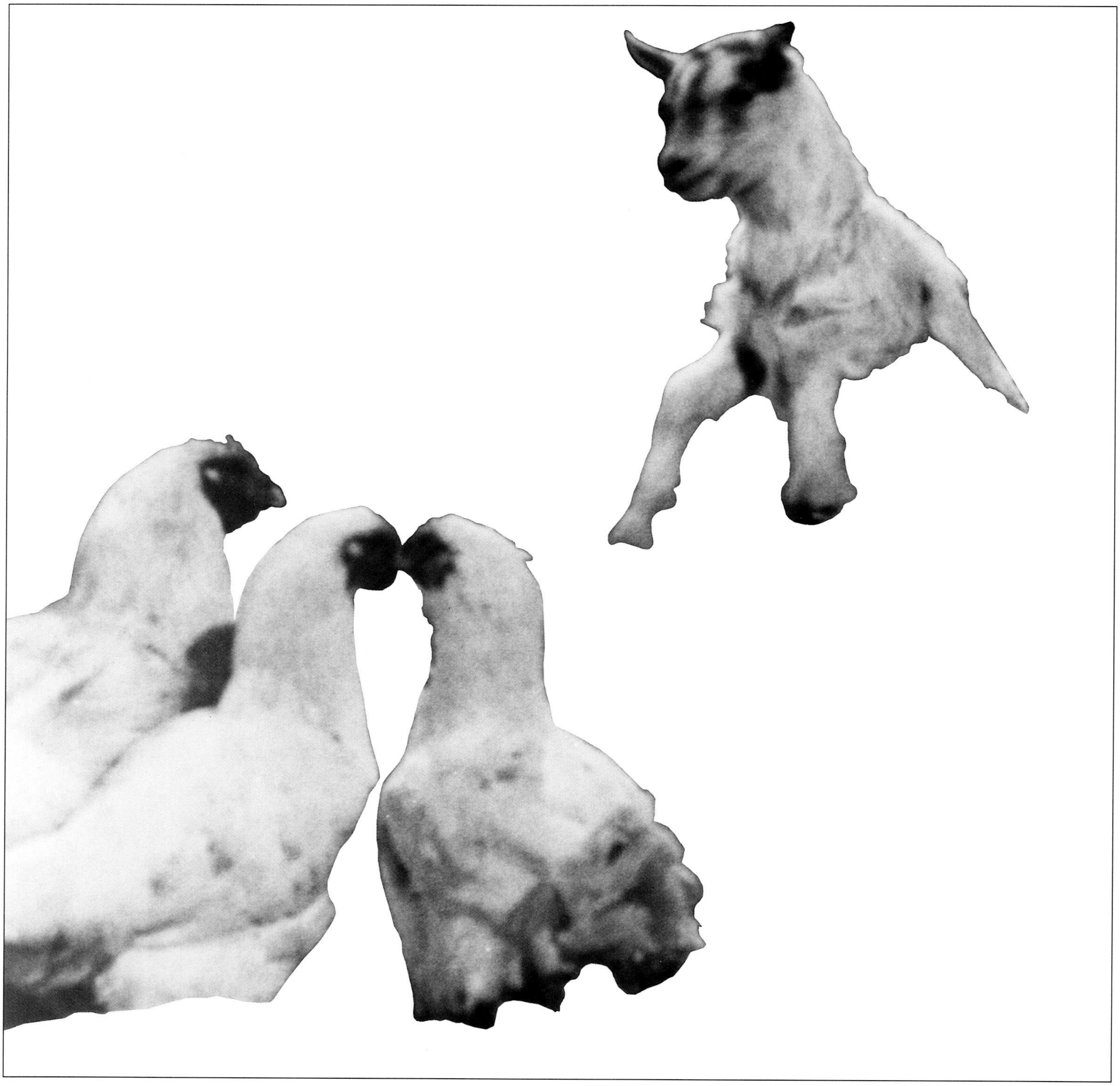

CHICKENS AND GOAT

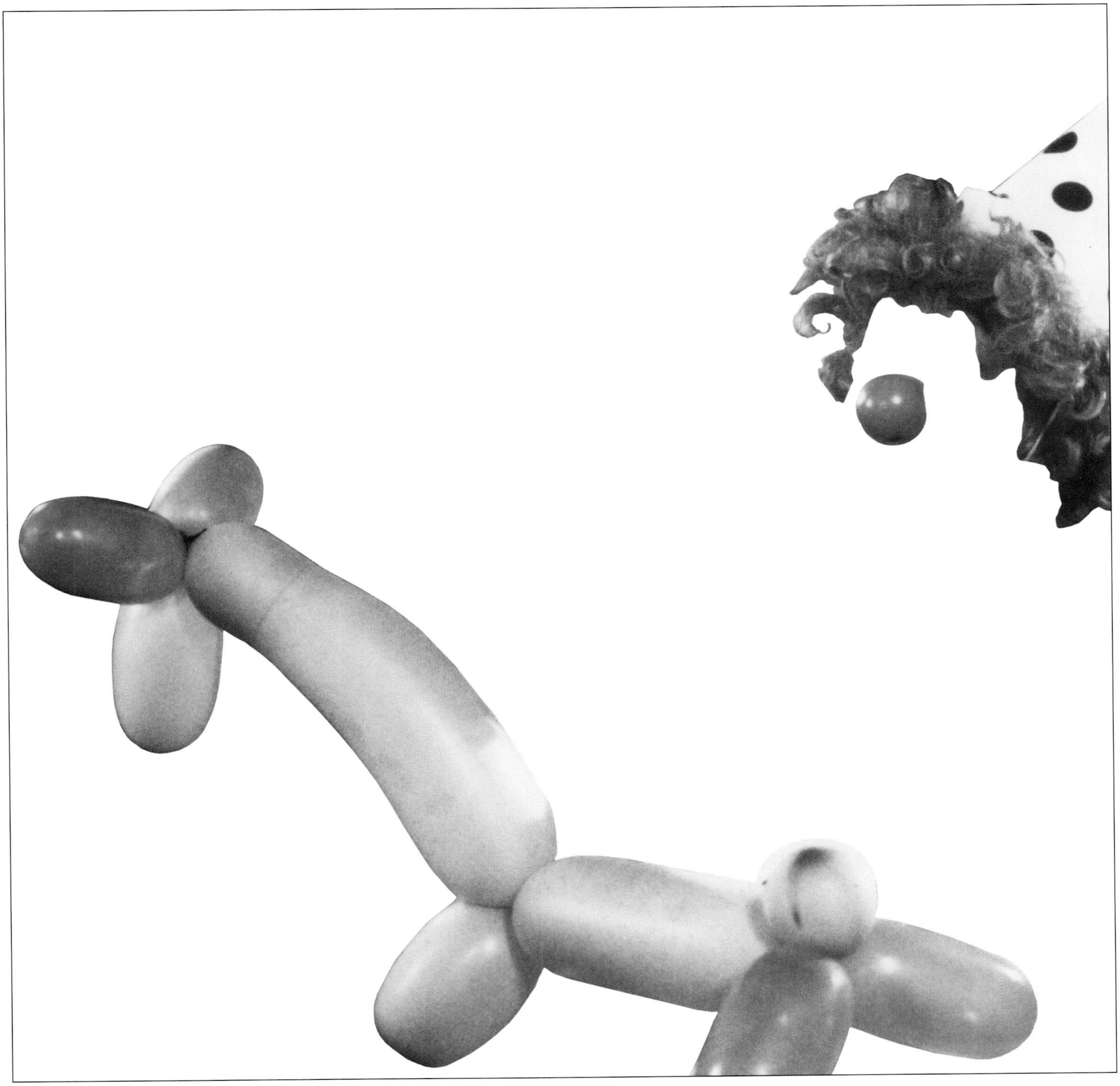

BALLOONS, HAIR, NOSE AND HAT

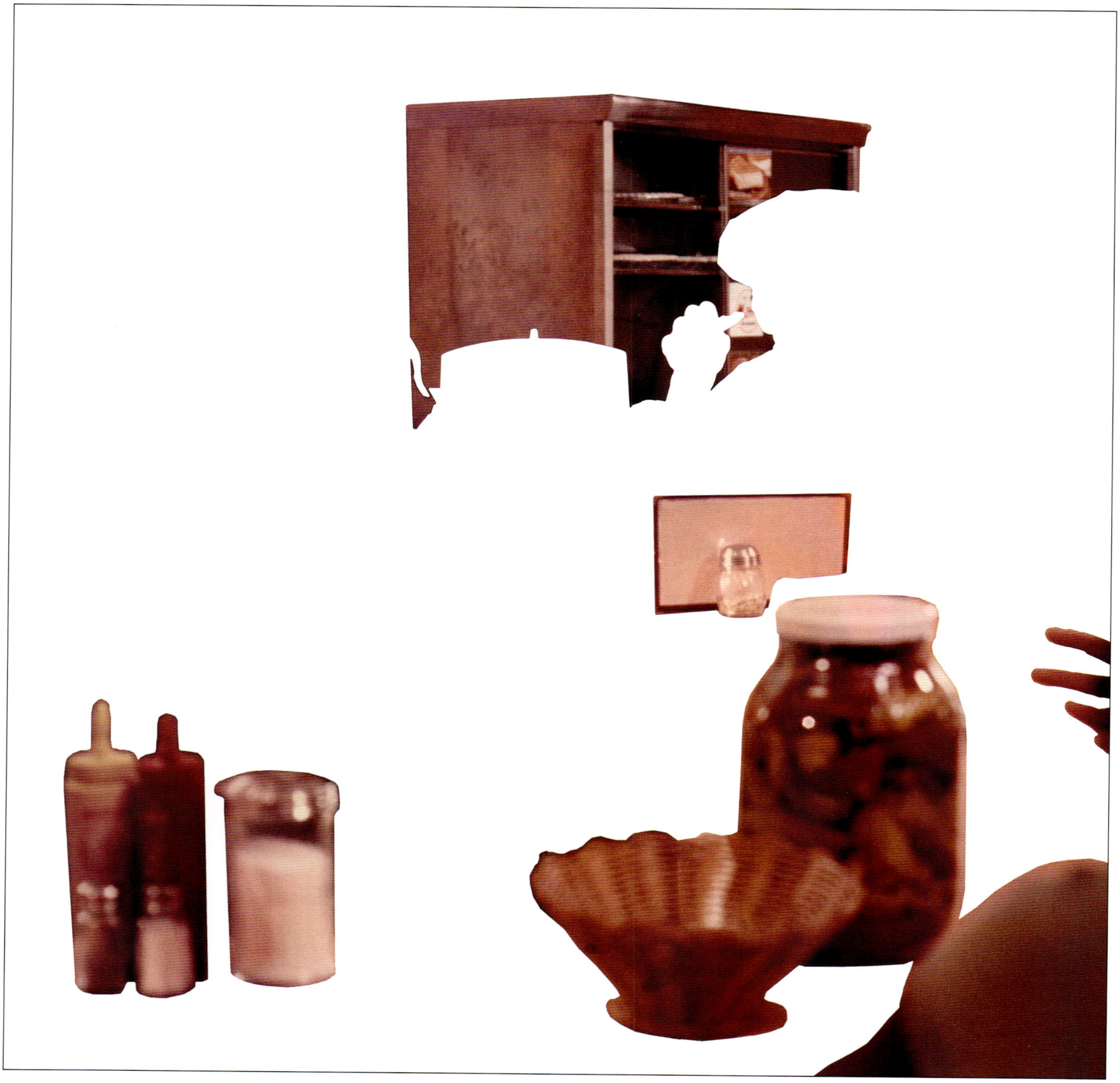

CONTAINERS, CABINET, MENU, SHOULDER AND FINGERS

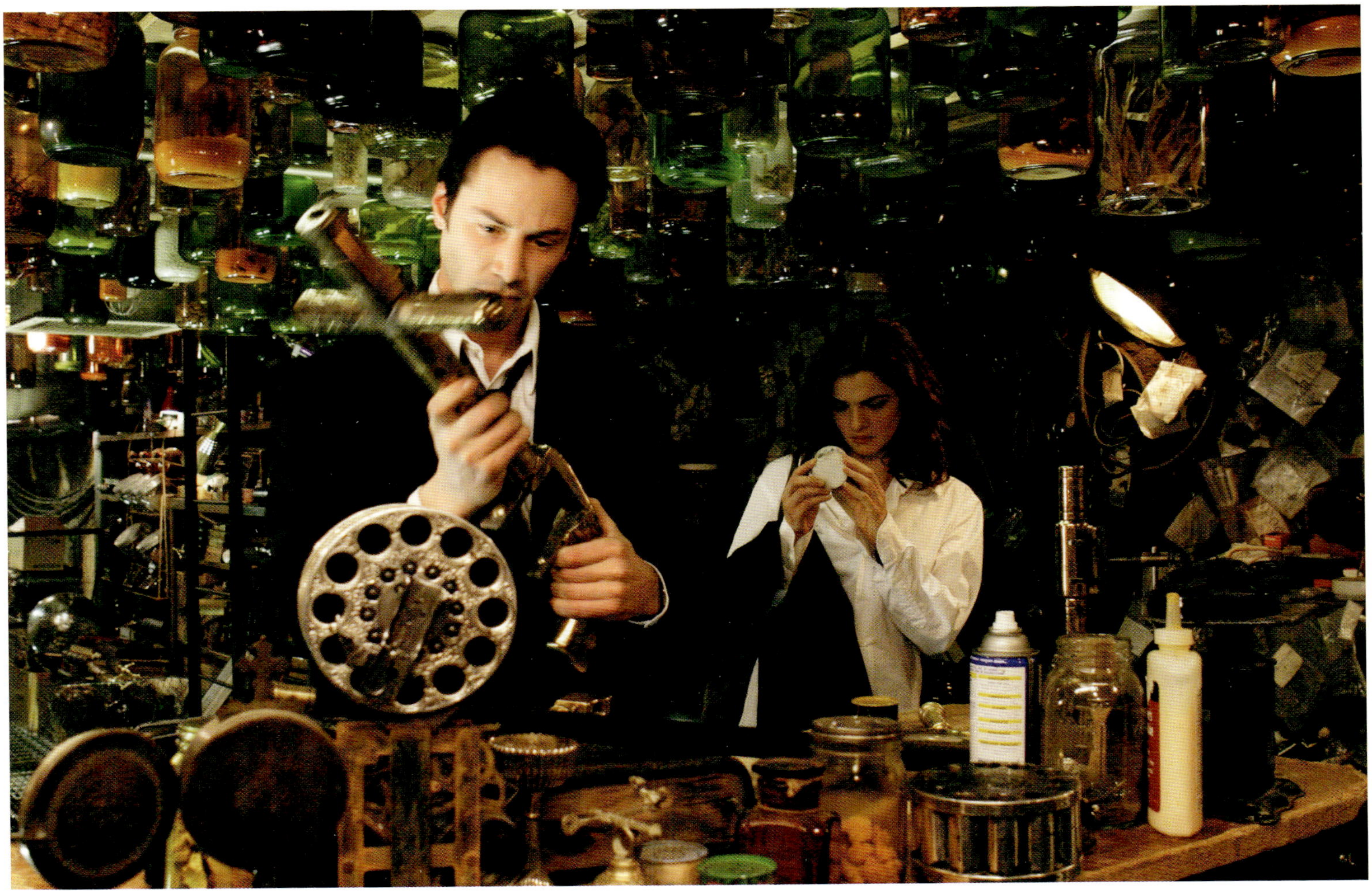

KEANU REEVES, RACHEL WEISZ, “CONSTANTINE”, WARNER BROTHERS, 2005

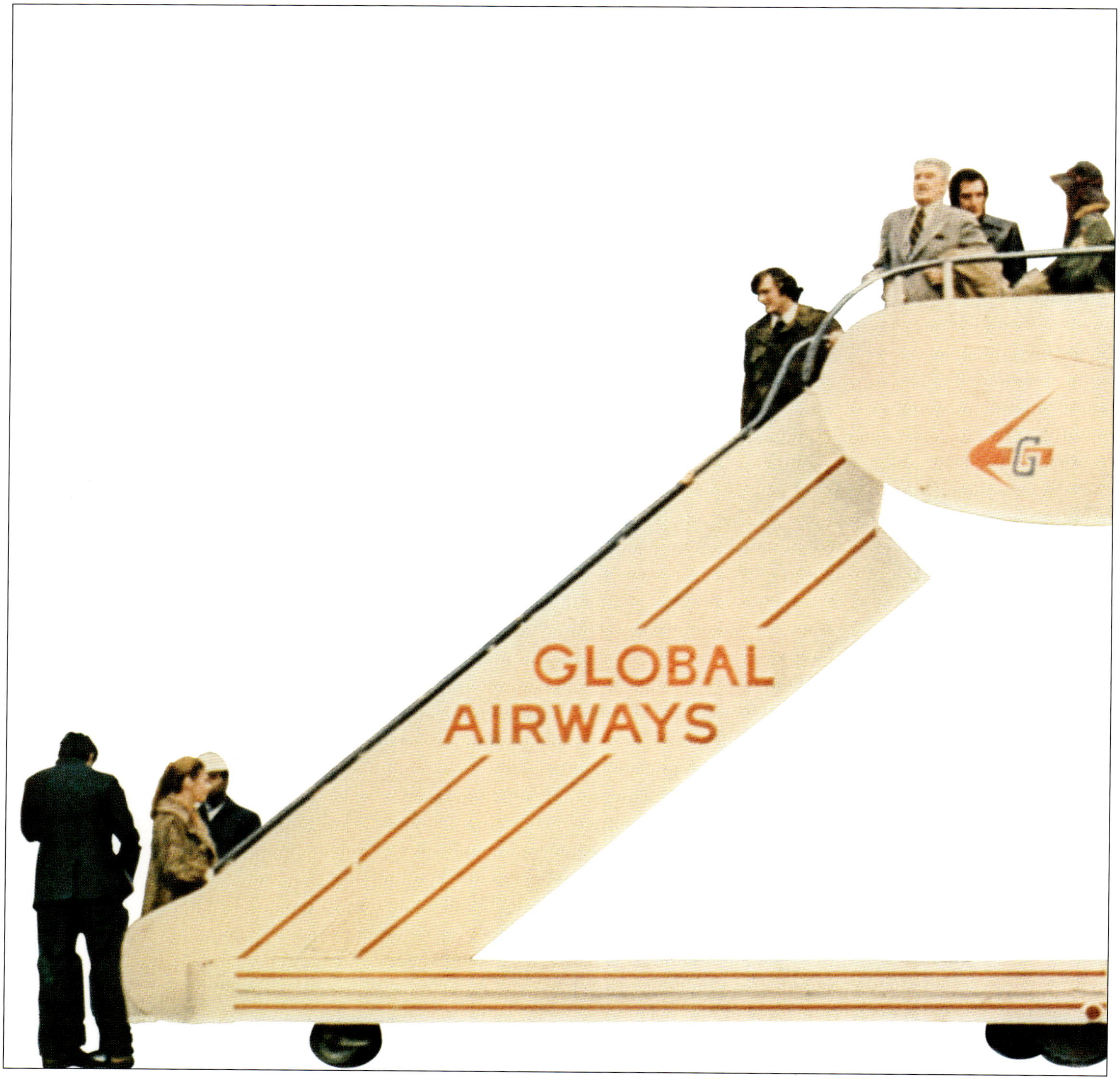


PERSONS AND RAMP

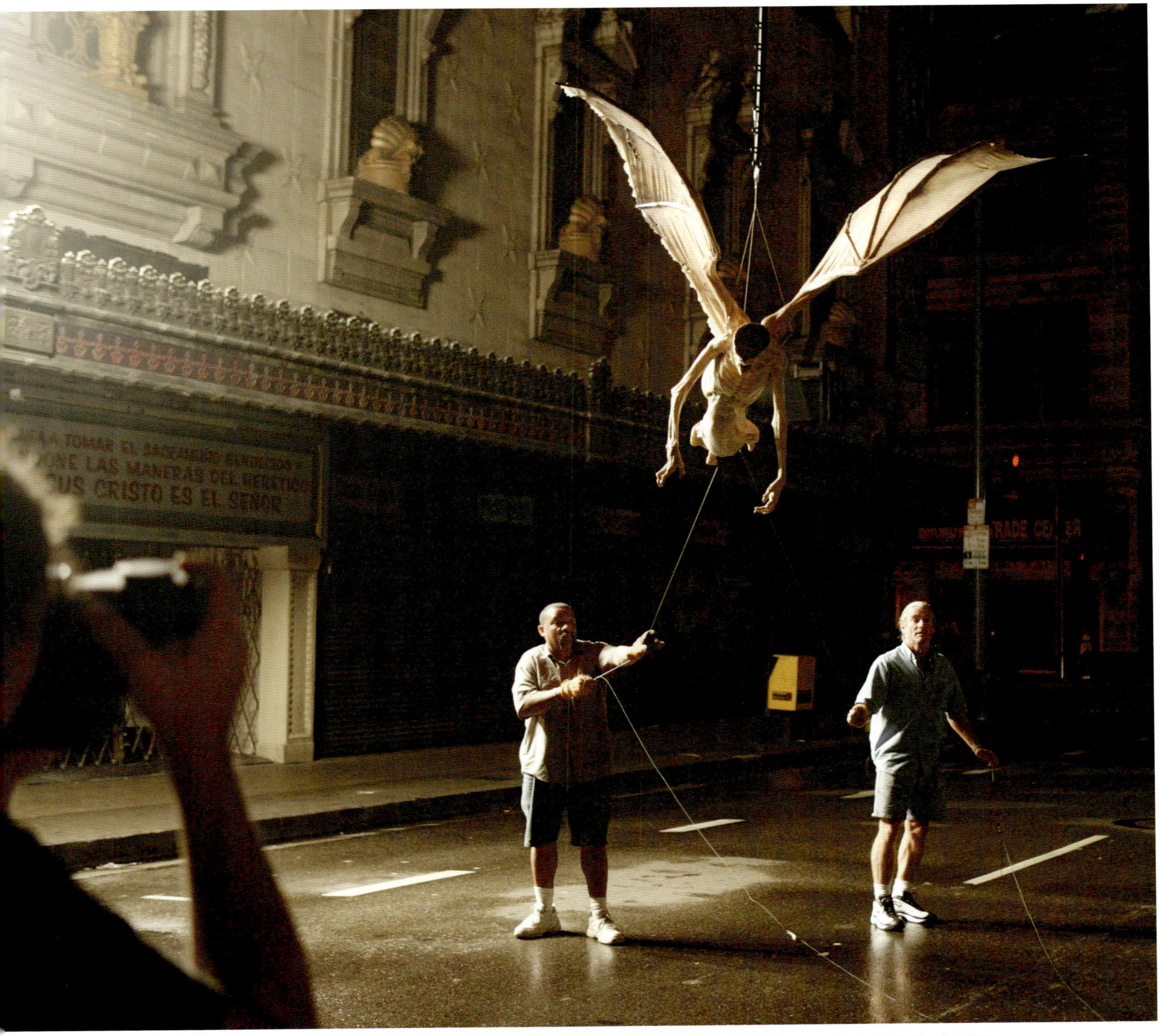


FX MEN AND PUPPET, "CONSTANTINE", WARNER BROTHERS, 2005

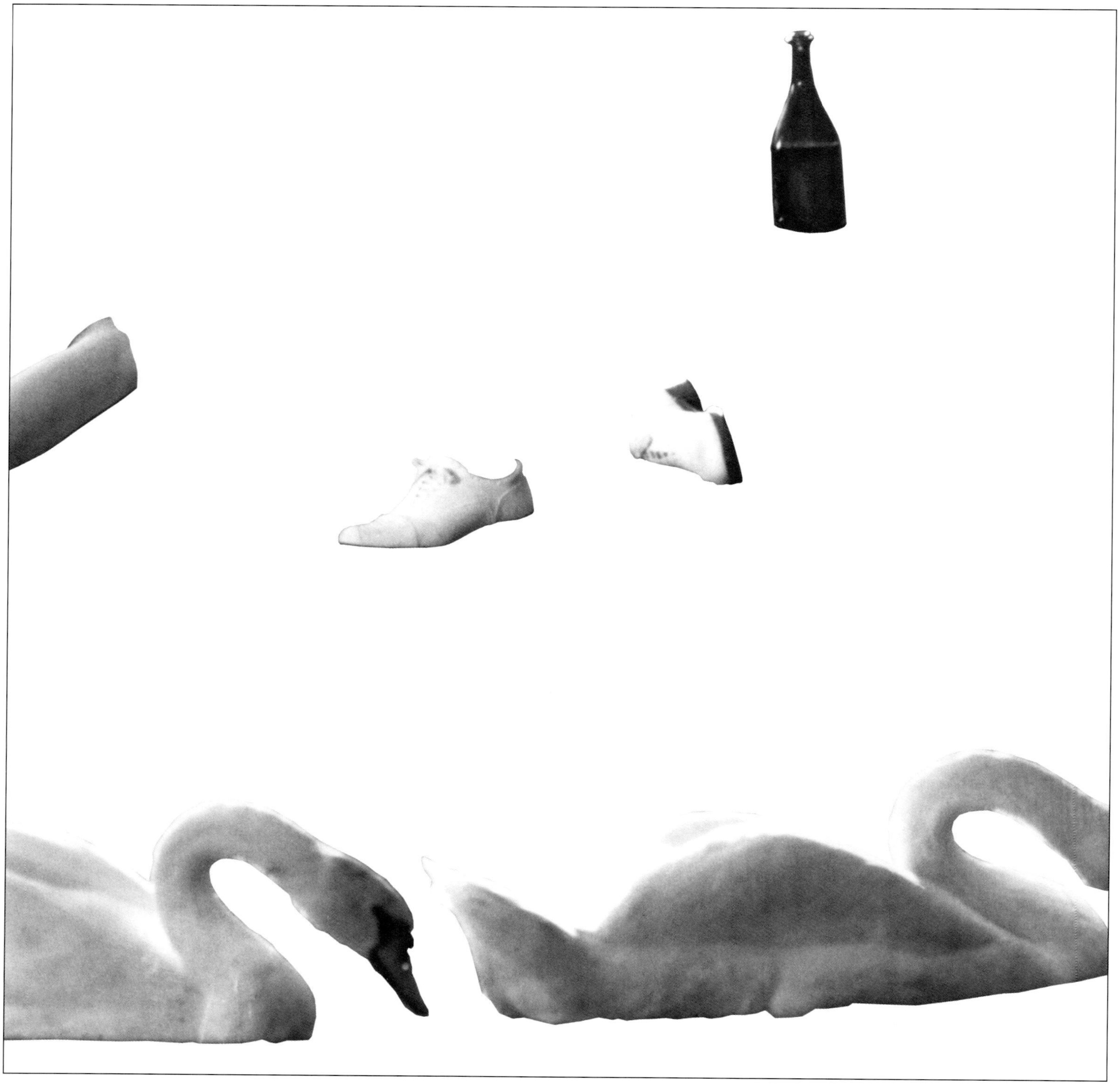

ARM, SWANS, SHOES AND BOTTLE

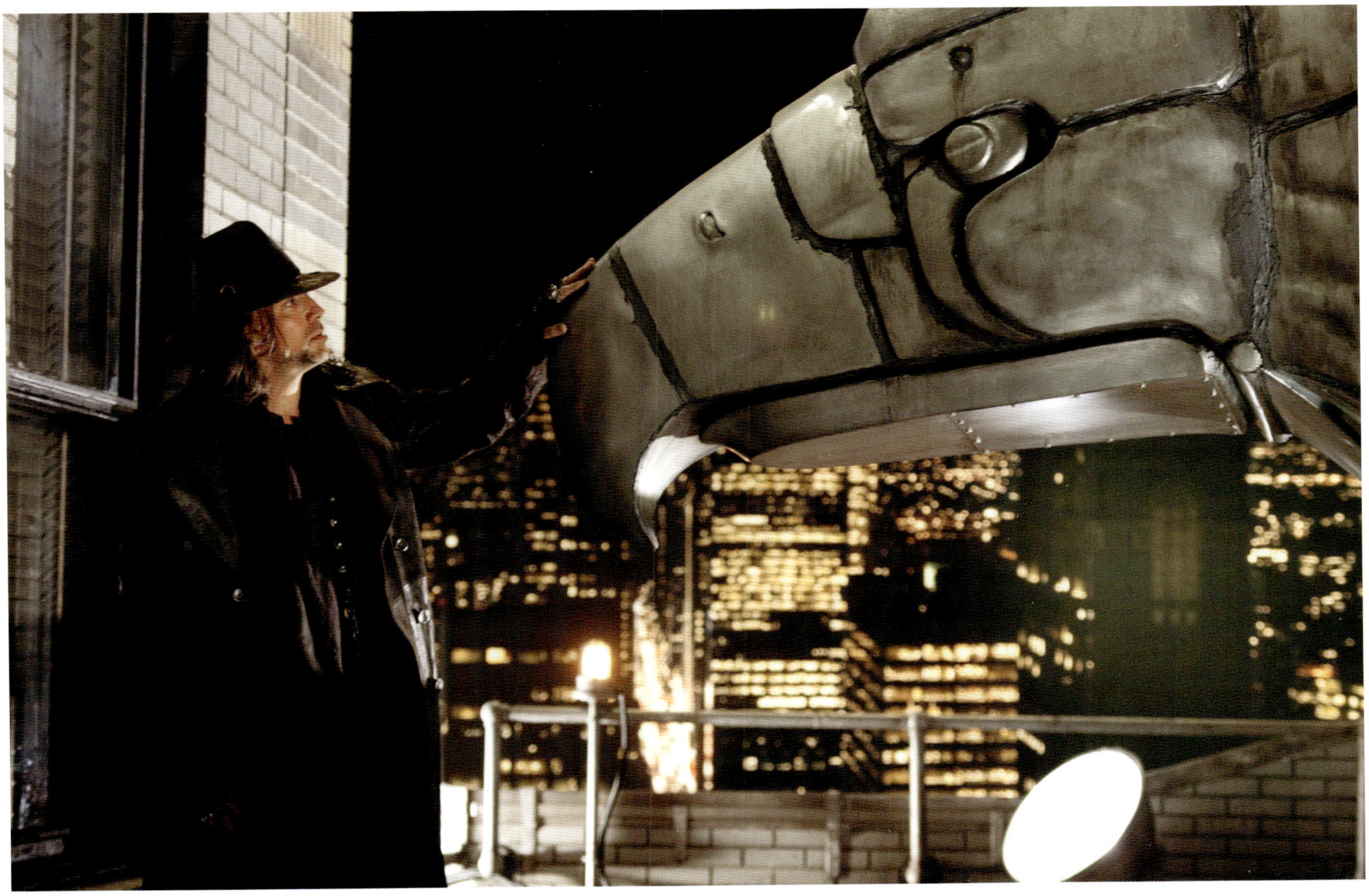

NICOLAS CAGE, “THE SORCERER’S APPRENTICE,” DISNEY ENTERPRISES, 2009

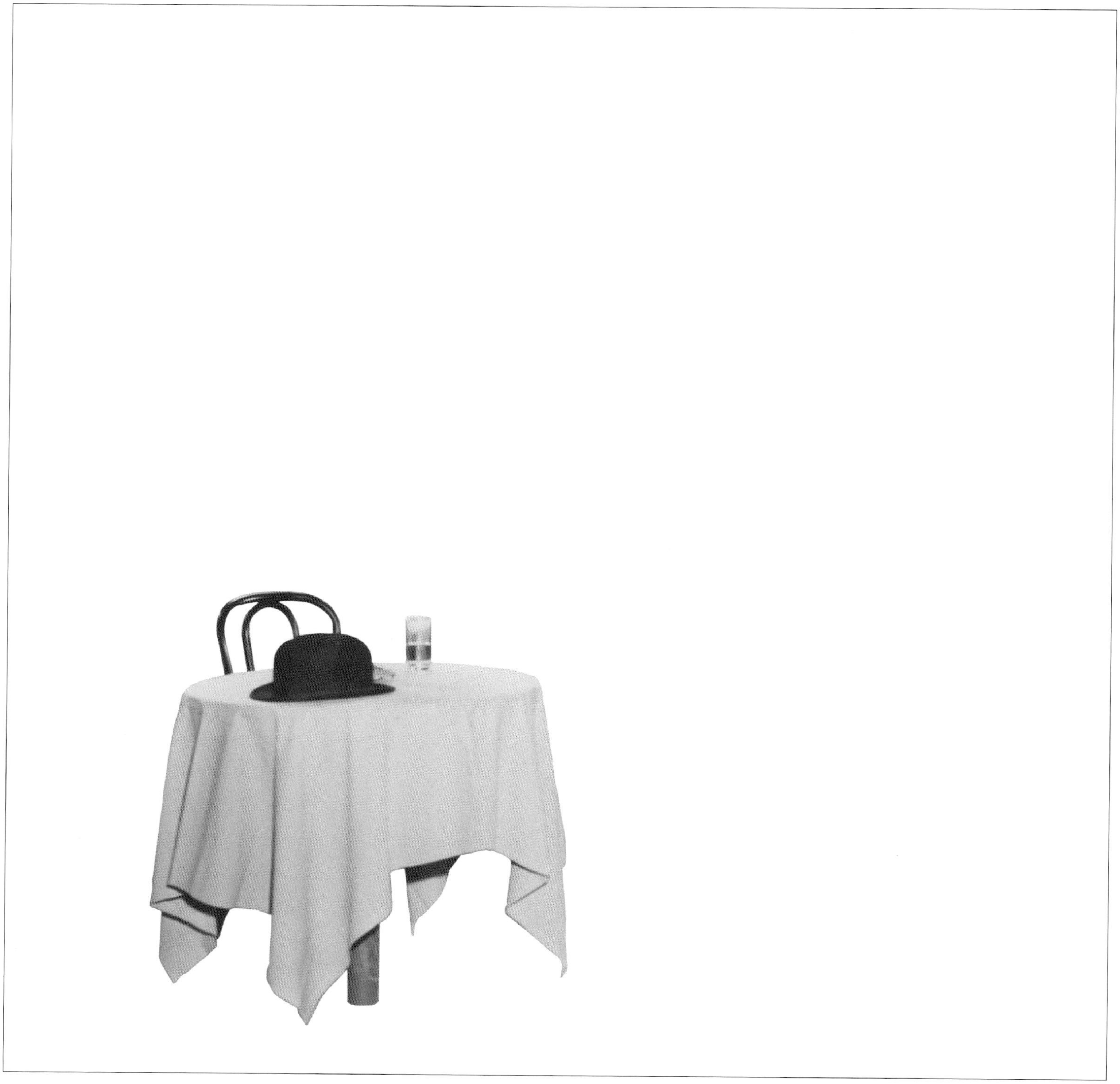

TABLE, CHAIR, HAT AND GLASS

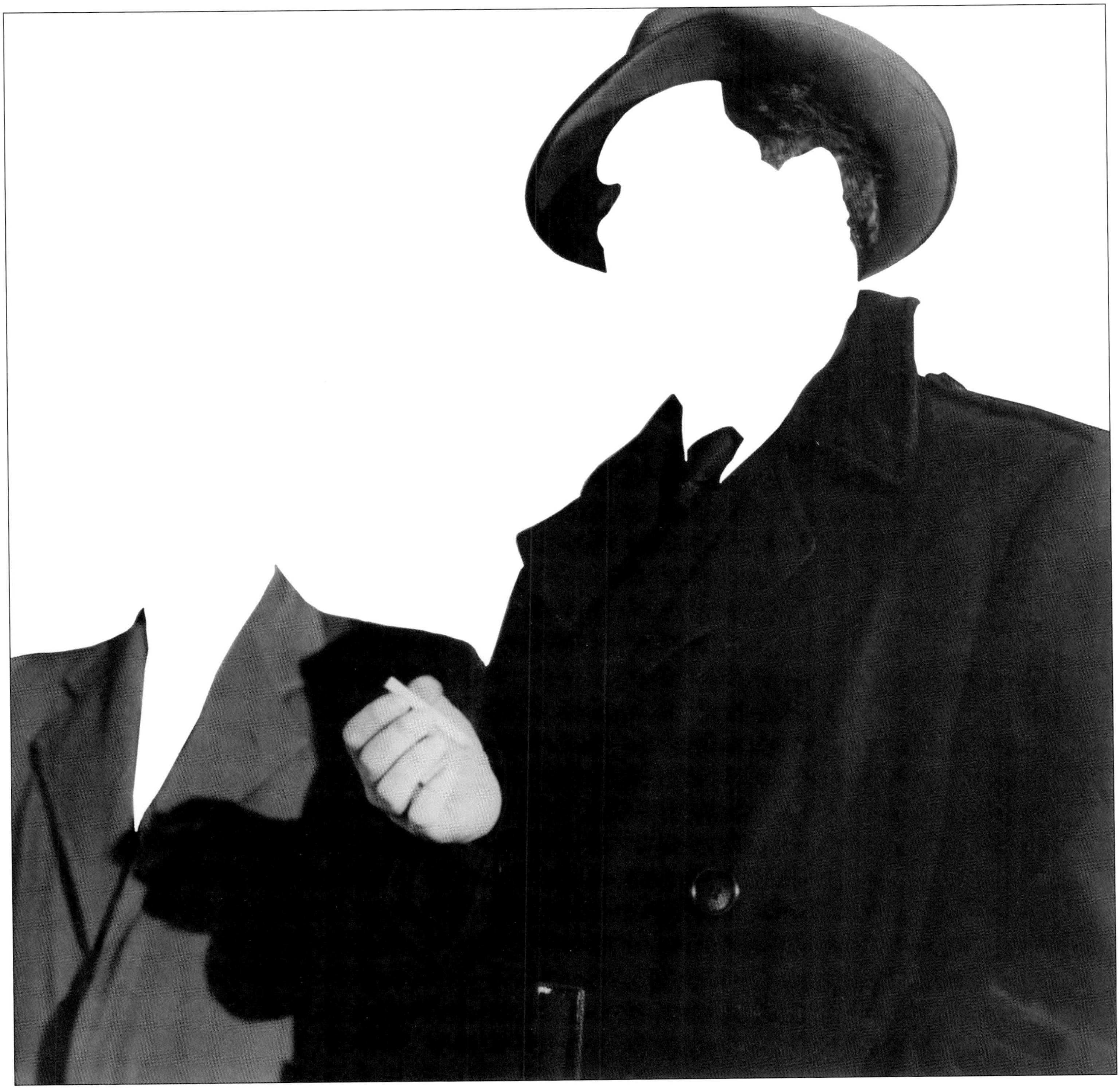

COATS, HAND, CIGARETTE AND HAT

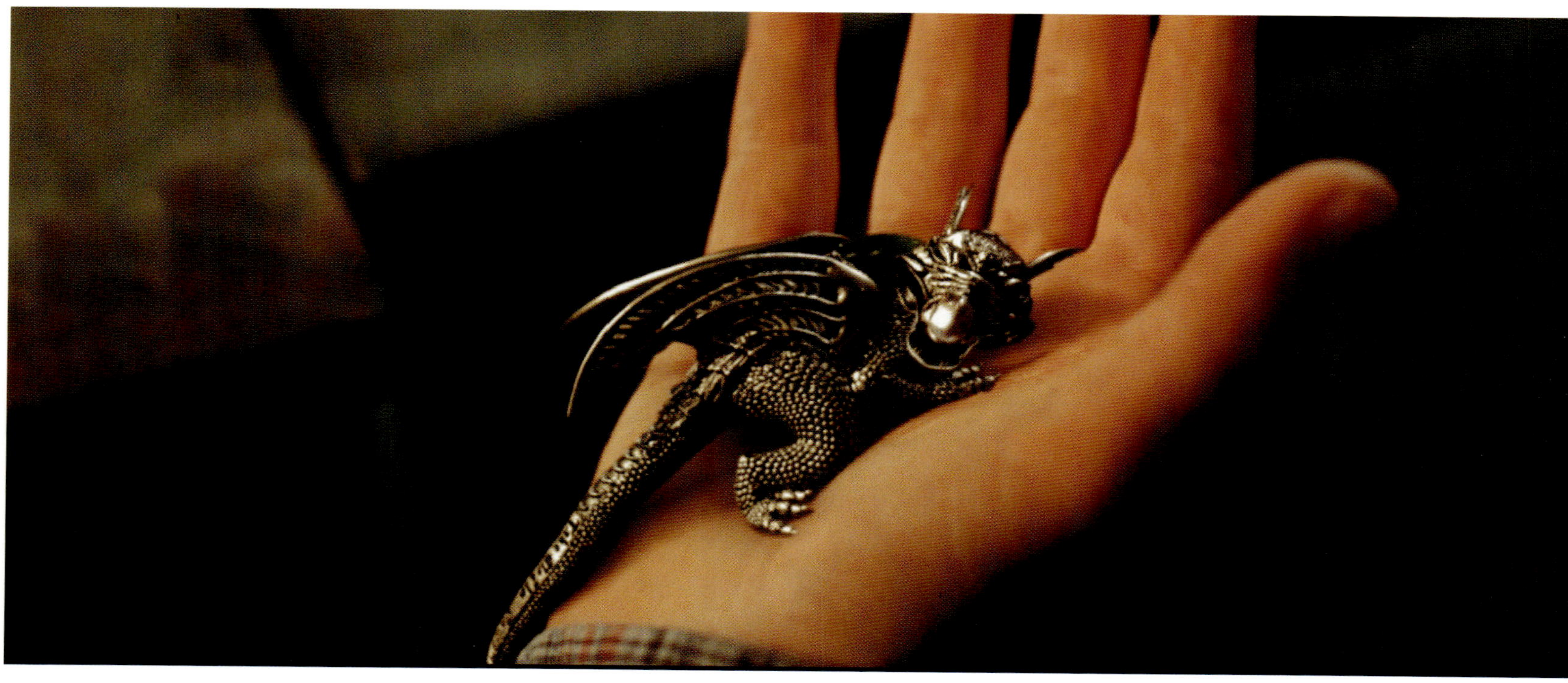

“THE SORCERER’S APPRENTICE,” DISNEY ENTERPRISES, 2009

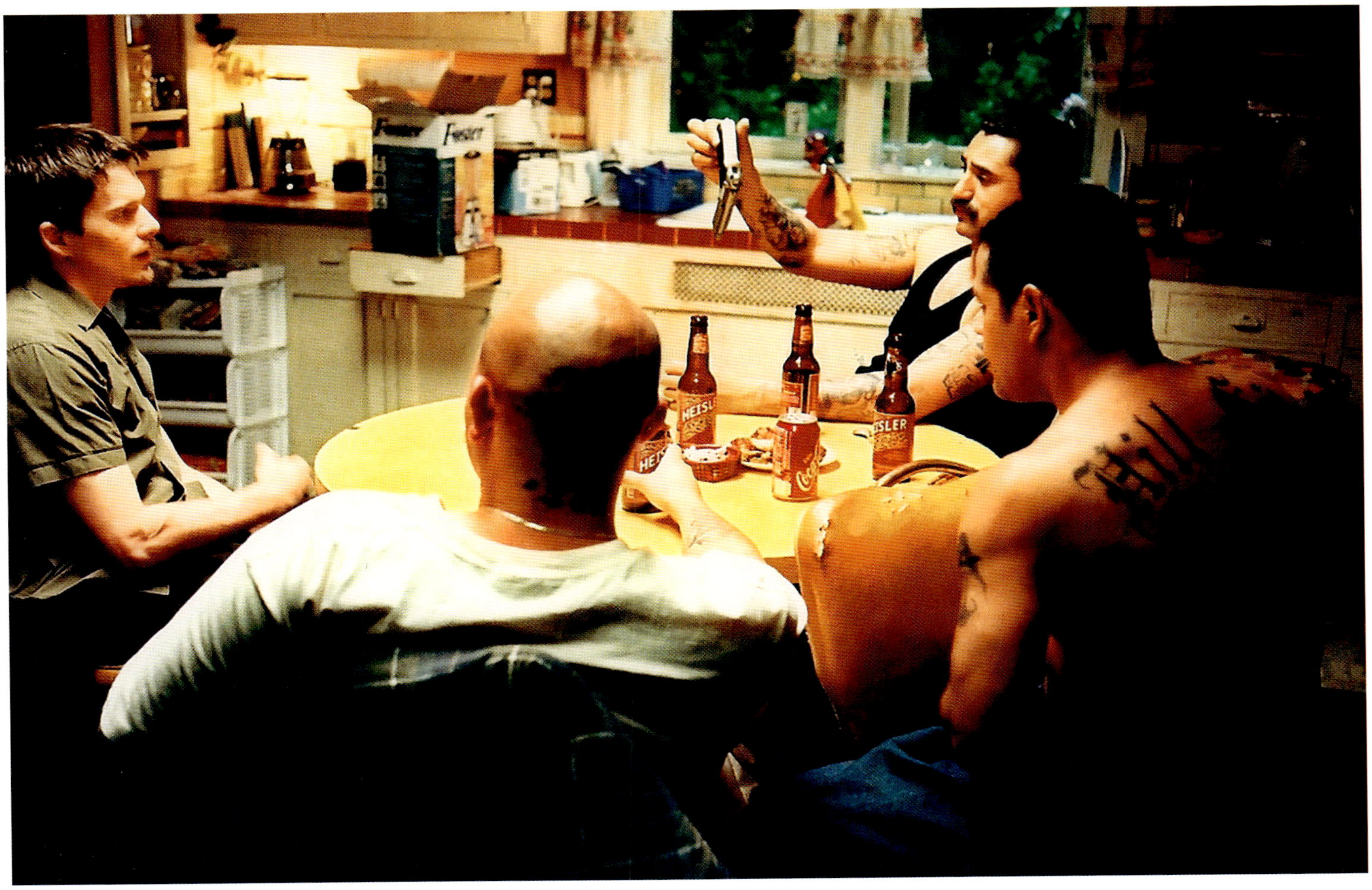

ETHAN HAWKE, RAYMOND CRUZ, “TRAINING DAY”, WARNER BROTHERS, 2001

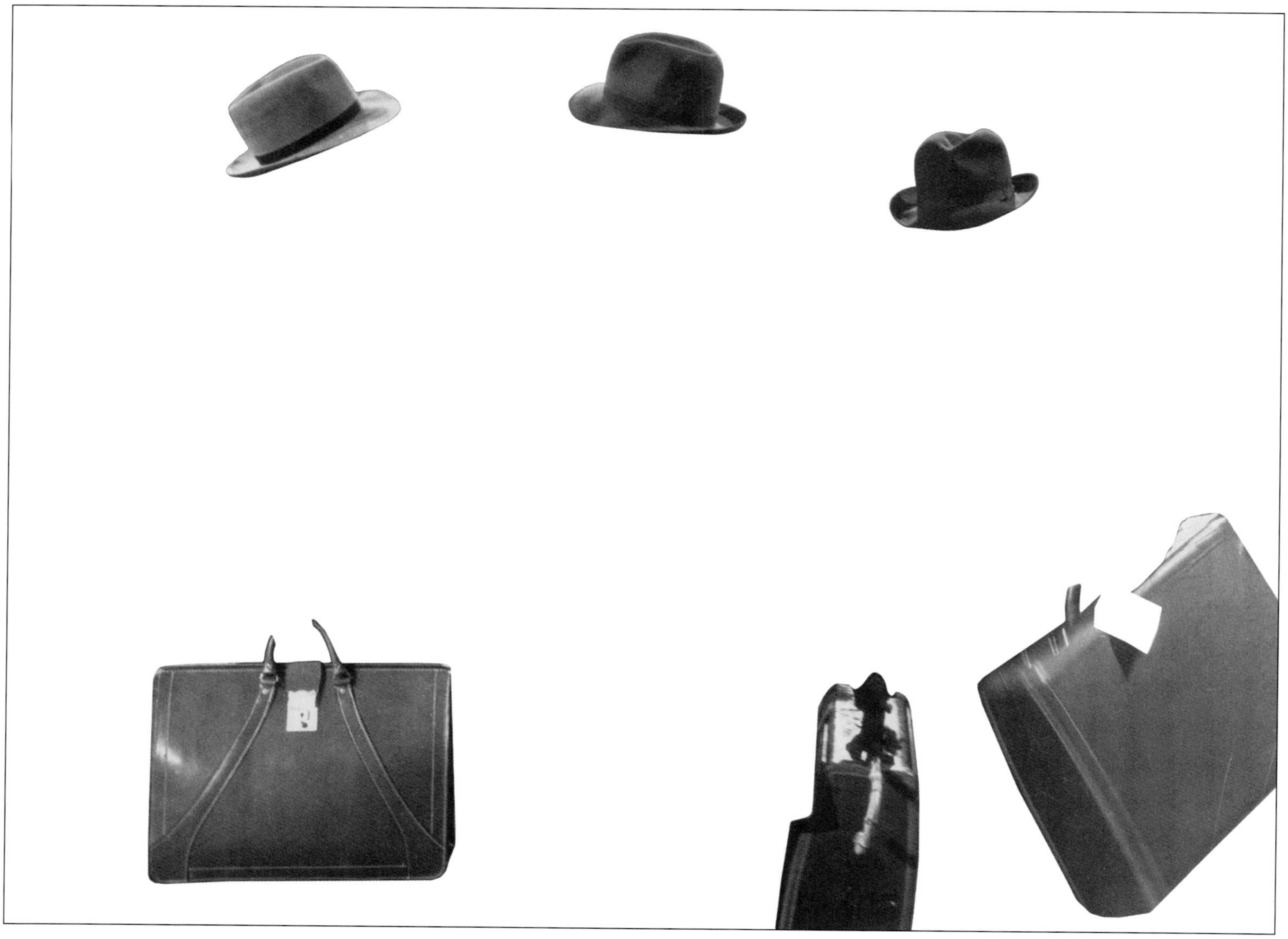

HATS AND BRIEFCASES

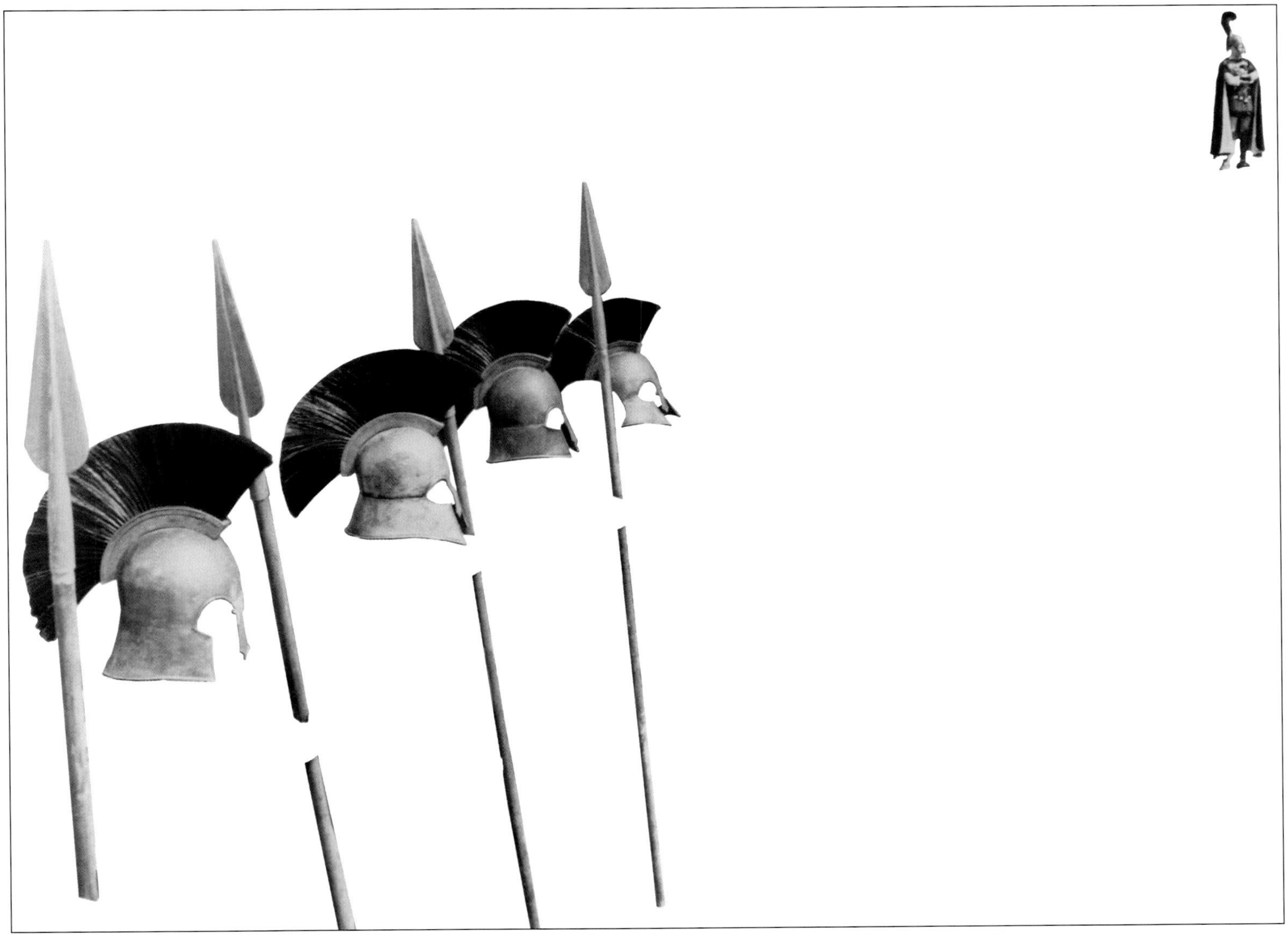

SPEARS, HELMETS AND PERSON

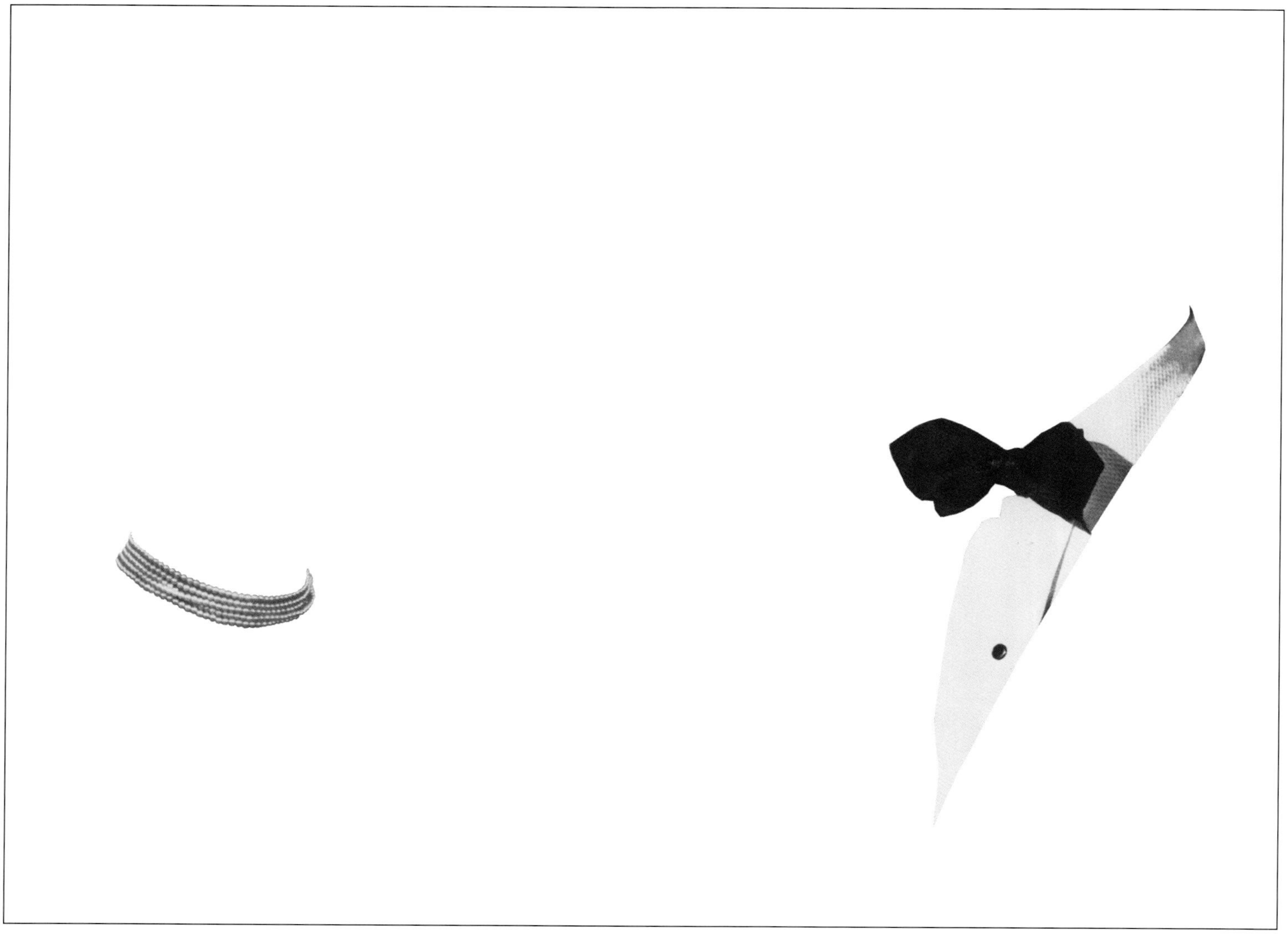

NECKLACE, BOW TIE AND PART OF SHIRT (WITH STUD)

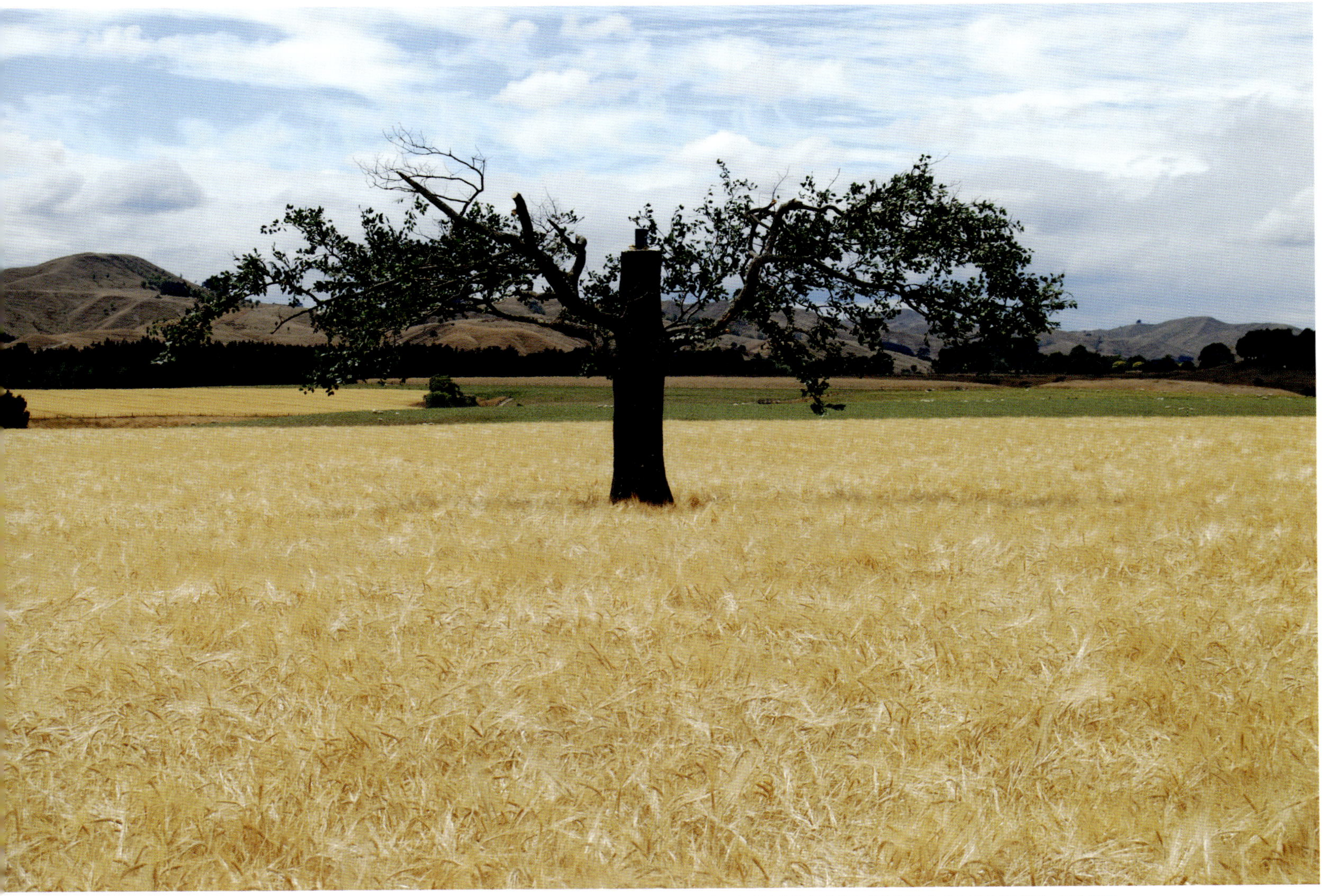

“THE LOVELEY BONES”, DREAMWORKS/PARAMOUNT, 2009

"THE SORCERER'S APPRENTICE", DISNEY ENTERPRISES, 2009

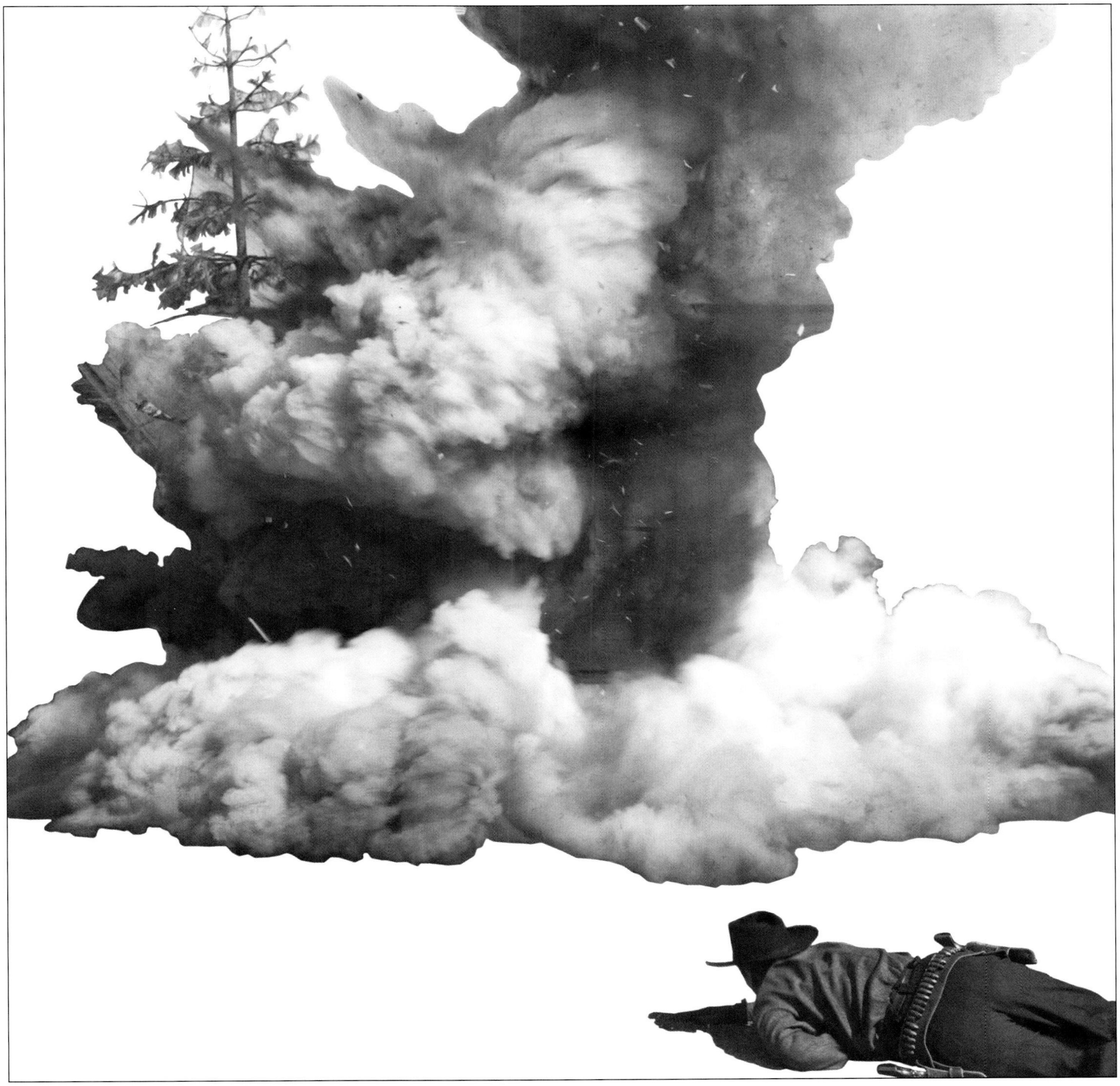

FIRE, TREE, SHADOW AND PERSON

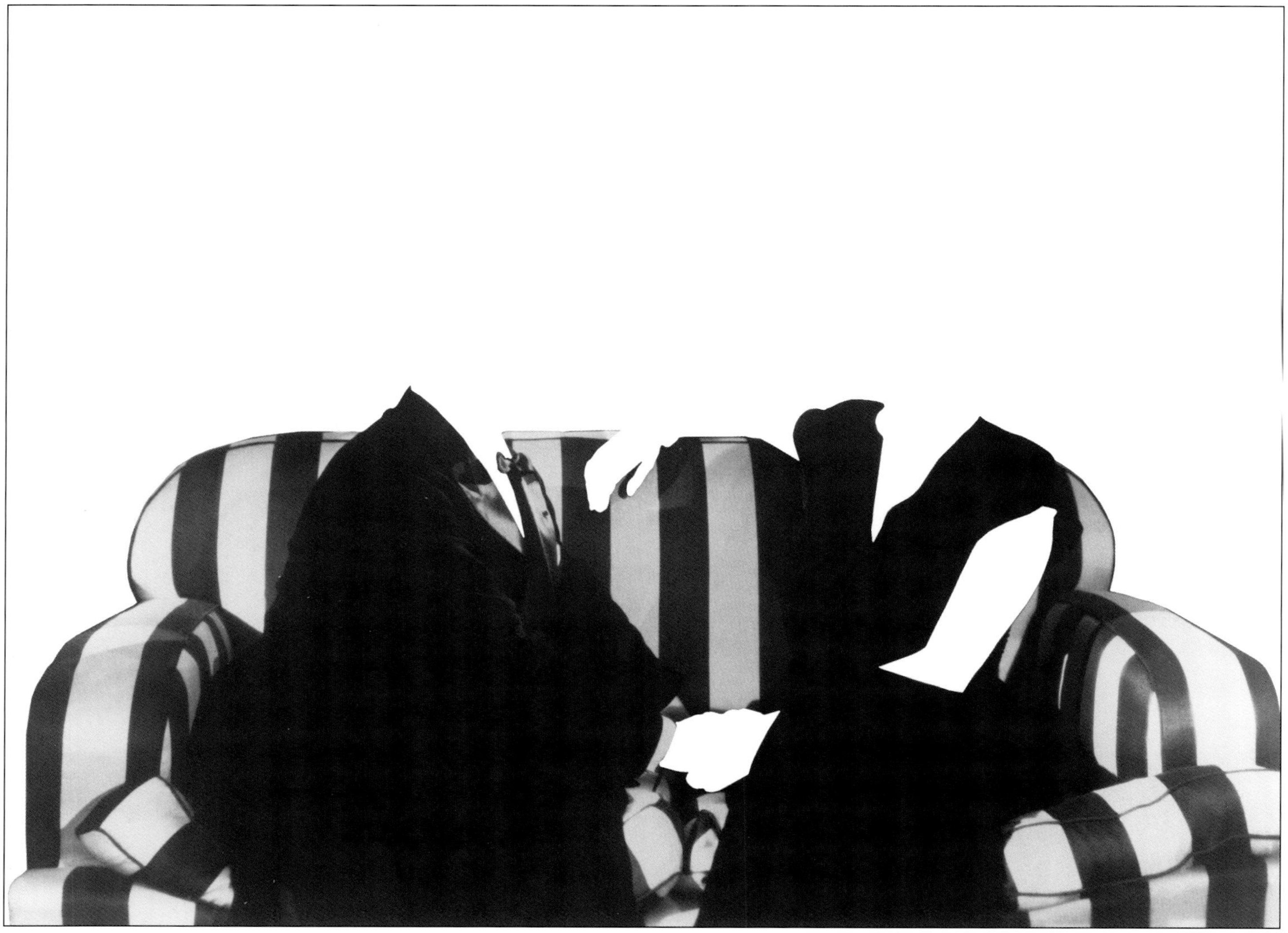

COUCH, SUIT AND DRESS

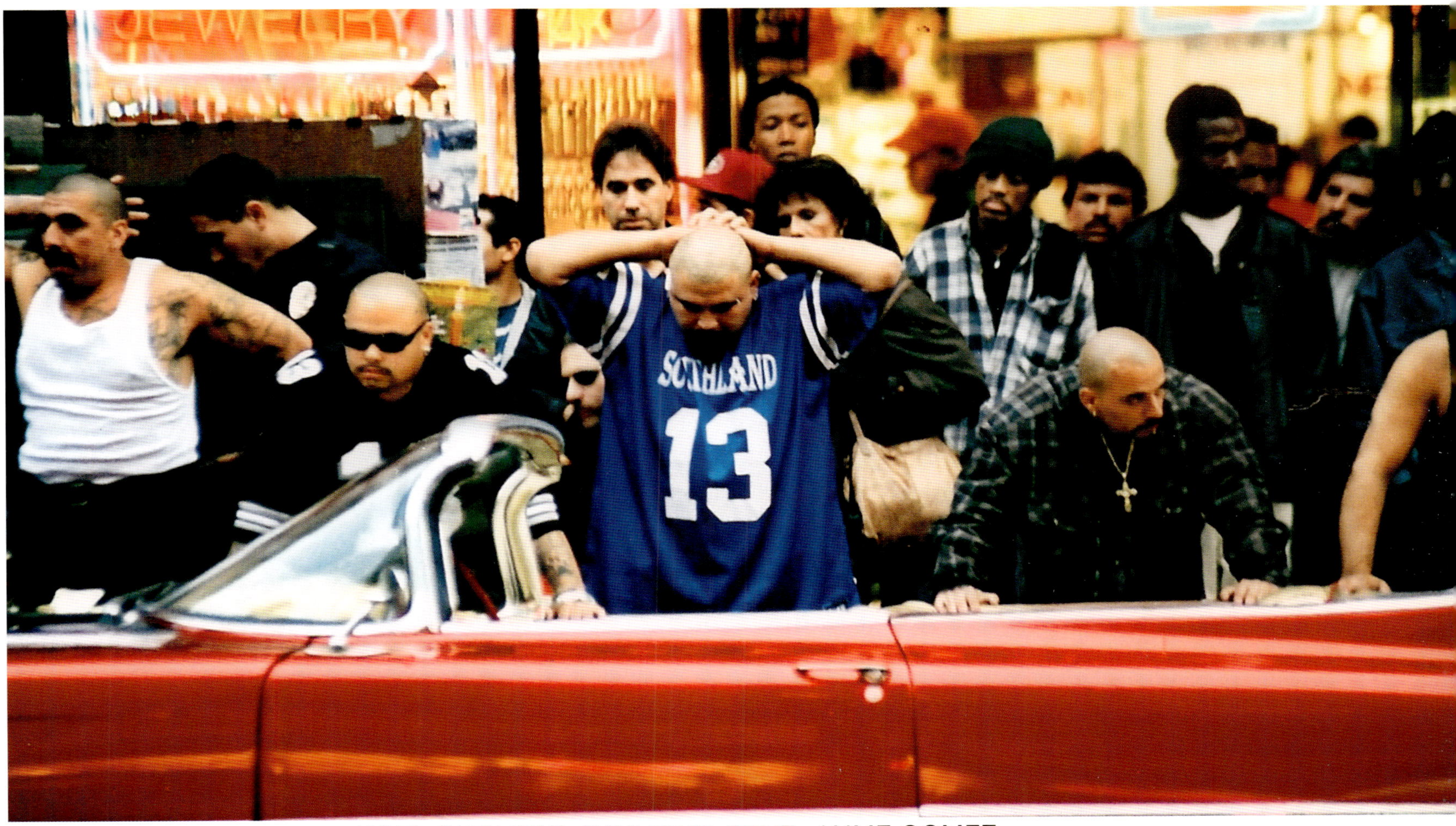


NOEL GUGLIEMI, RAYMOND CRUZ, JAIME GOMEZ,
"TRAINING DAY", WARNER BROTHERS, 2001

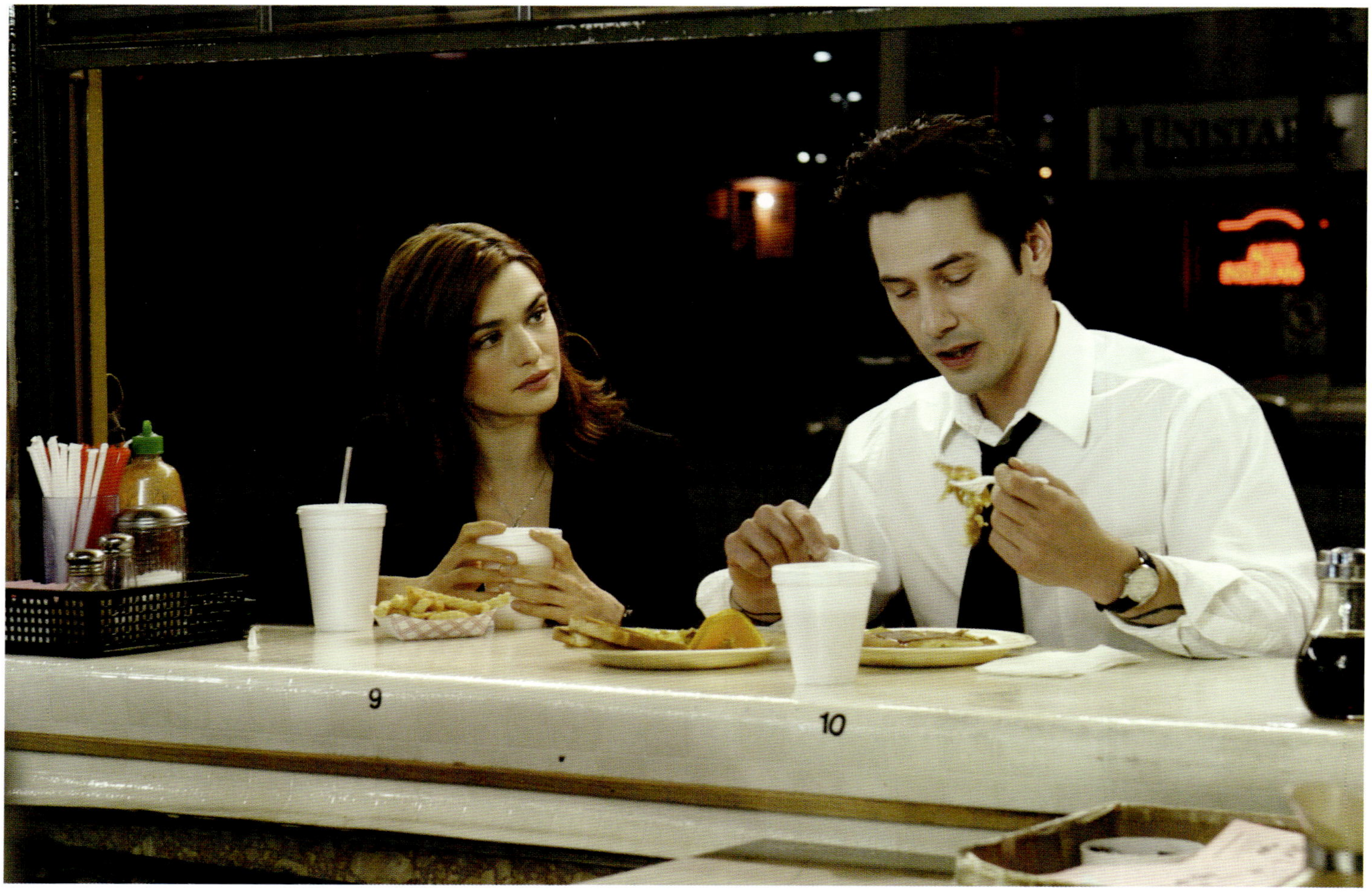

RACHEL WEISZ, KEANU REEVES, “CONSTANTINE”, WARNER BROTHERS, 2005

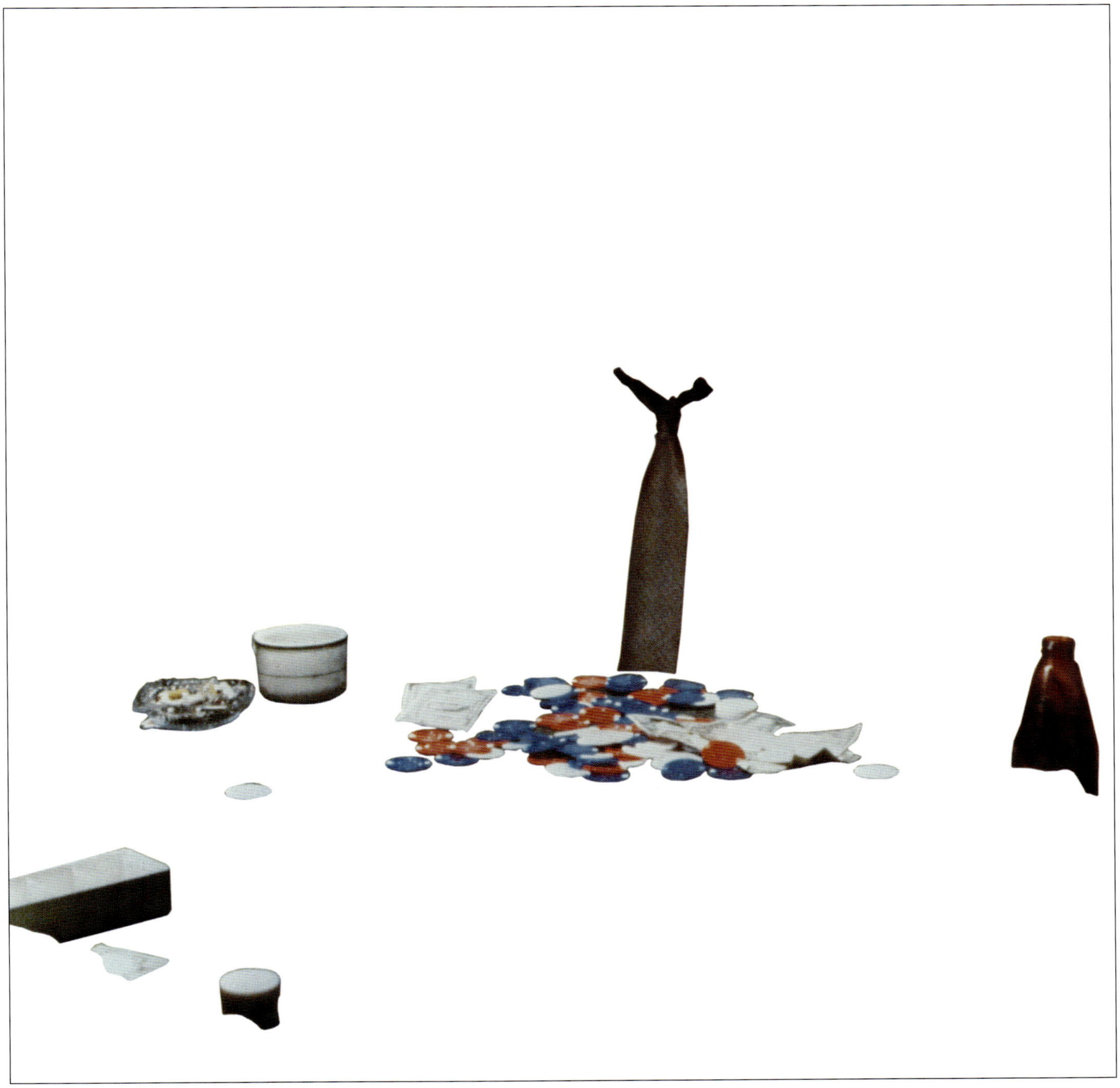

ASHTRAY, CUP, MONEY, POKER CHIPS, NECKTIE AND BOTTLE

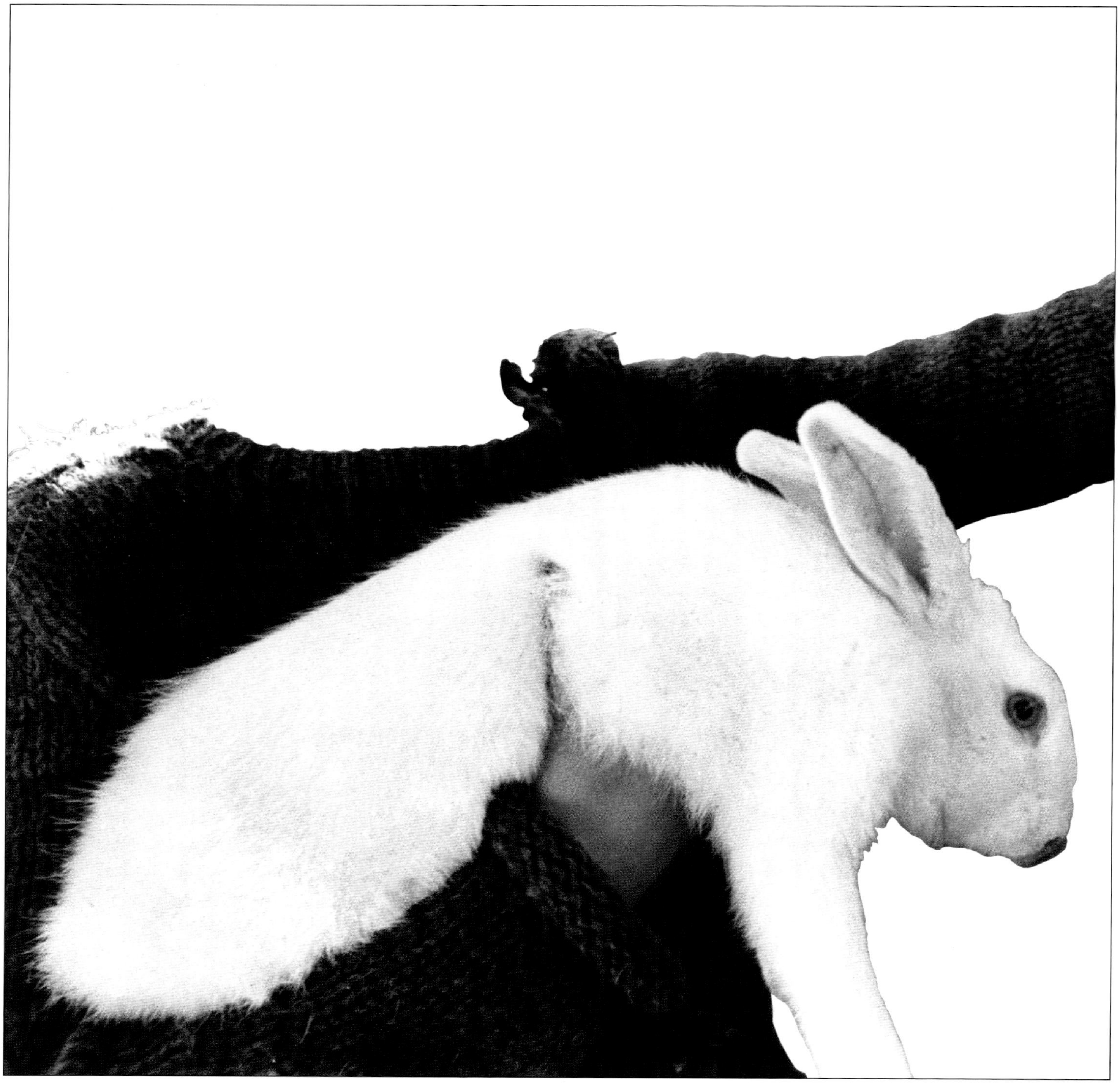

SWEATER AND RABBIT

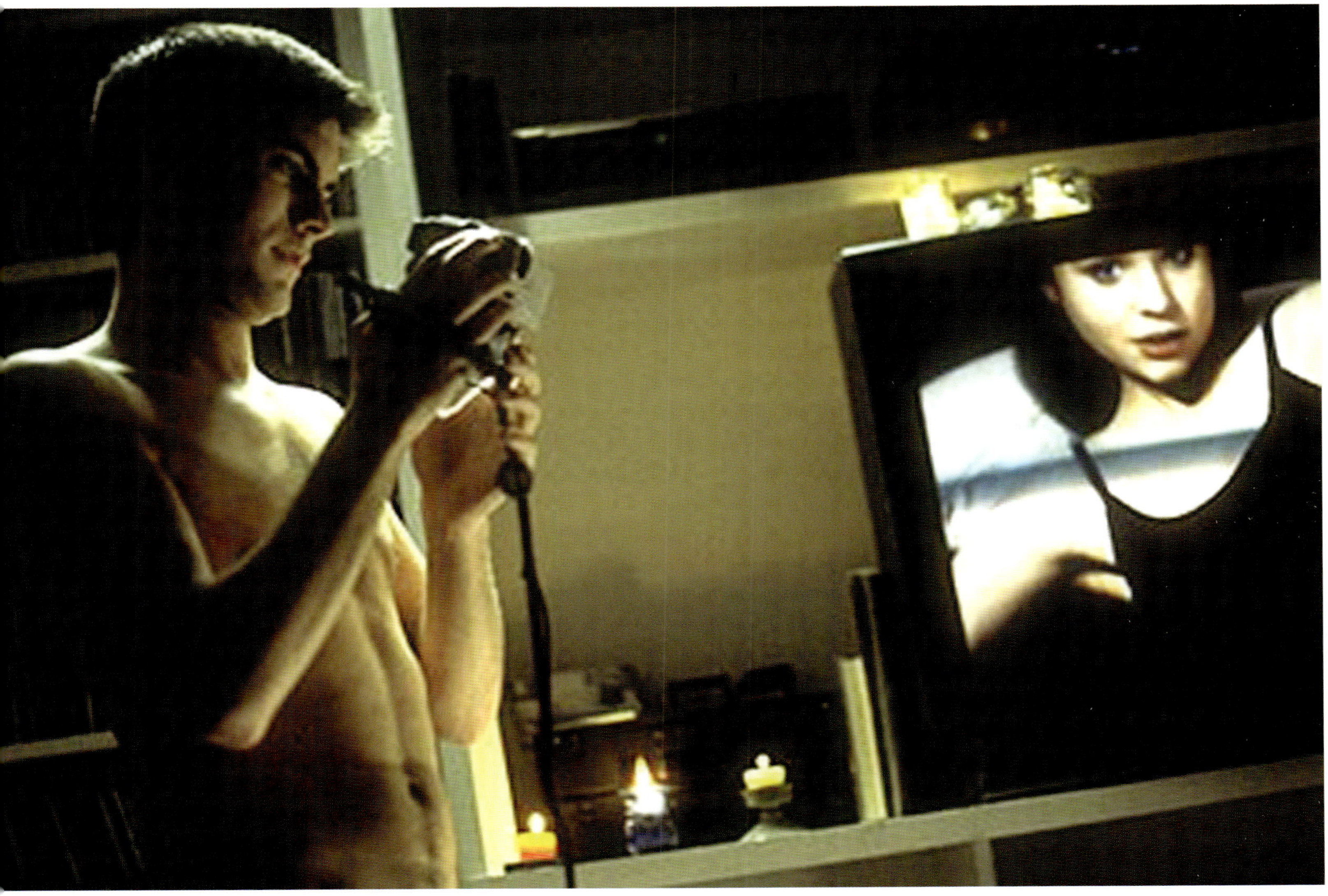

WES BENTLEY, THORA BIRCH, “AMERICAN BEAUTY”,
DREAMWORKS/PARAMOUNT, 1999

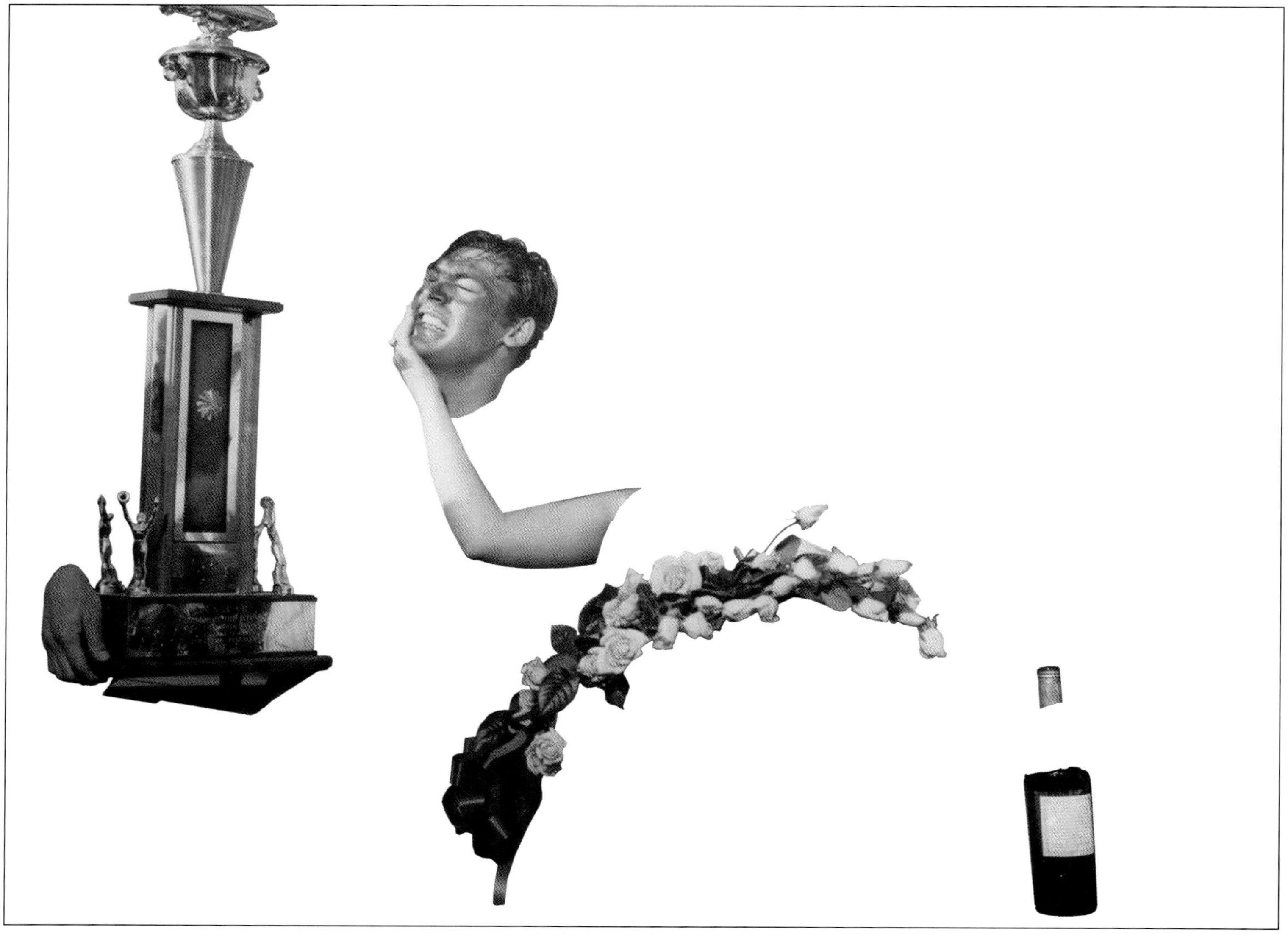

TROPHY, HEAD, ARM, GARLAND AND BOTTLE

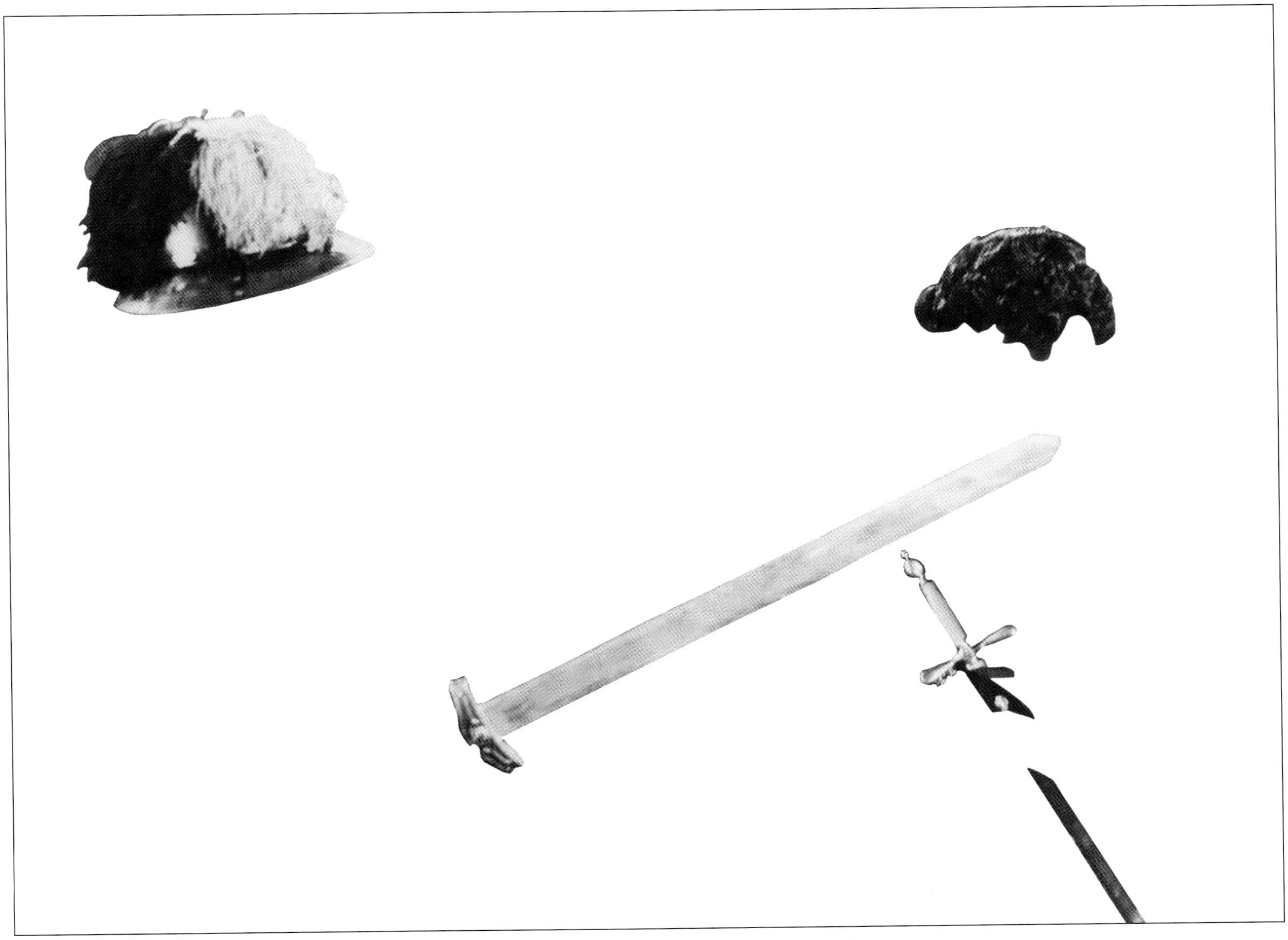

HELMET, SWORDS AND HAIR

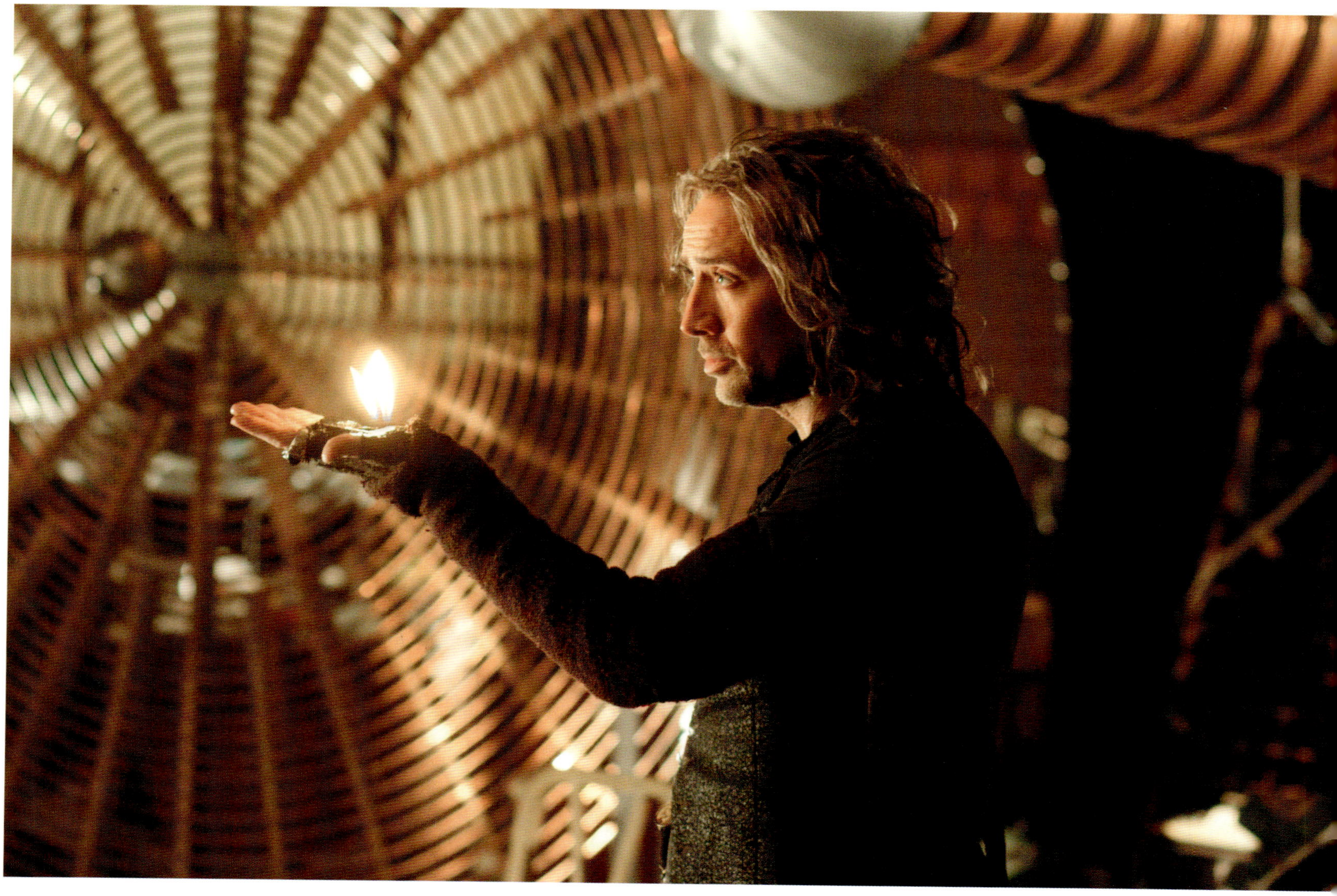

NICOLAS CAGE, “THE SORCERER’S APPRENTICE,” DISNEY ENTERPRISES, 2009

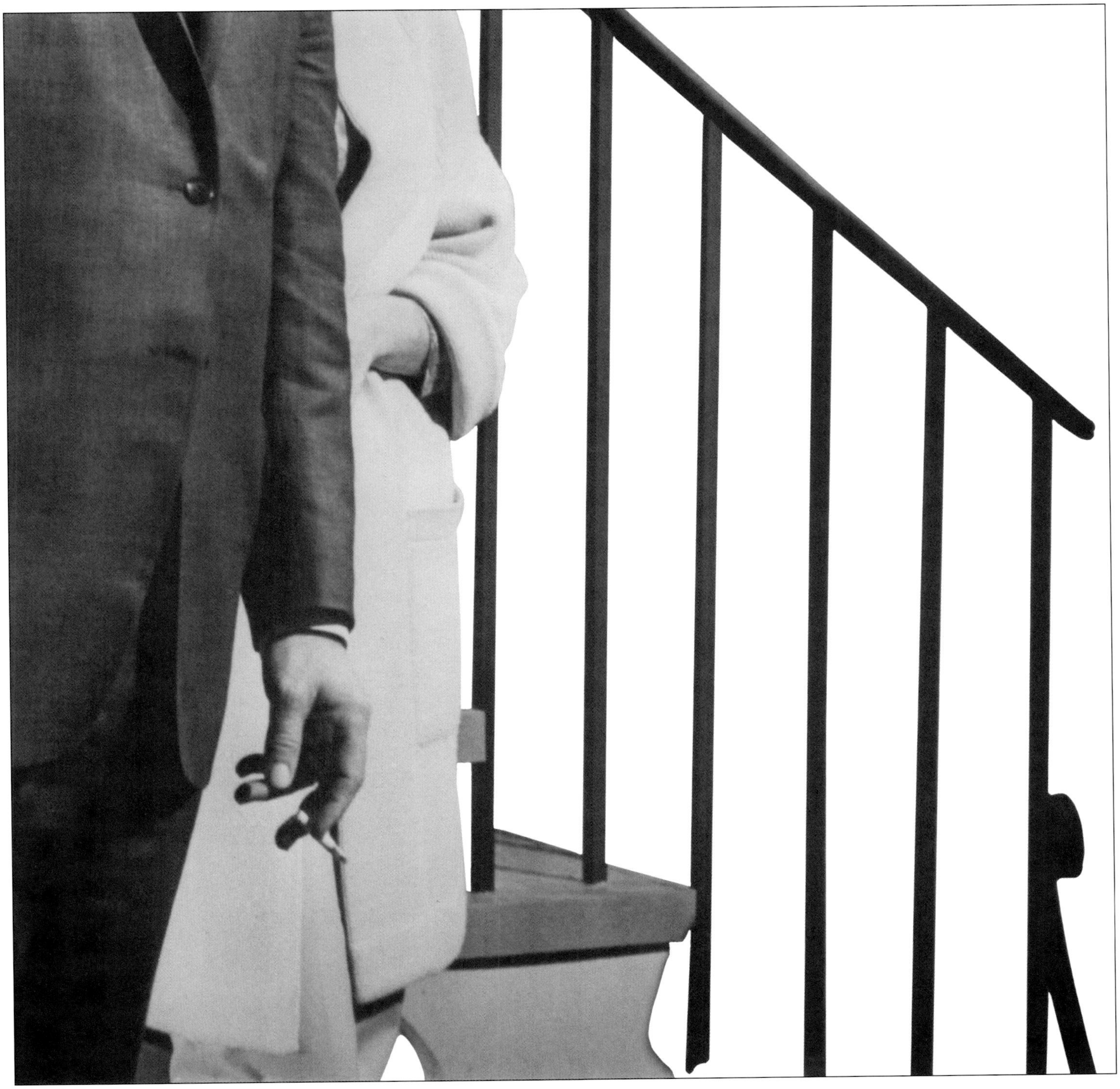

PERSONS, CIGARETTE AND STAIRWAY

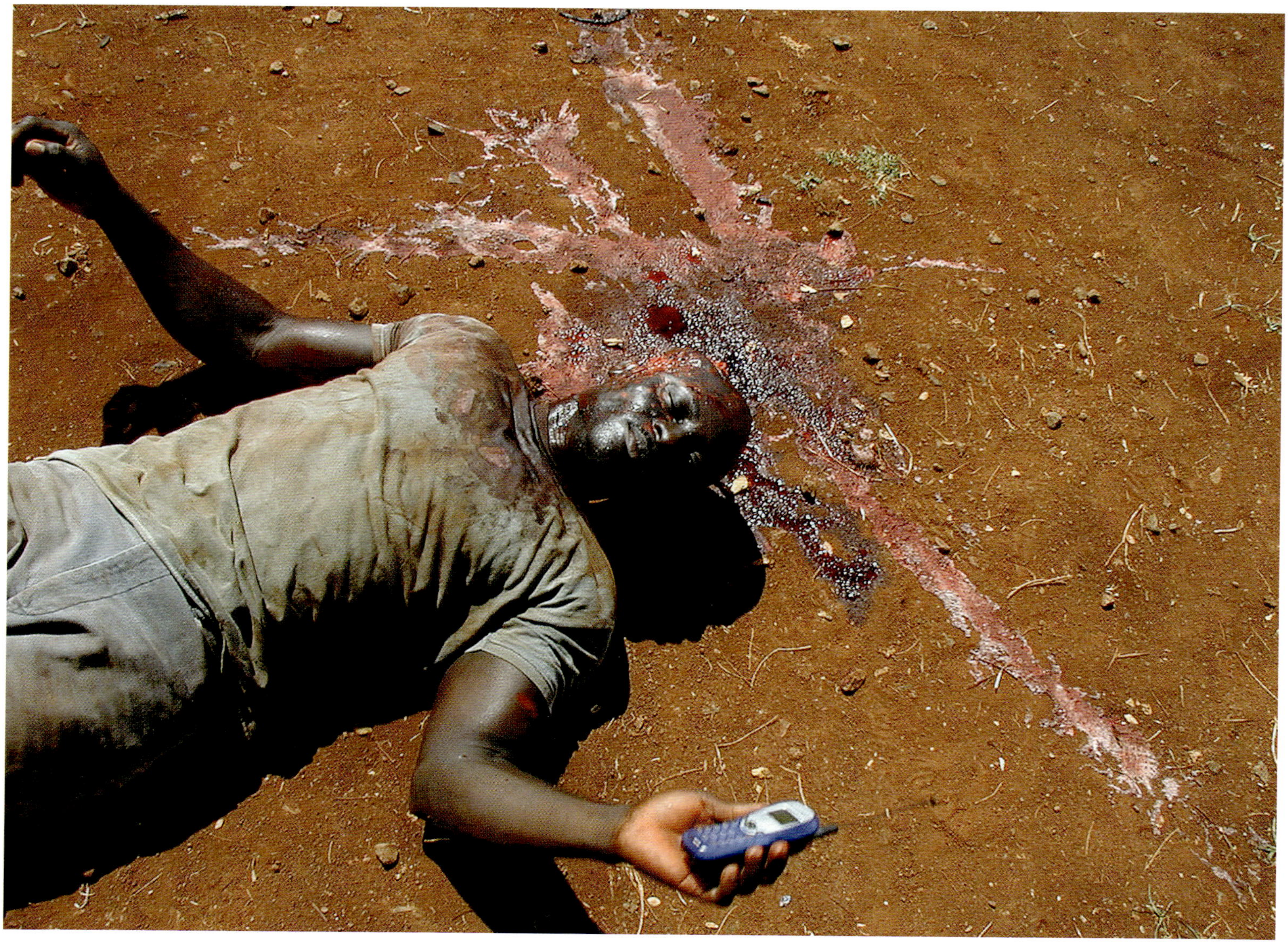

DEAD BODY, “TEARS OF THE SUN”, SONY/TRISTAR, 2003

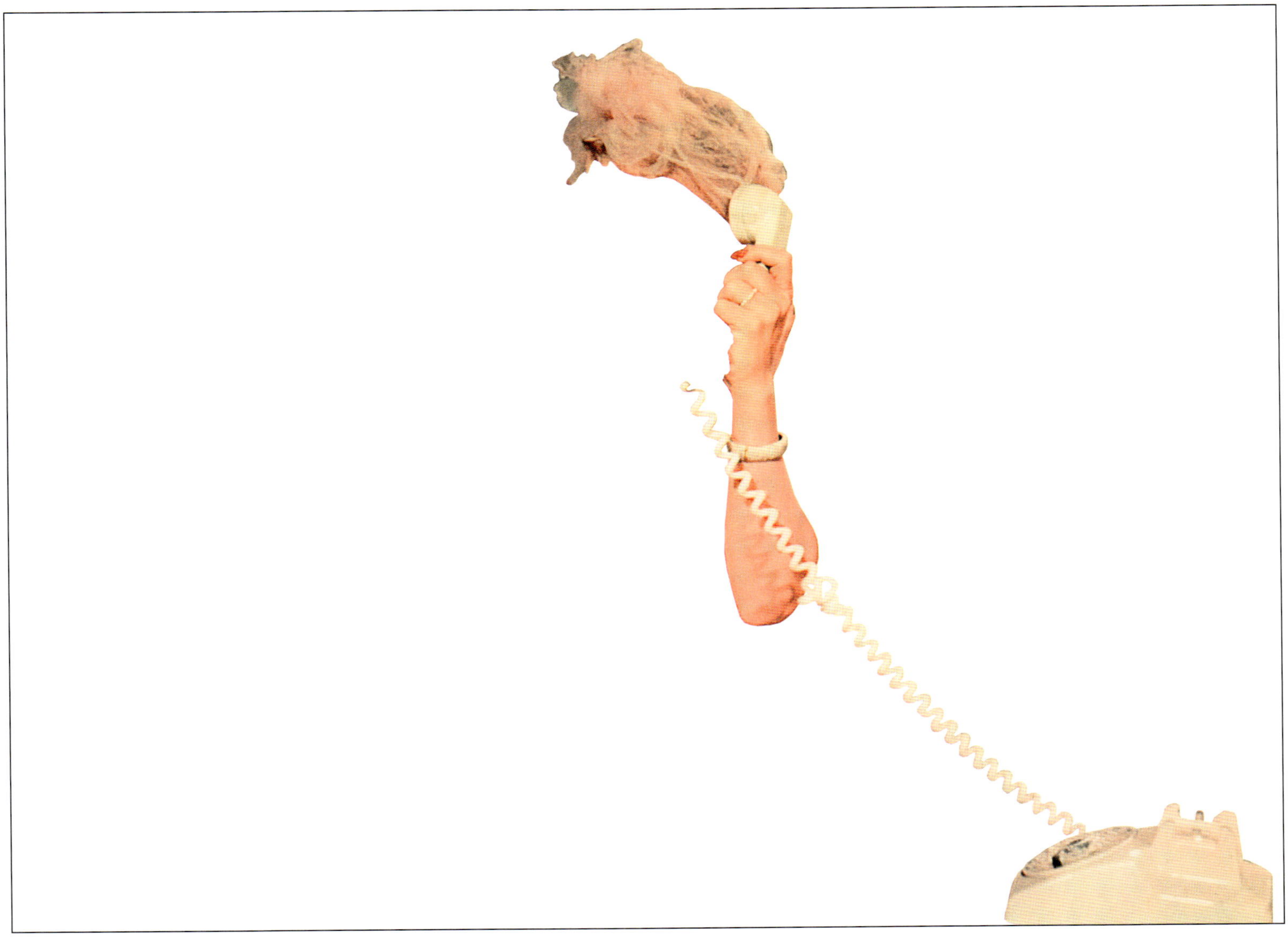

SNOOD, PHONE AND ARM

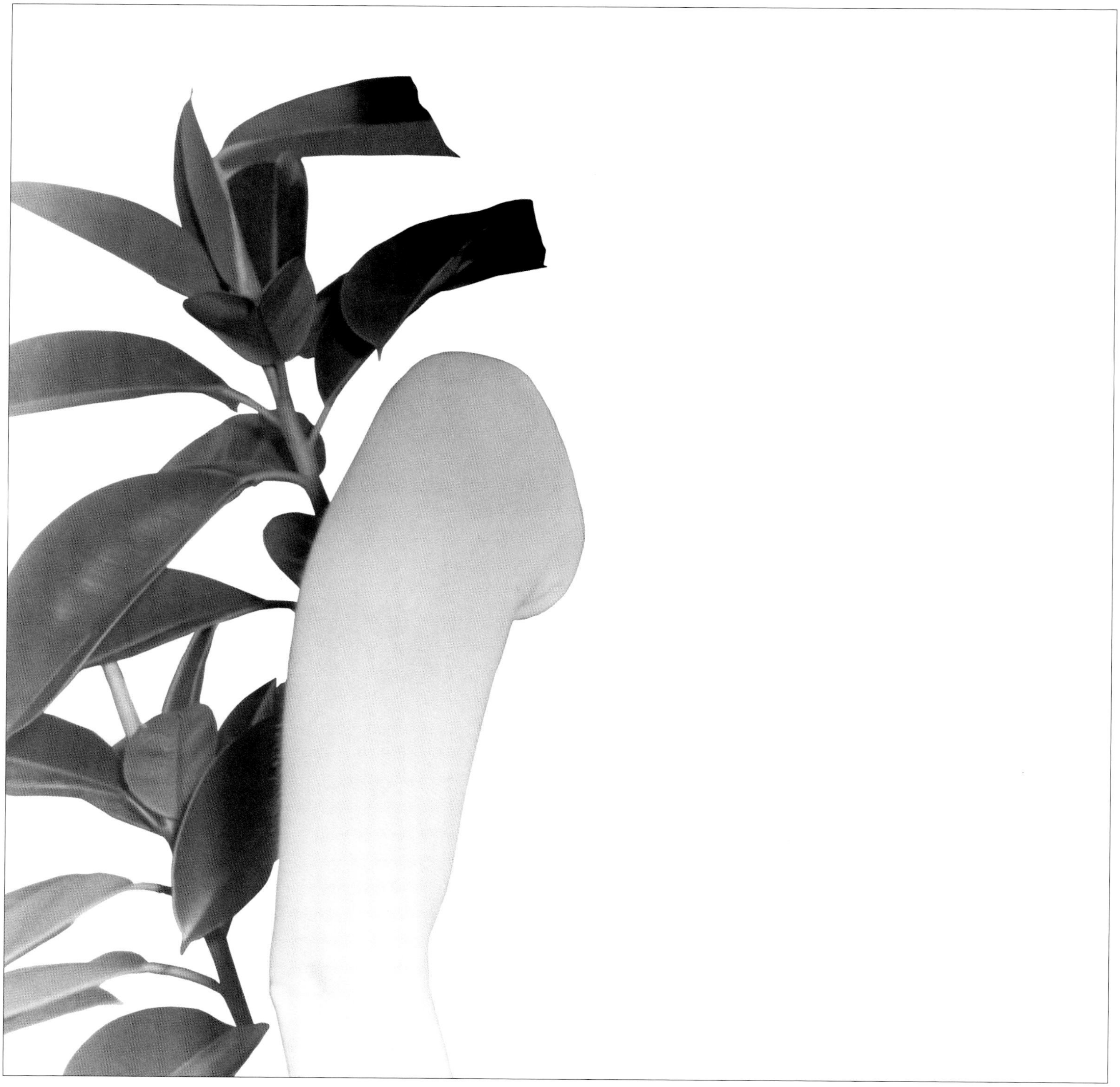

PLANT AND ARM

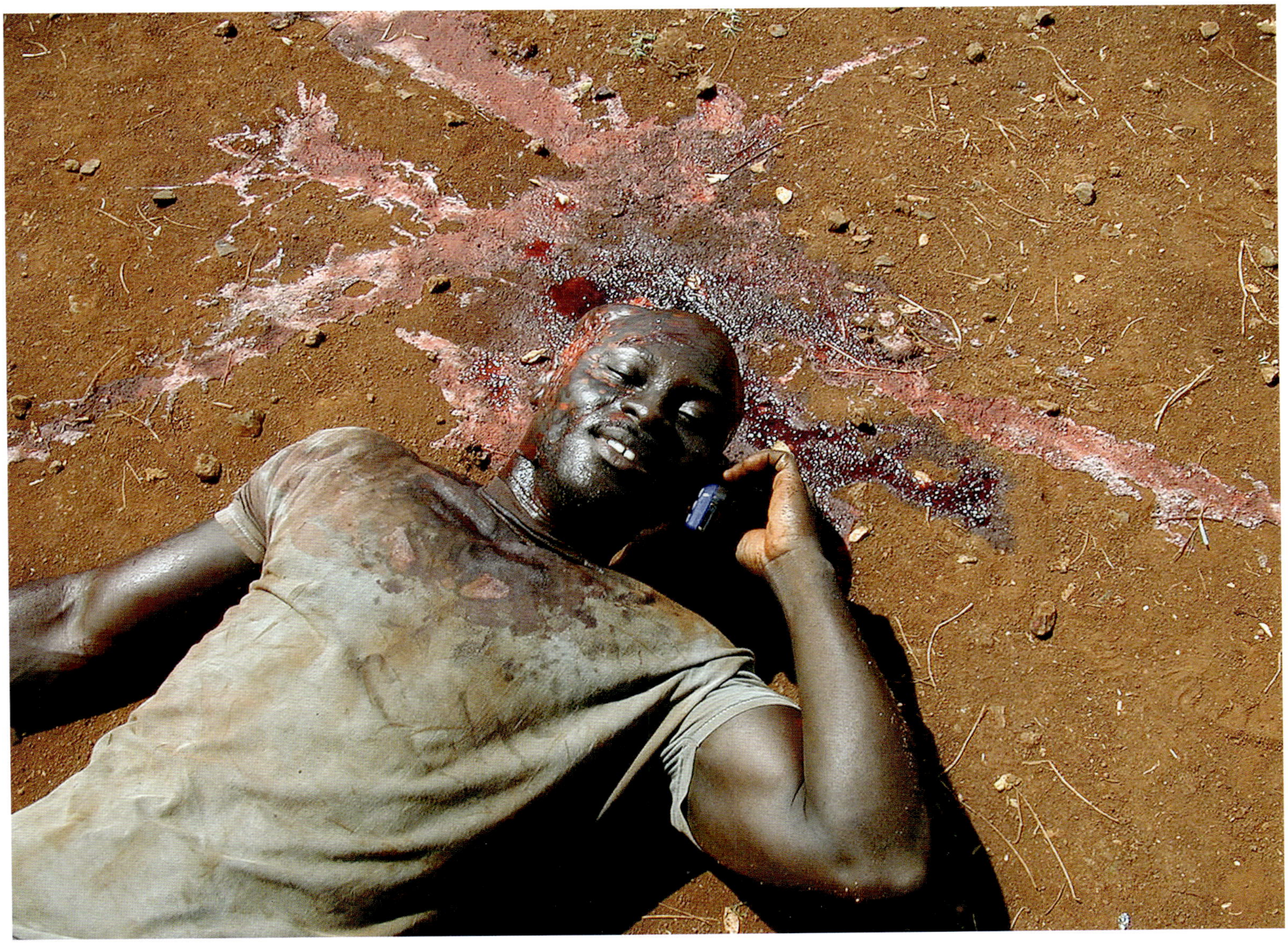

DEAD BODY, “TEARS OF THE SUN”, SONY/TRISTAR, 2003

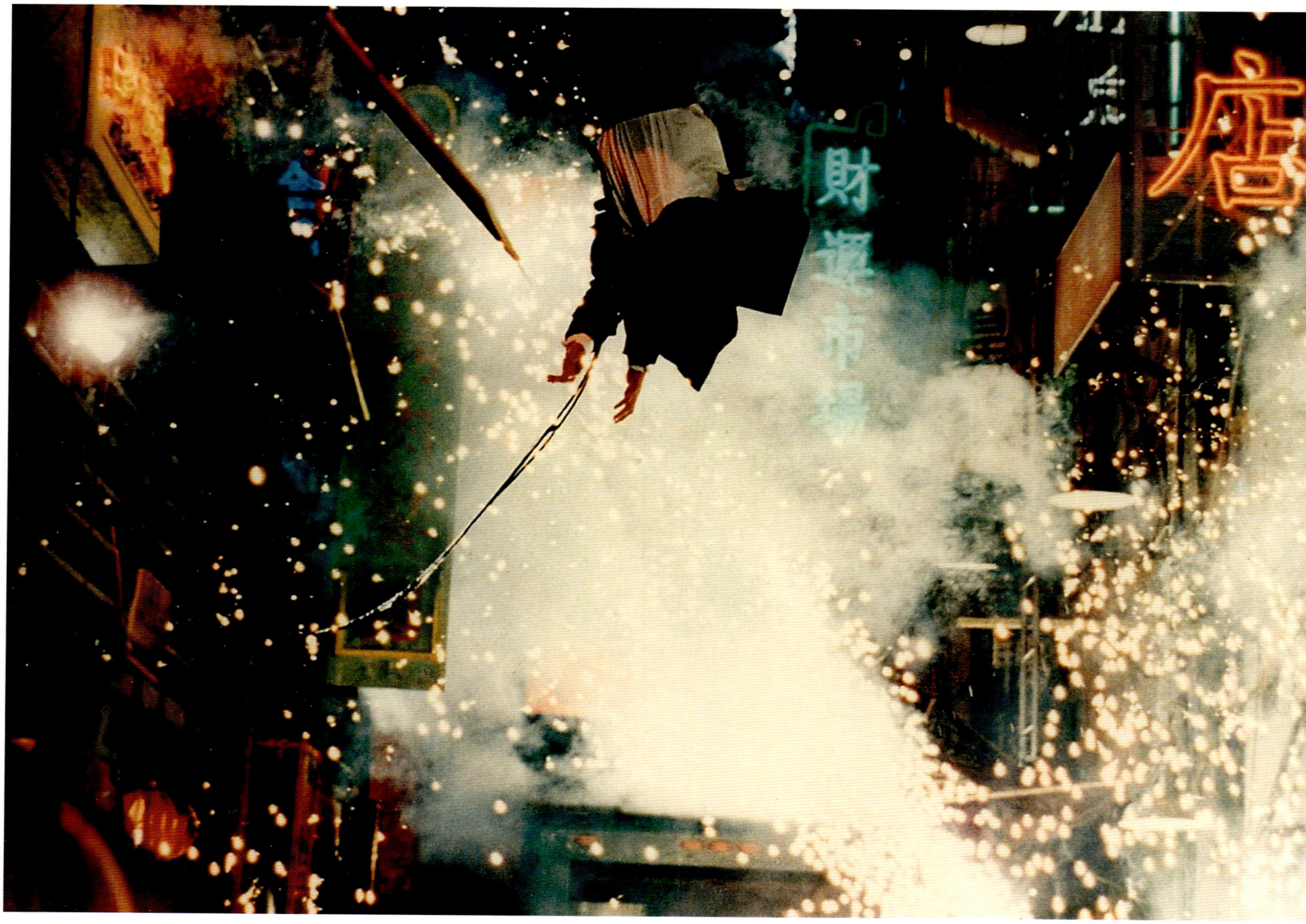


"THE REPLACEMENT KILLERS", SONY/TRISTAR, 1998

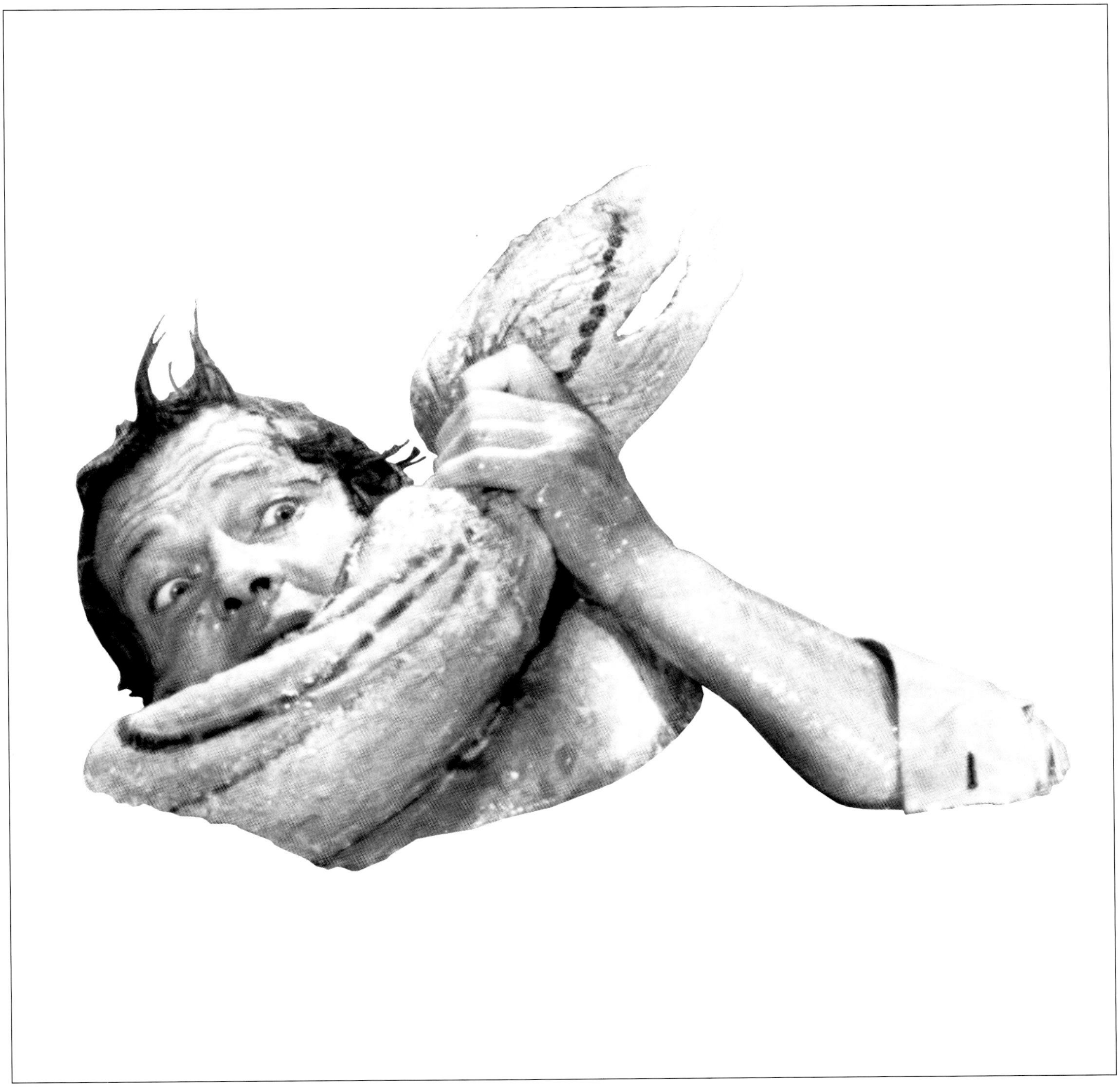

PERSON AND SERPENT

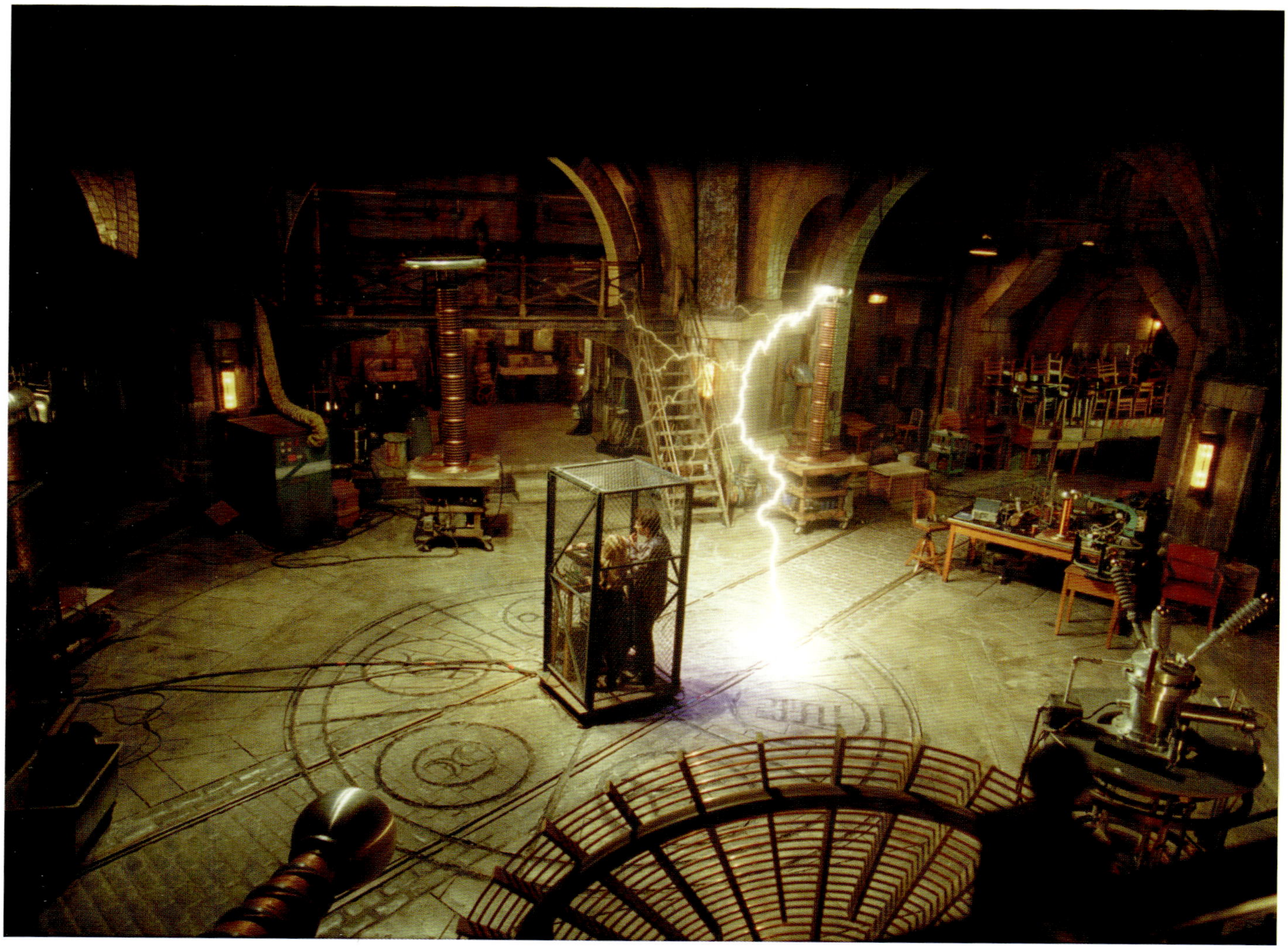

“THE SORCERER’S APPRENTICE”, DISNEY ENTERPRISES, 2009

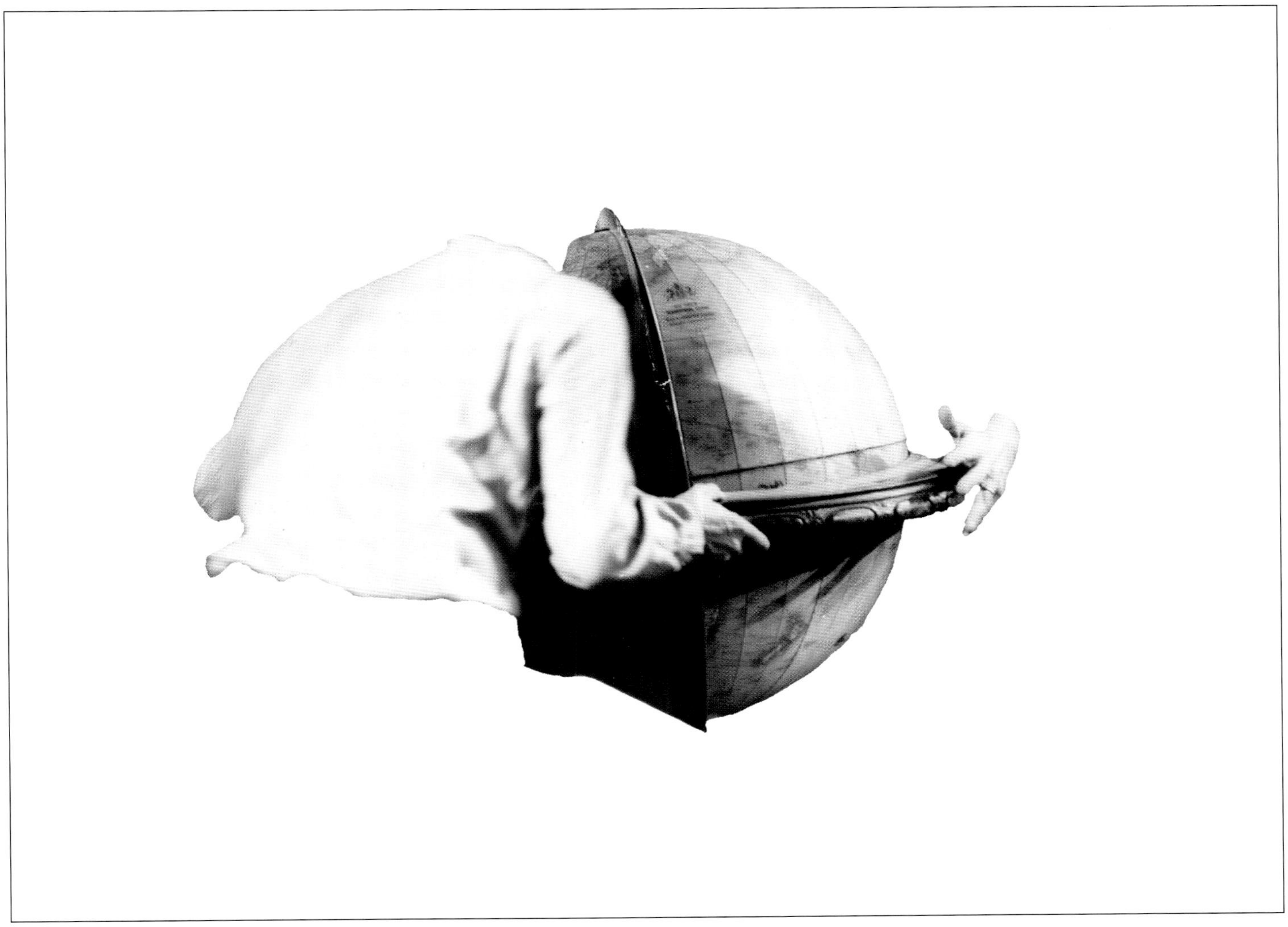

PERSON, GLOBE AND HAND

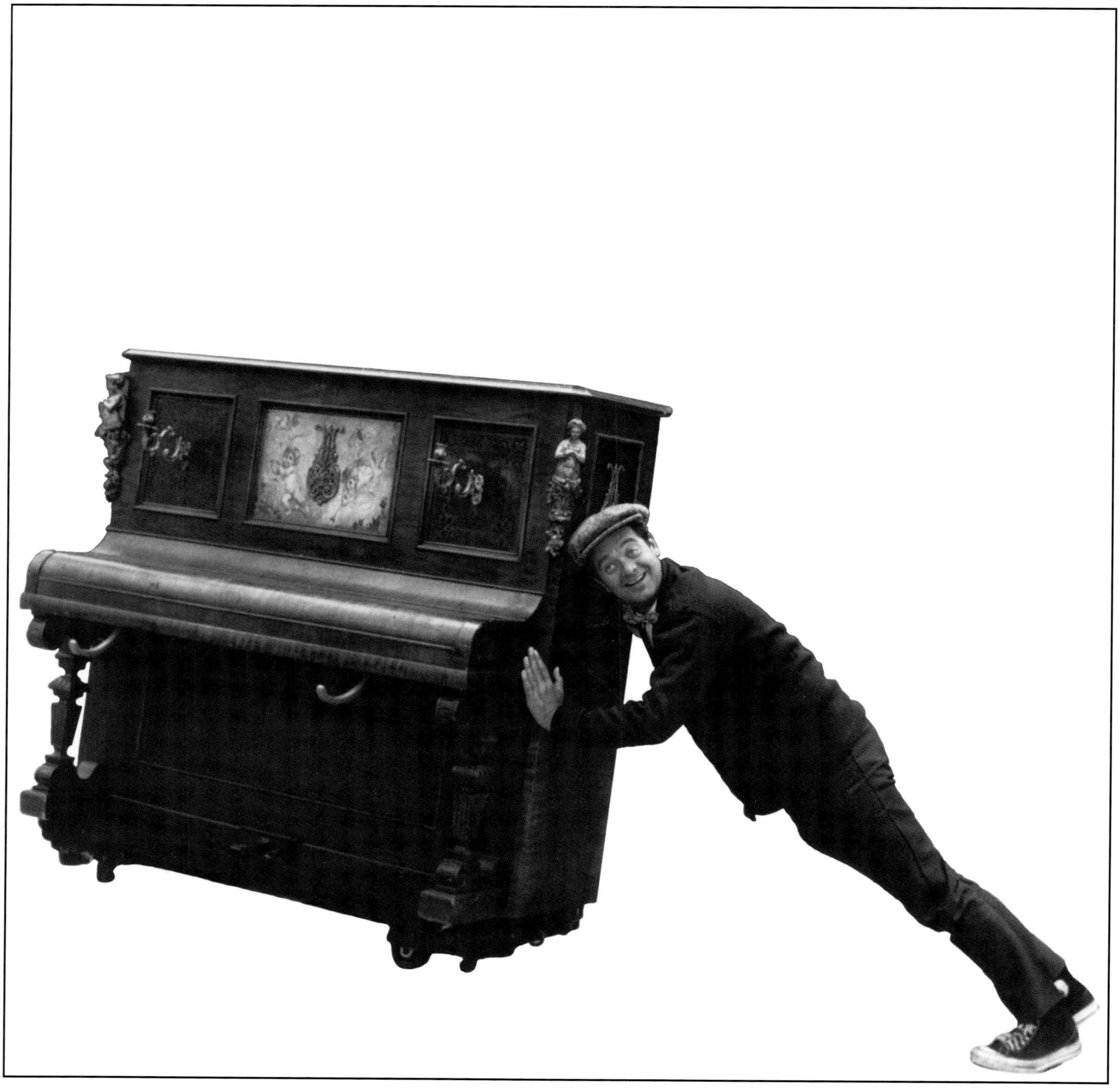

PIANO AND PERSON

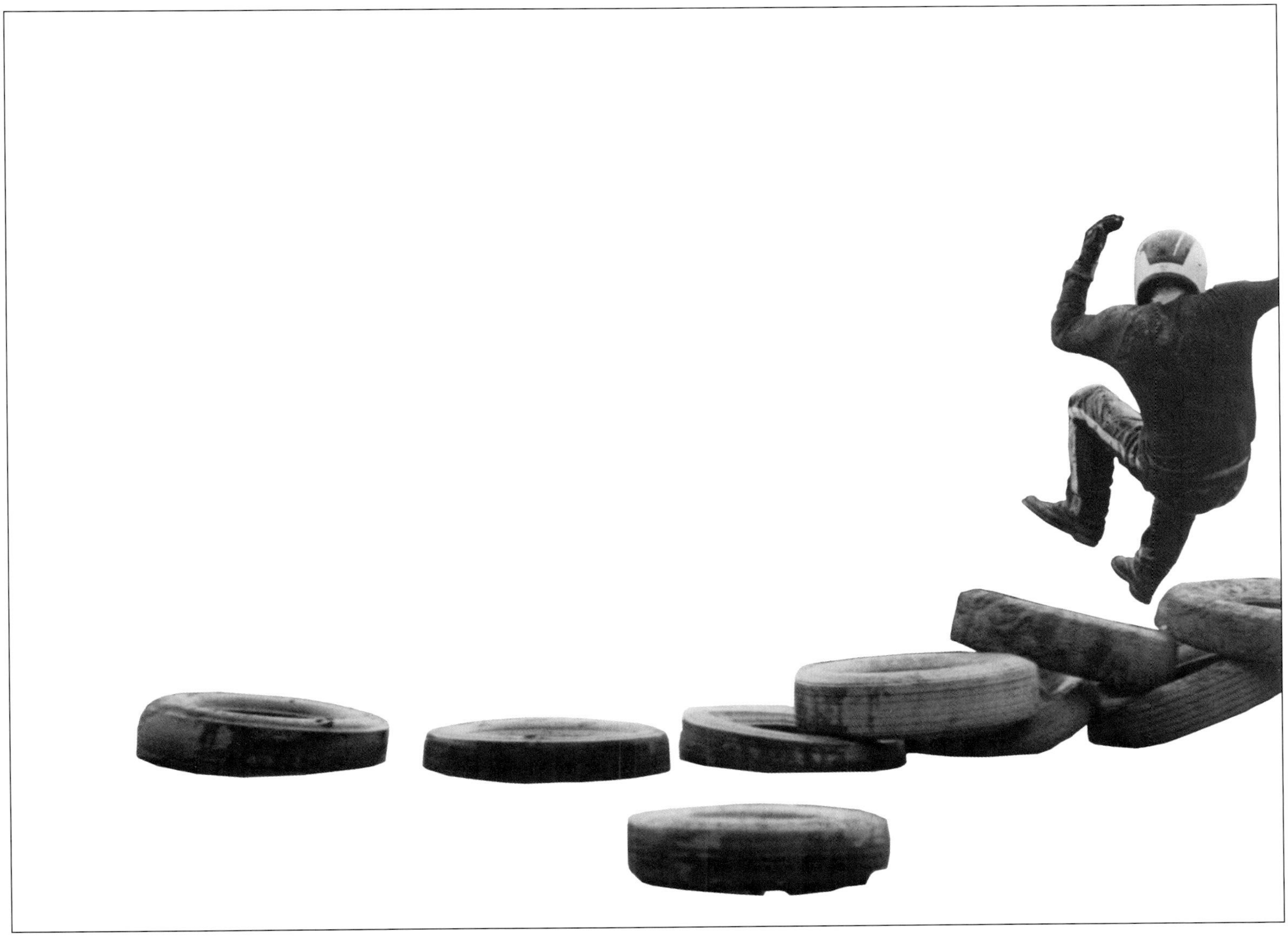

TIRES AND PERSON

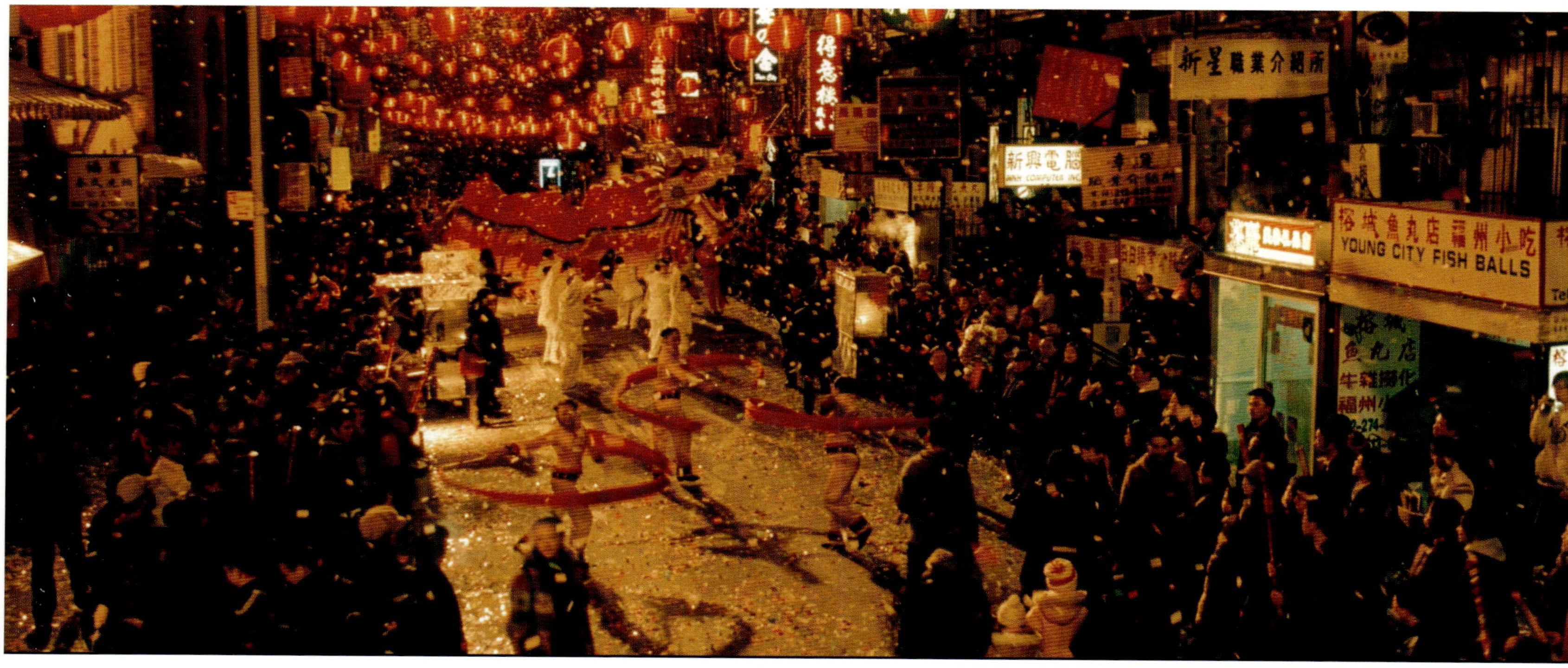


"THE SORCERER'S APPRENTICE", DISNEY ENTERPRISES 2009

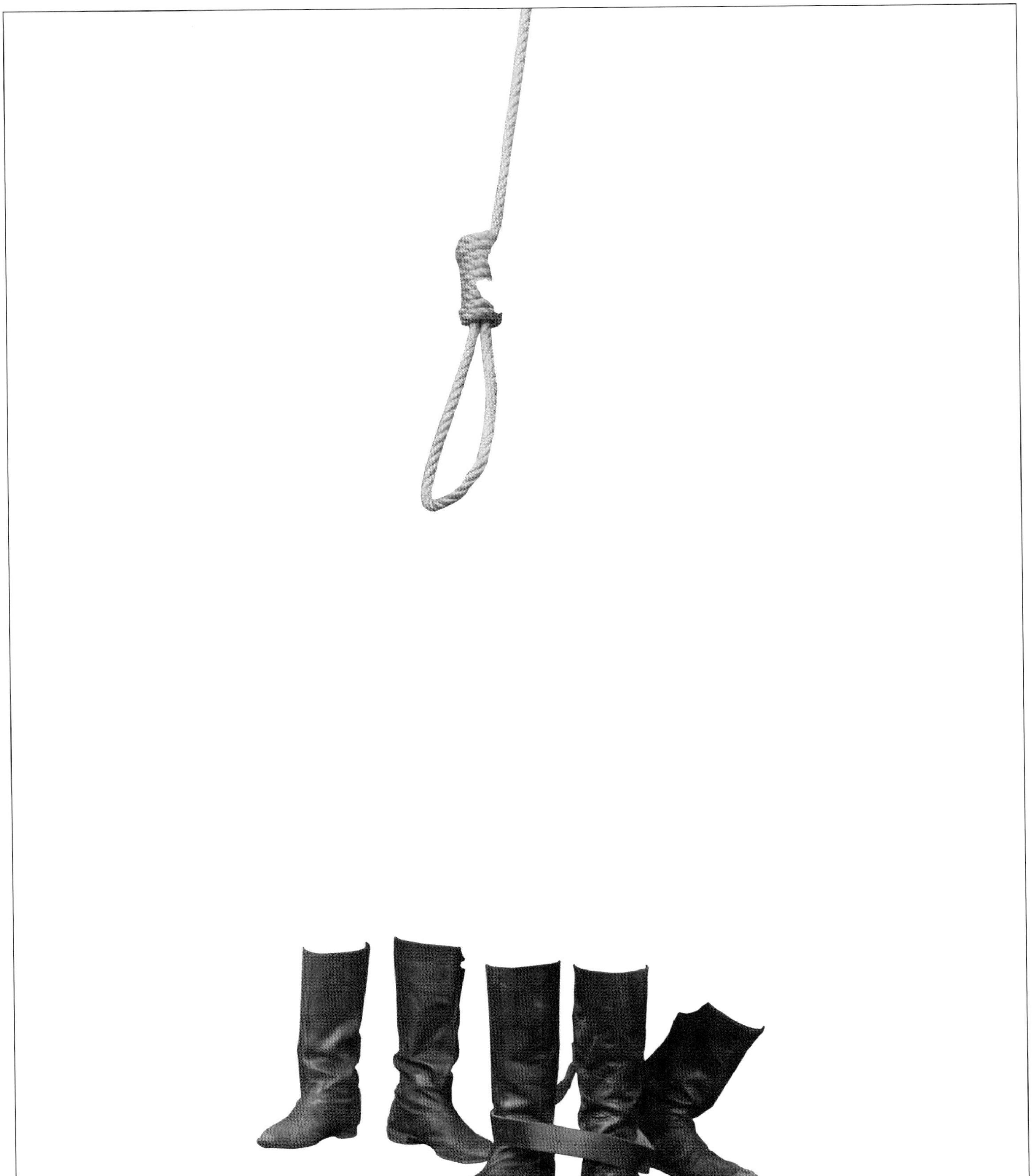

BOOTS, NOOSE AND BELT

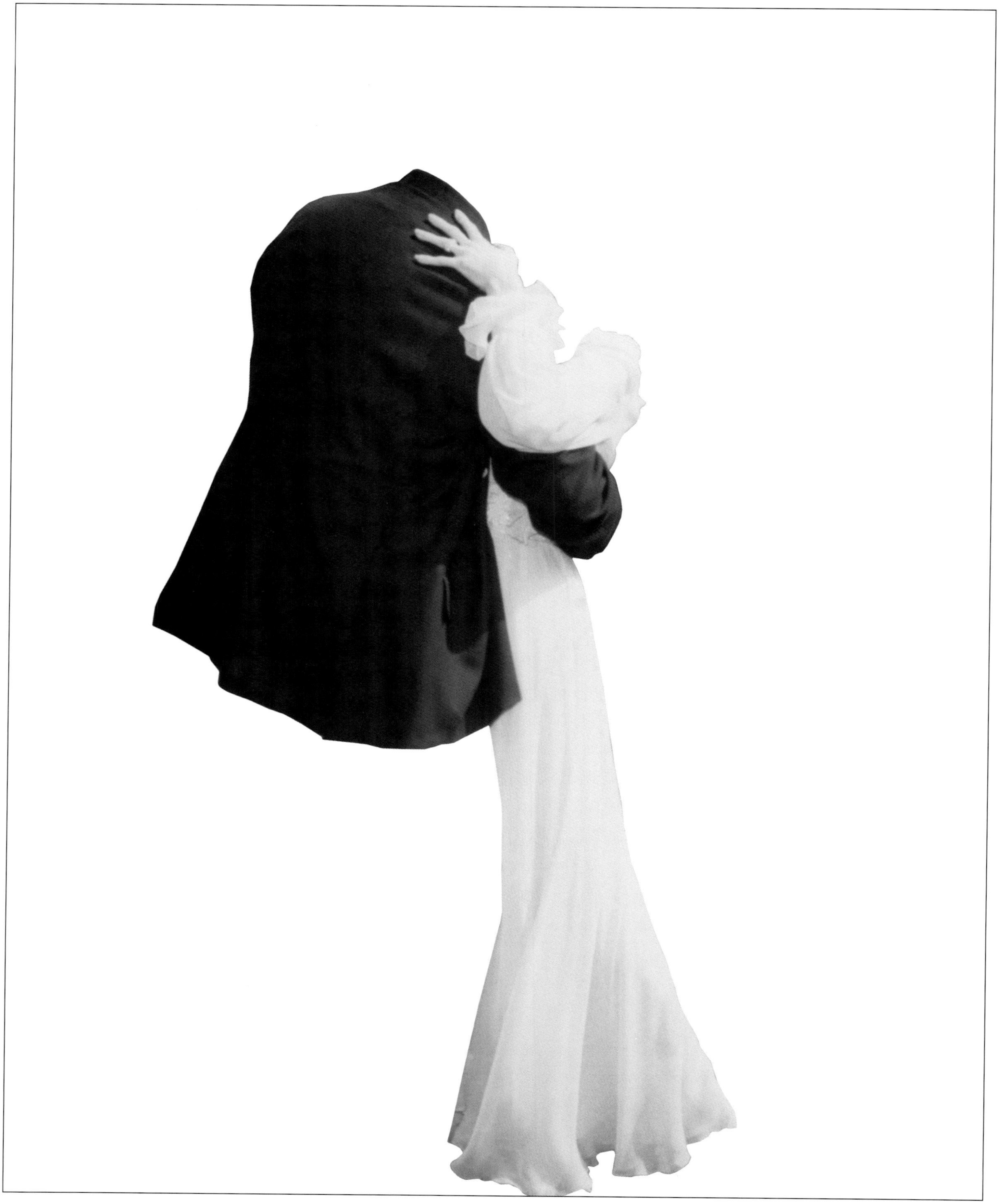

JACKET, DRESS AND HAND

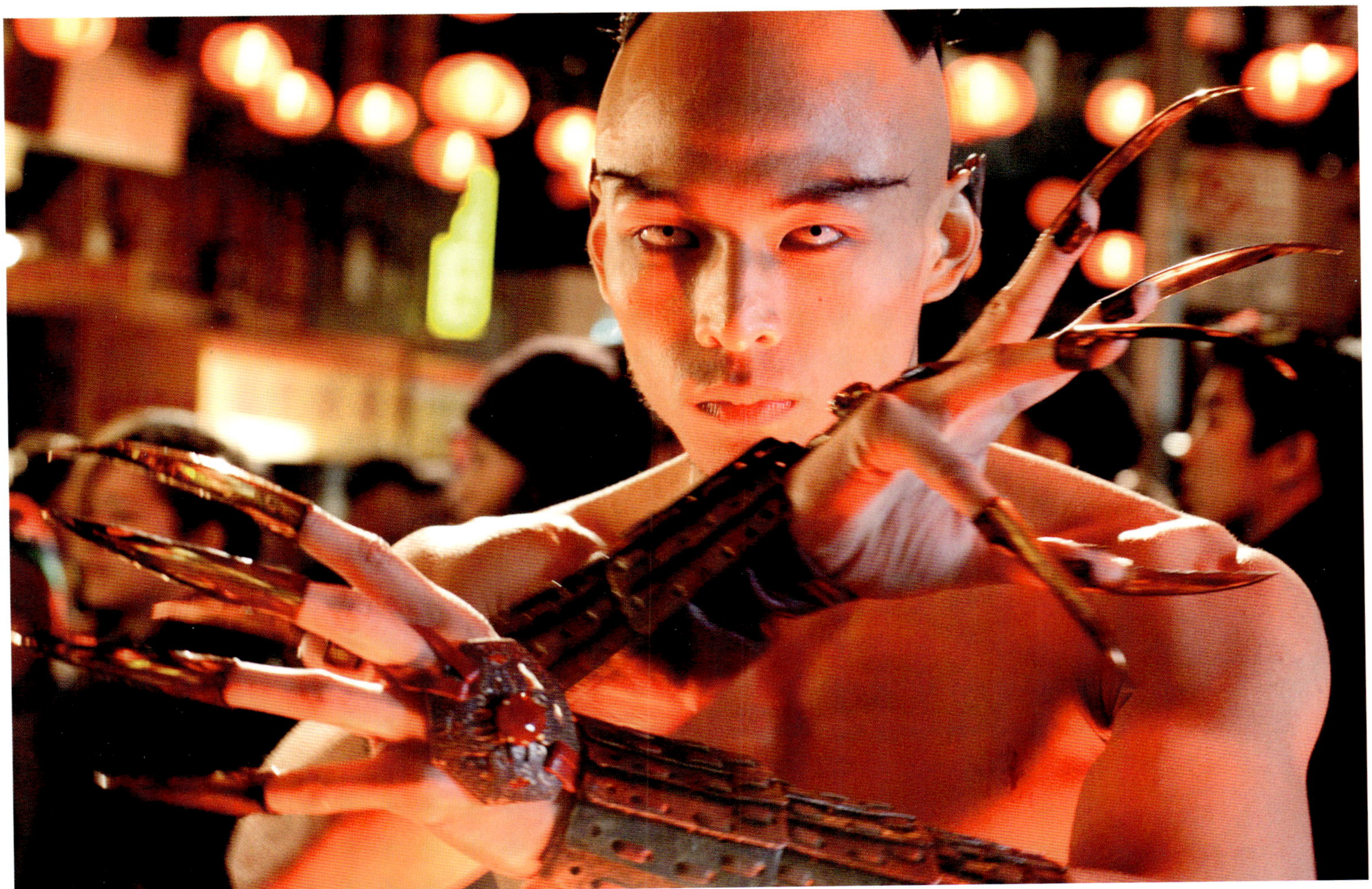

GREGORY WOO, “THE SORCERER’S APPRENTICE”, DISNEY ENTERPRISES, 2009

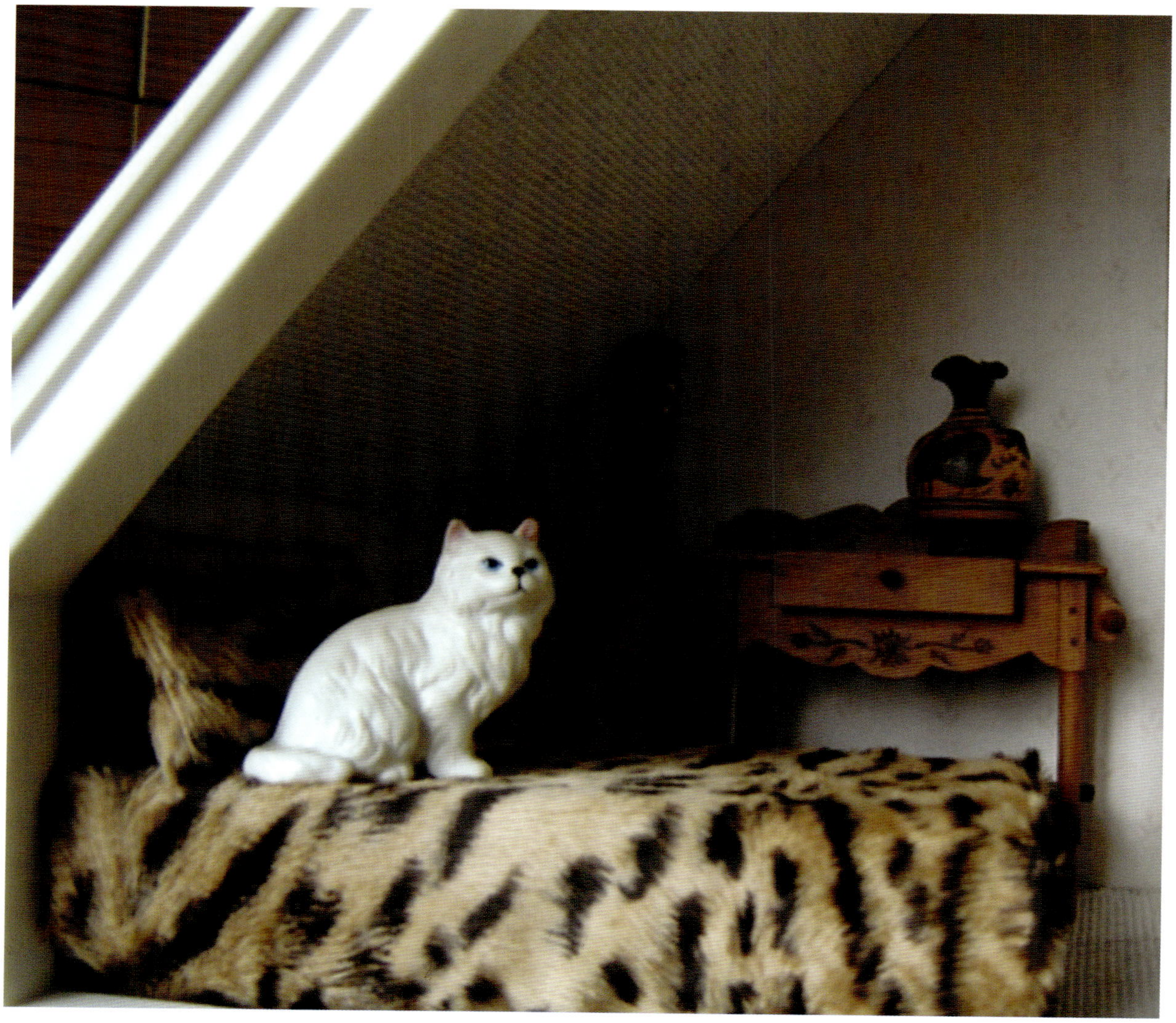

“THE LOVELEY BONES”, DREAMWORKS/PARAMOUNT, 2009

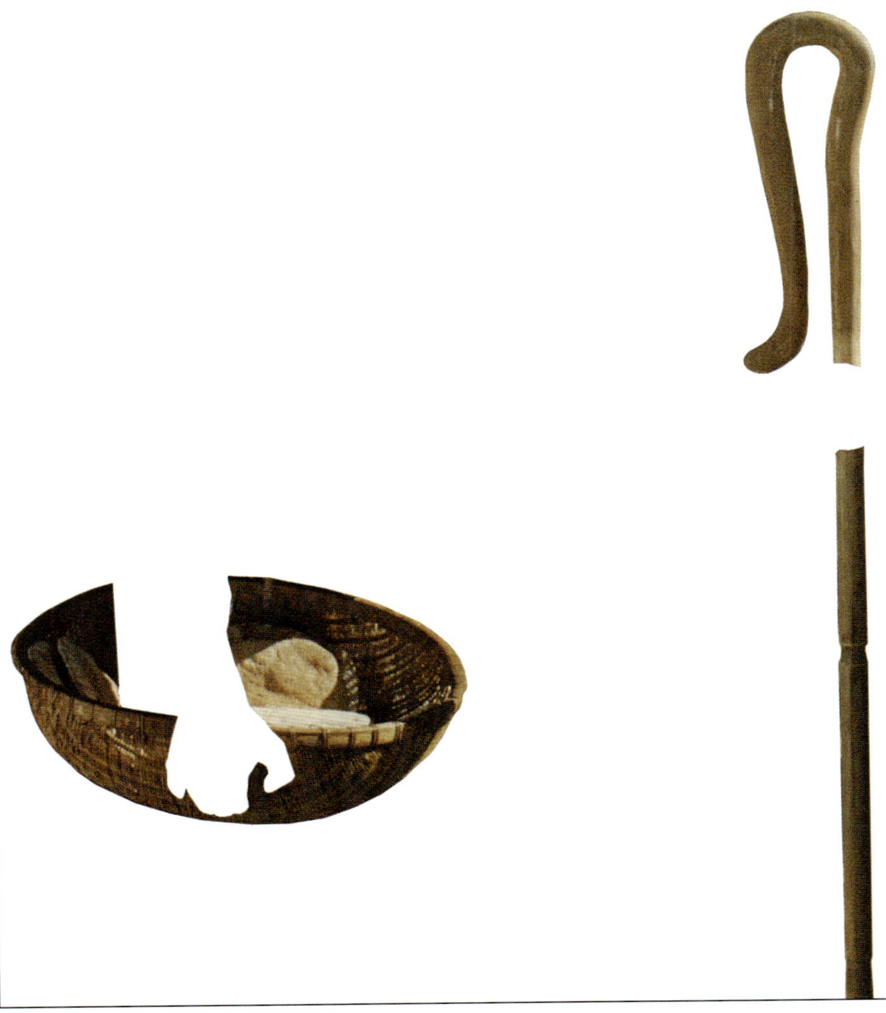

BASKET, BREAD AND SHEPHERD'S STAFF

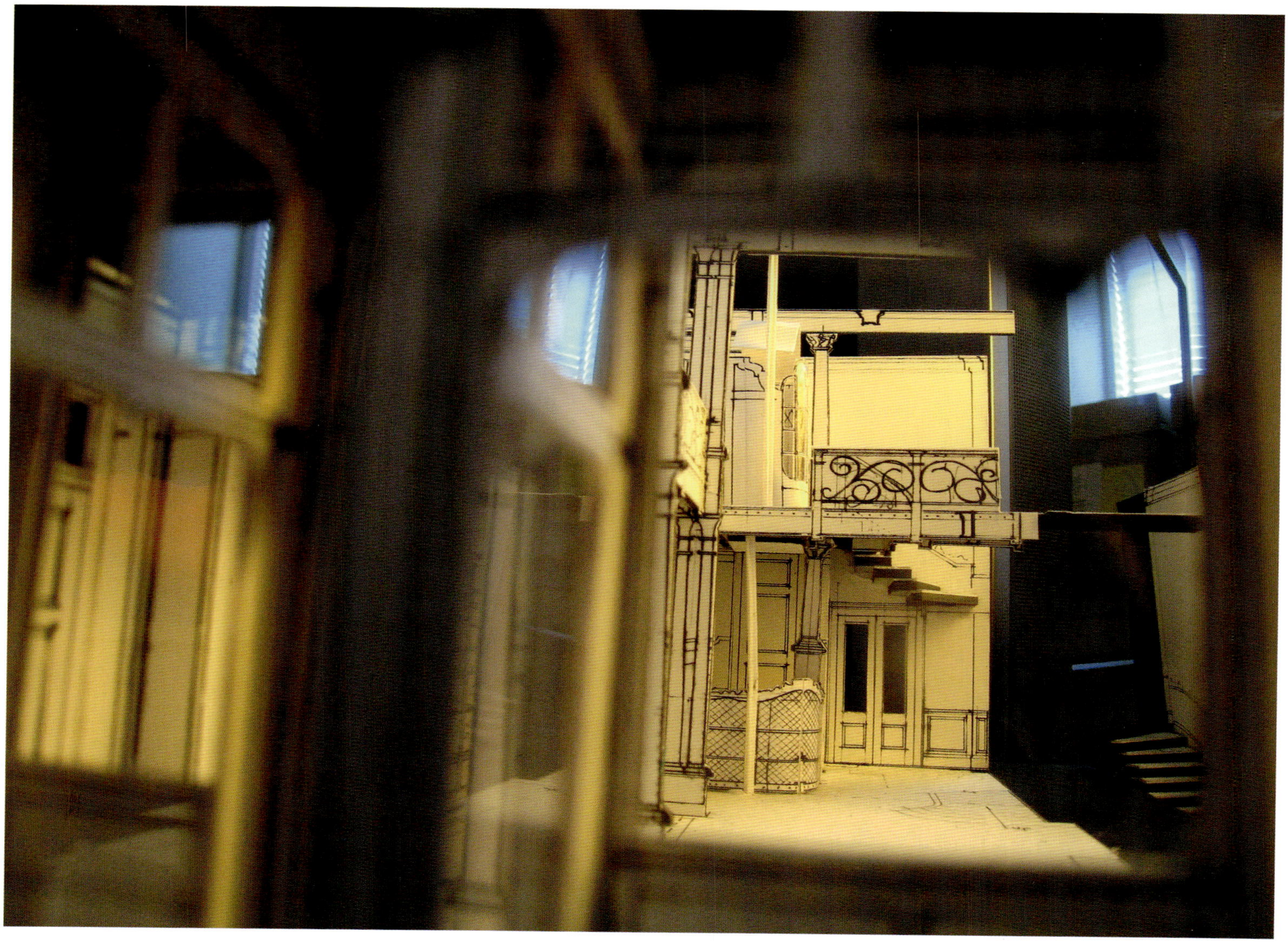

MISCELLANEOUS SET MODEL, “THE SORCERER’S APPRENTICE”, DISNEY ENTERPRISES, 2009

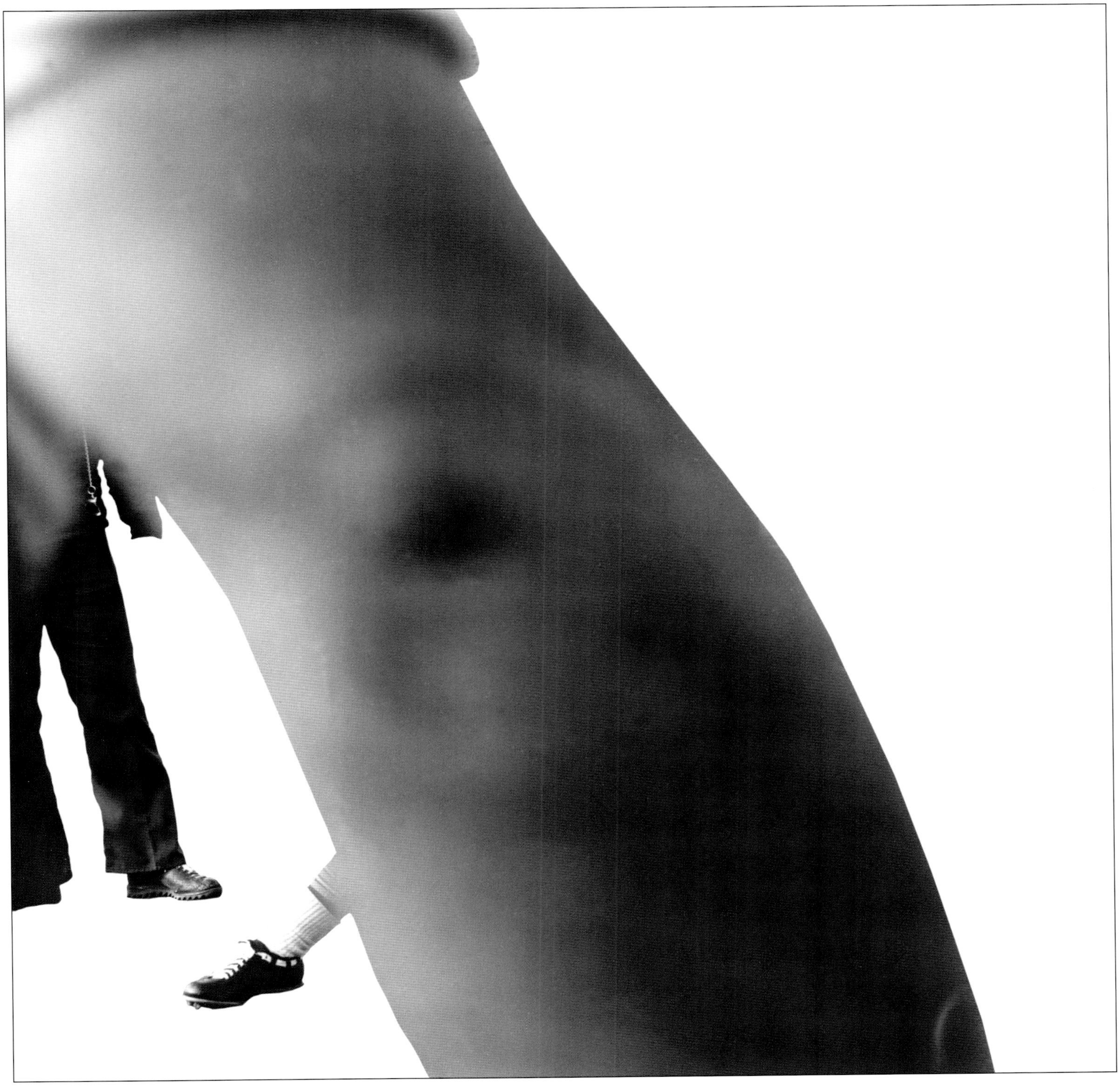

PERSON, FOOT AND ELBOW

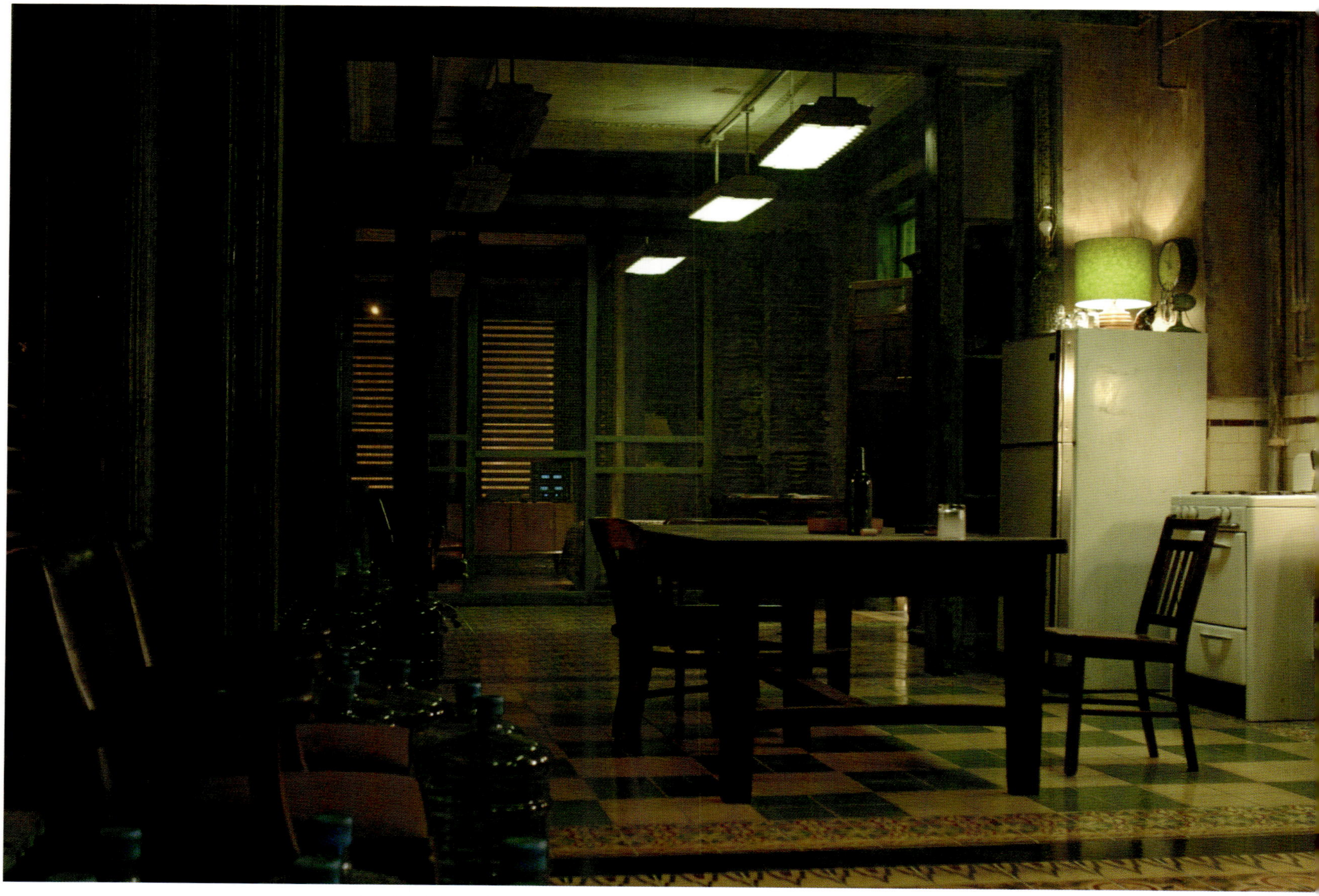

“CONSTANTINE”, WARNER BROTHERS, 2005

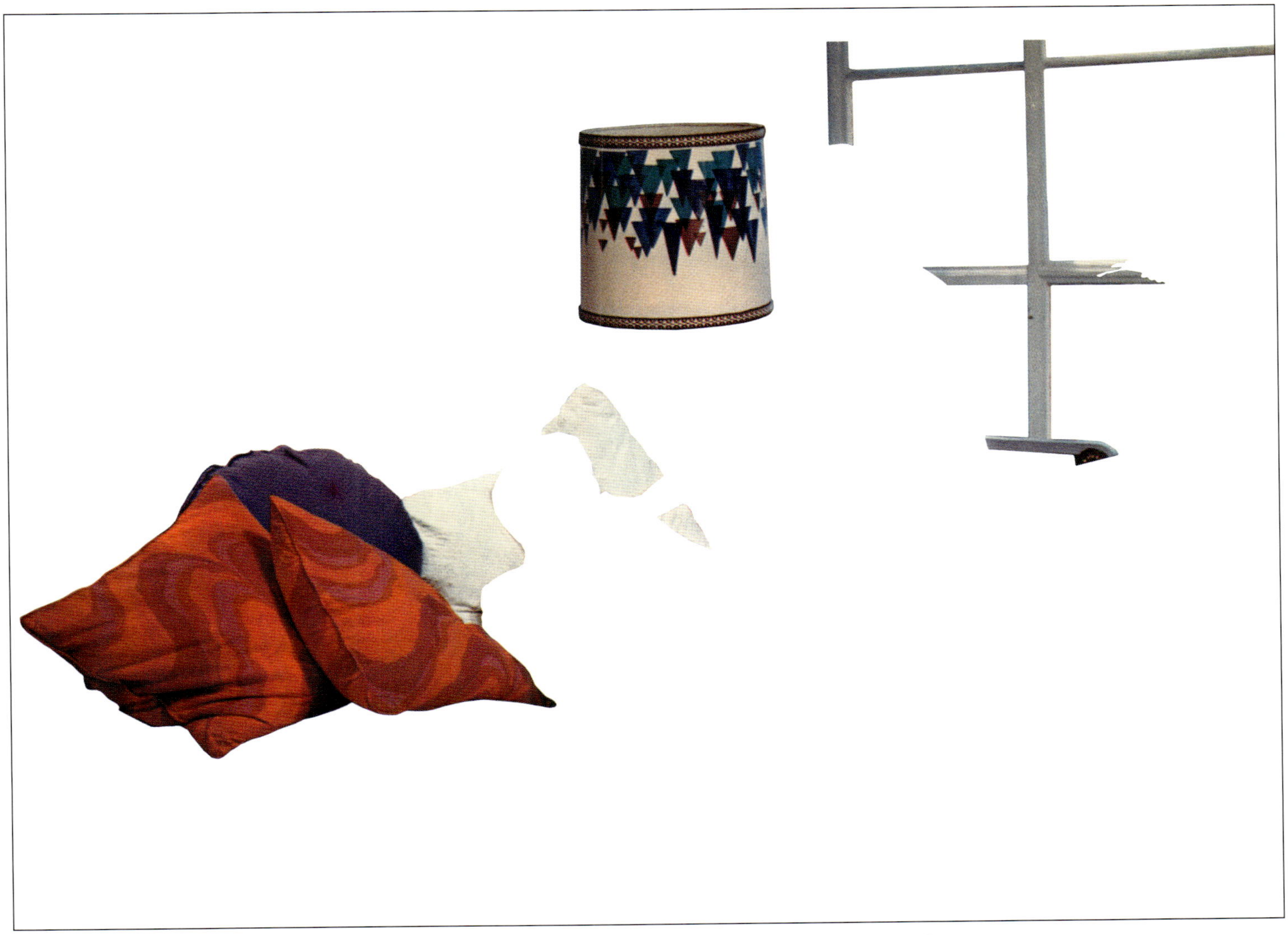

PILLOWS, LAMP SHADE AND SHELVING

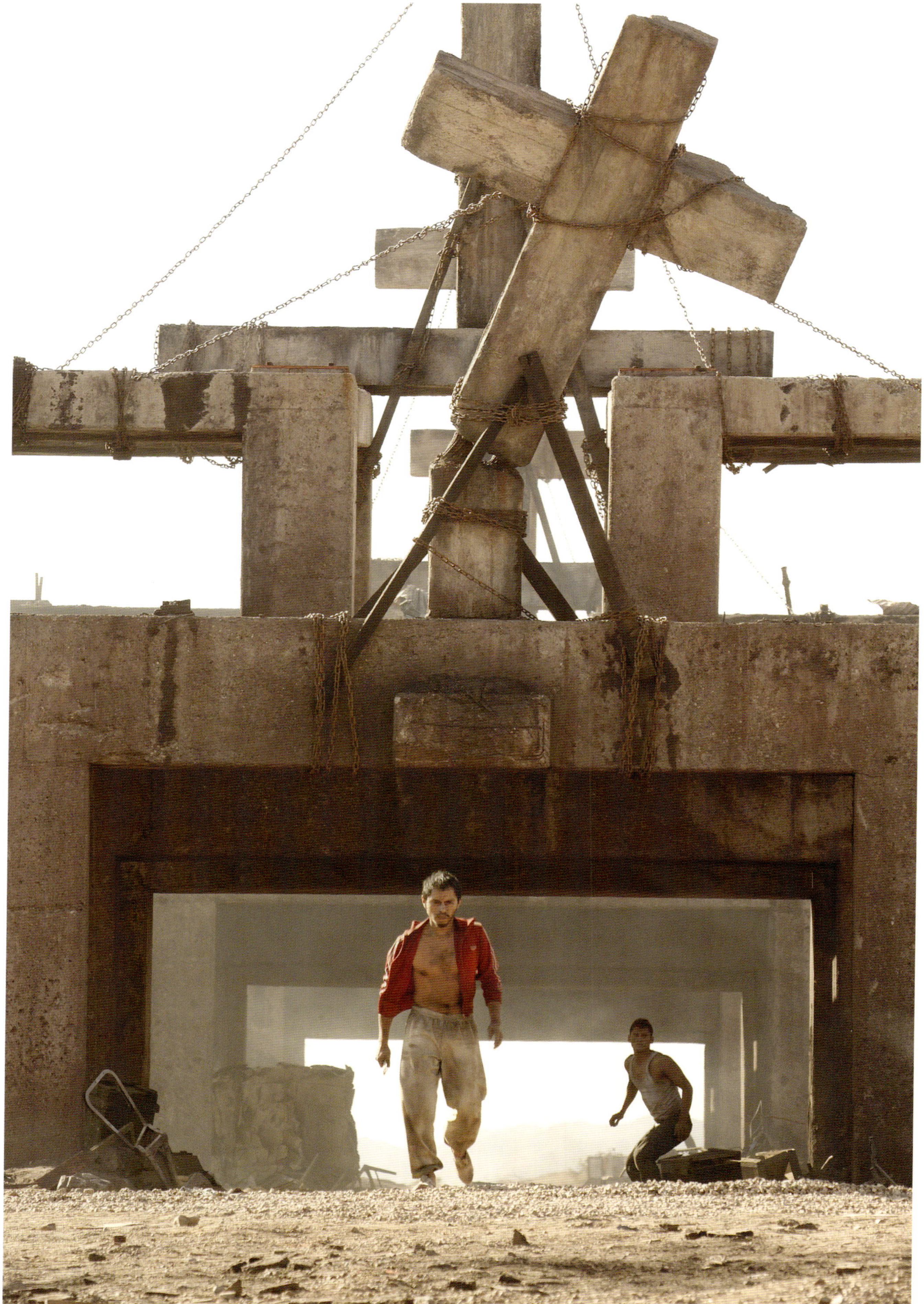

JESSE RAMIREZ, “CONSTANTINE”, WARNER BROTHERS, 2005

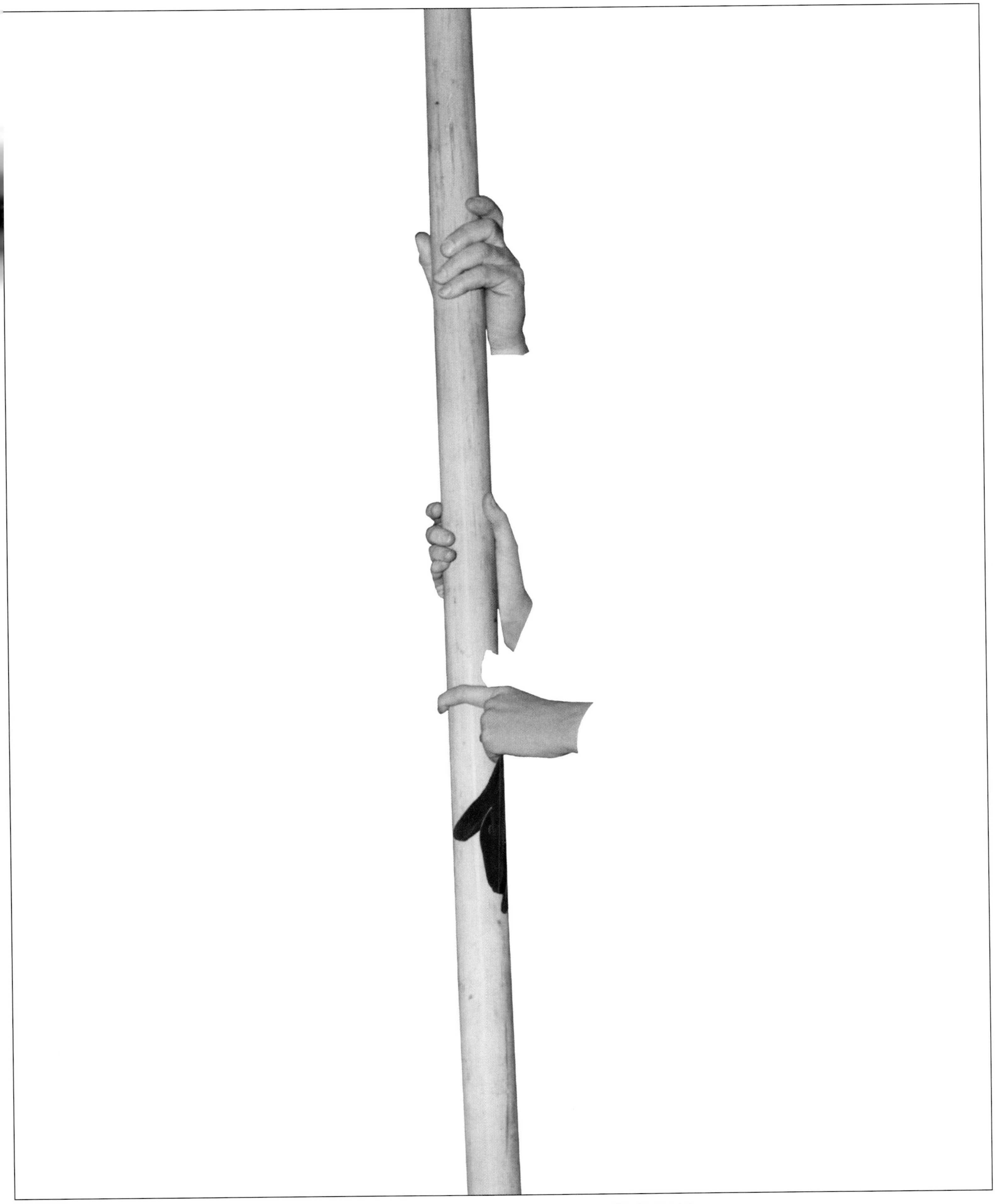

HANDS, GLOVE AND POLE

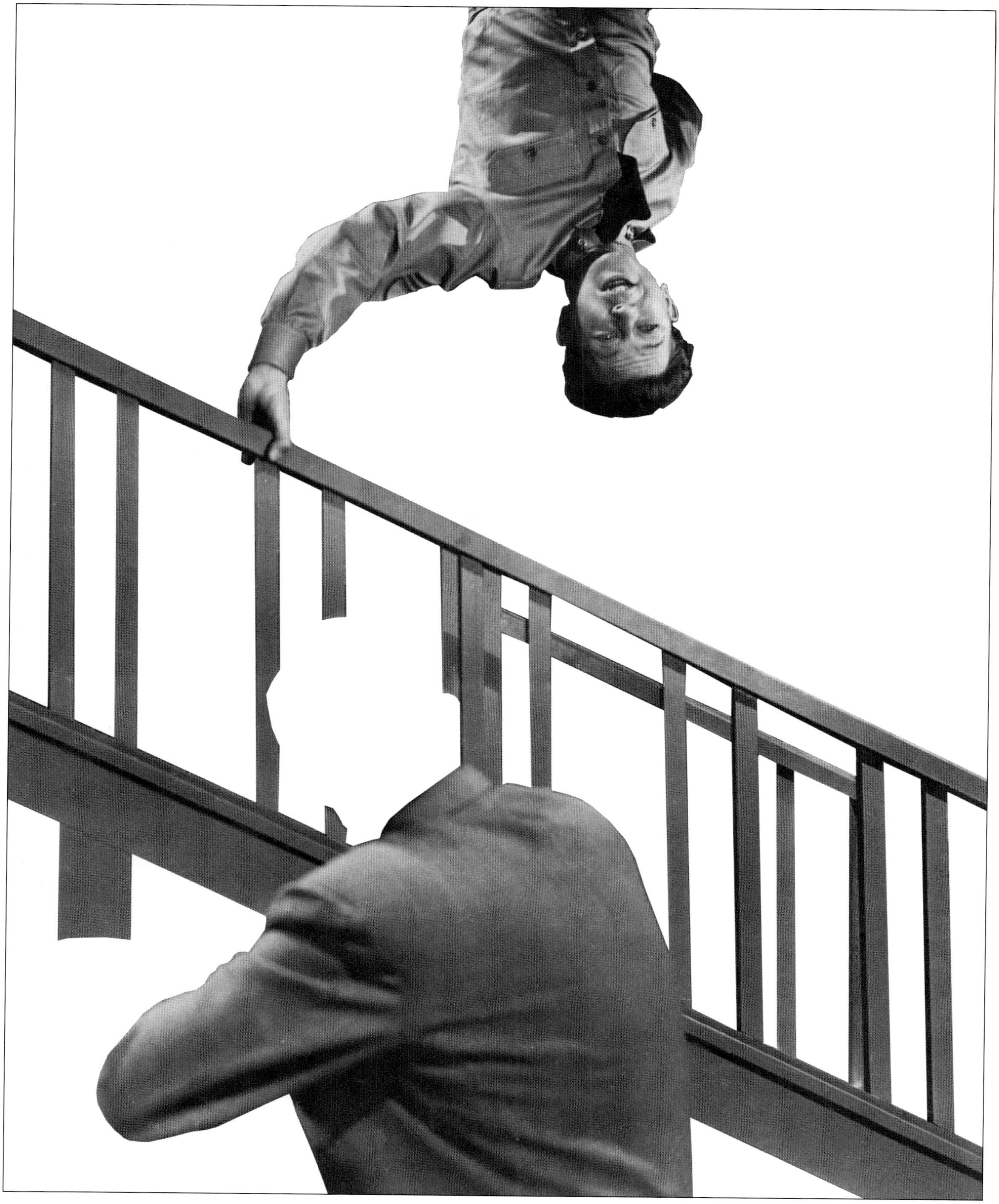

STAIRWAY, COAT AND PERSON

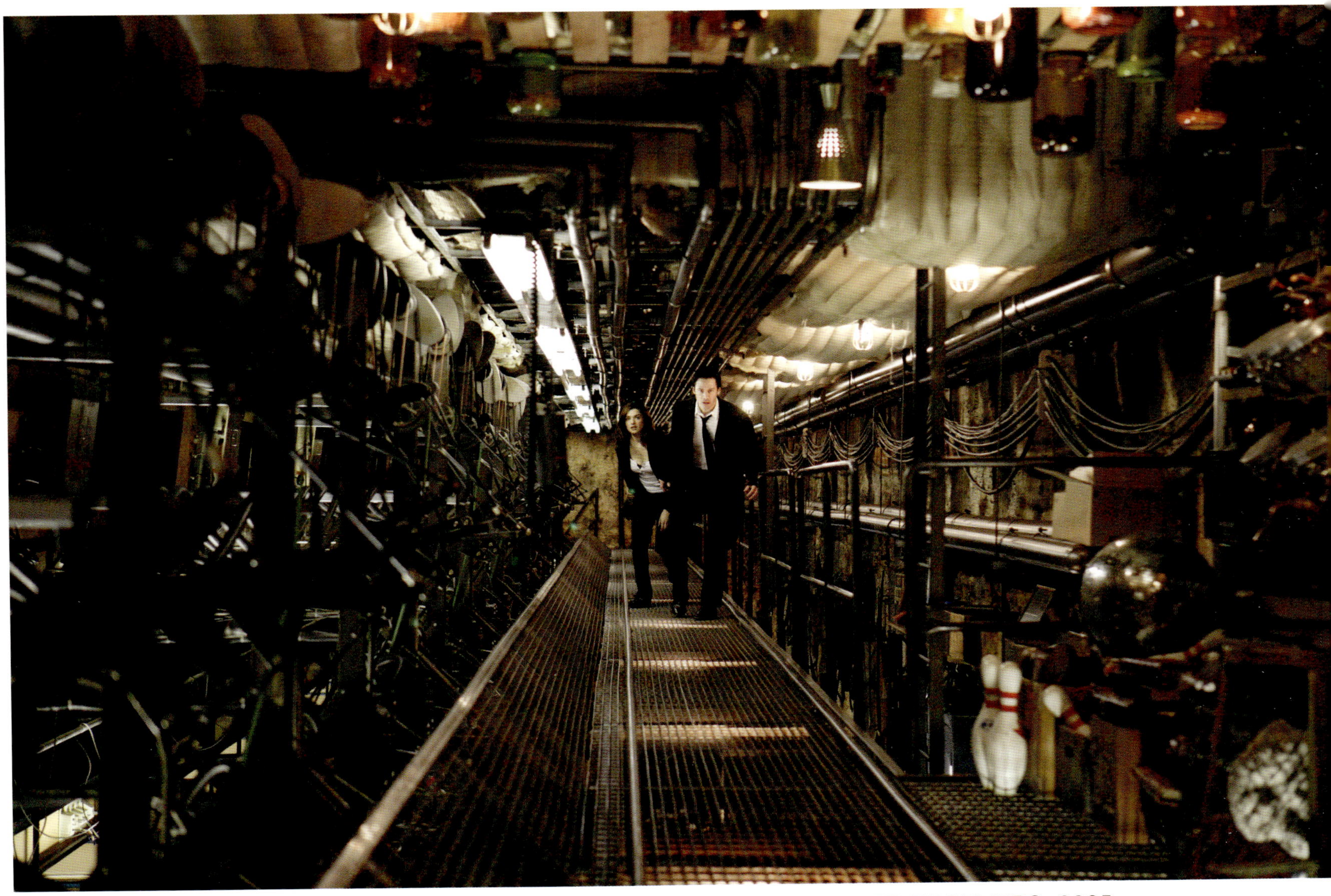

RACHEL WEISZ, KEANU REEVES, “CONSTANTINE”, WARNER BROTHERS, 2005

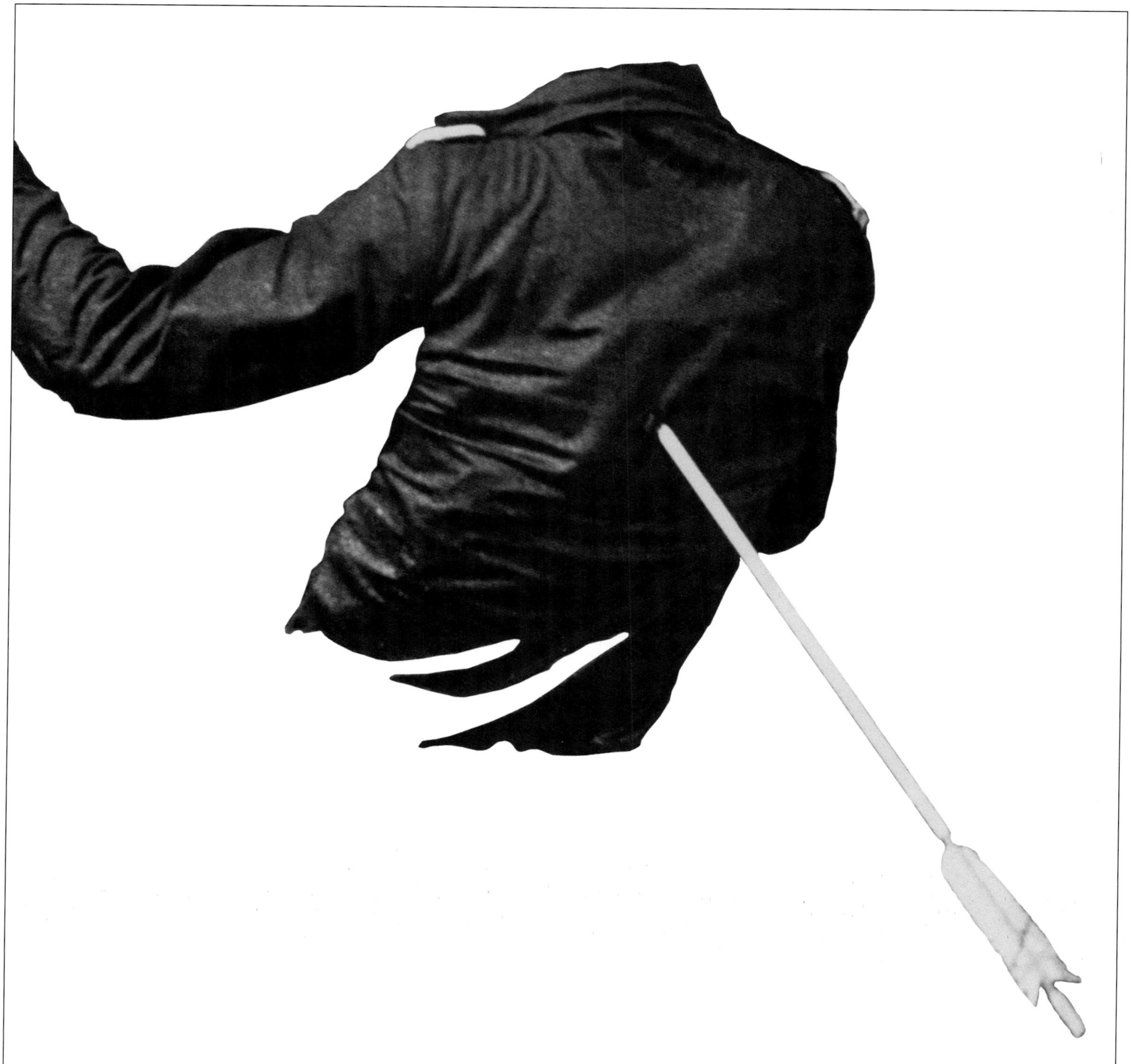

JACKET AND ARROW

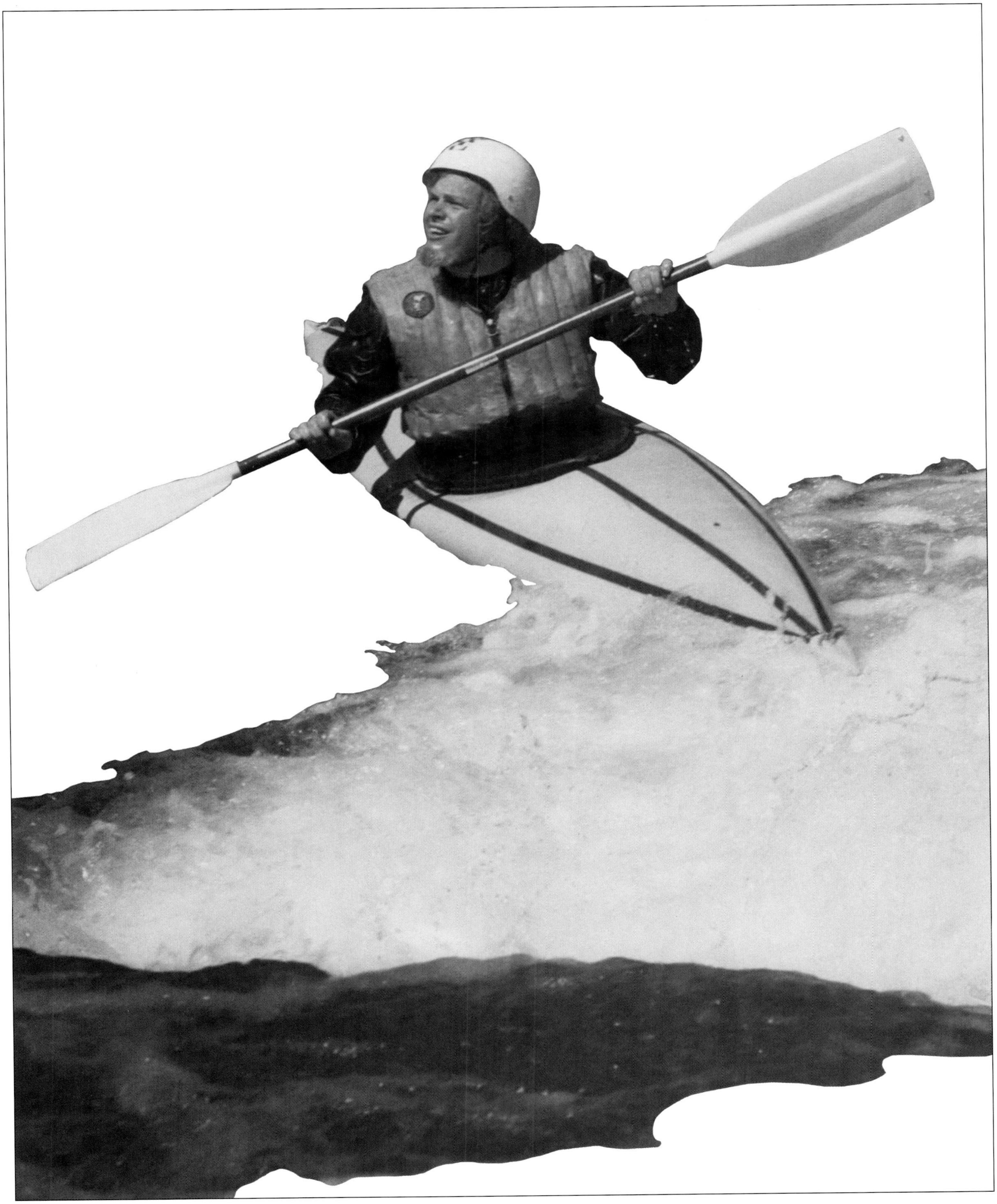

WATER, PADDLE, KAYAK AND PERSON

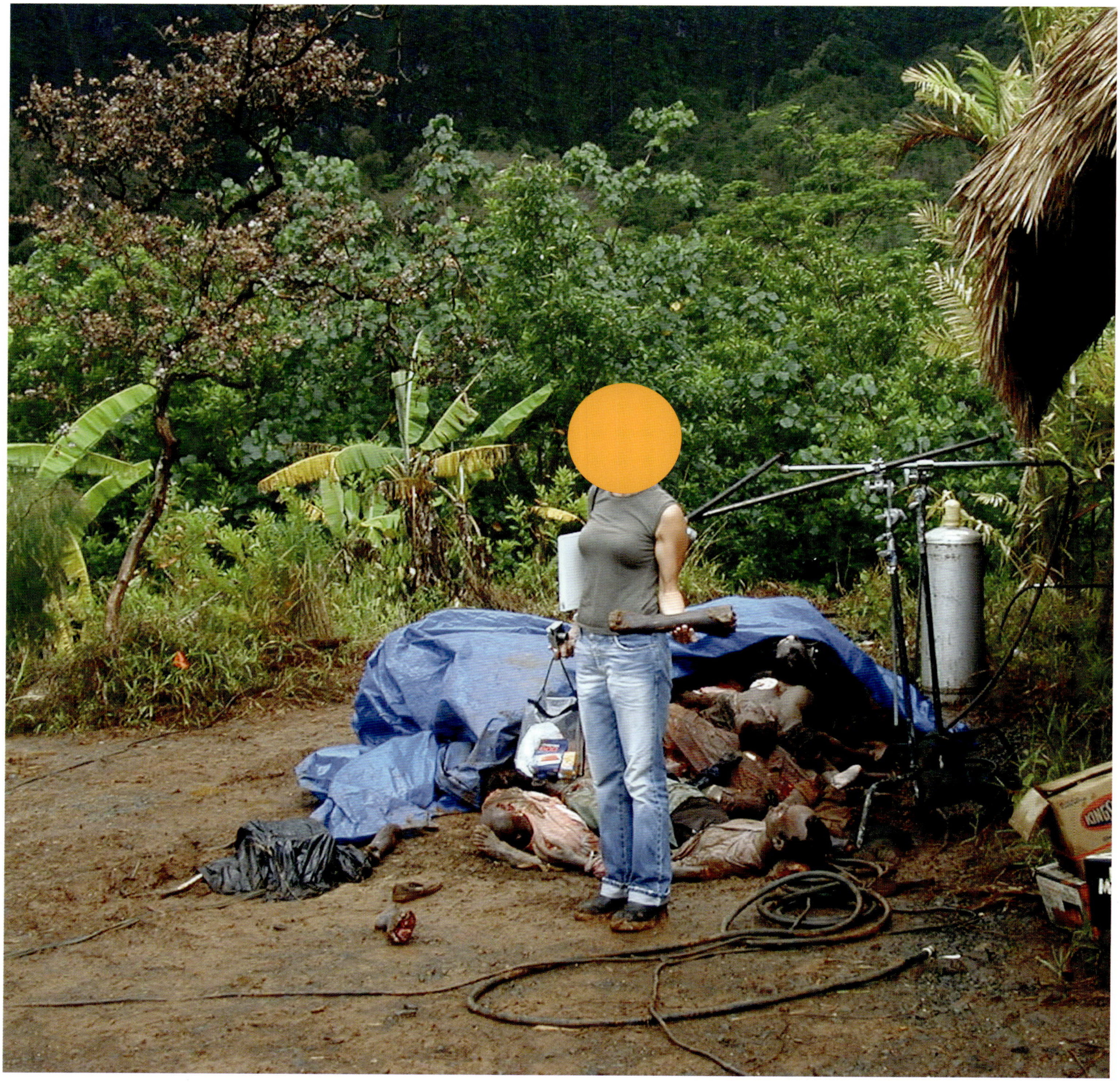

"TEARS OF THE SUN", SONY/TRISTAR, 2003

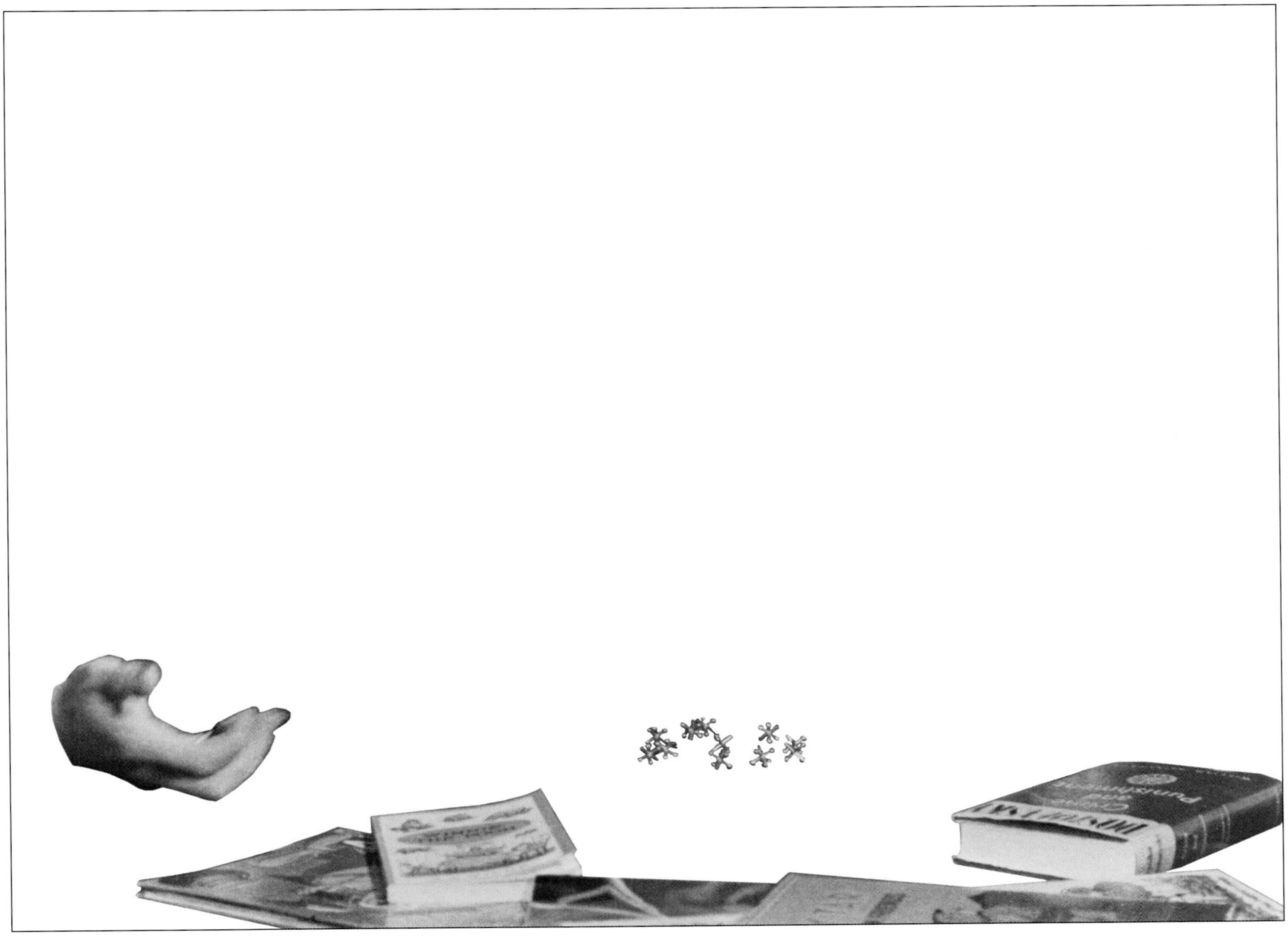

HAND, BOOKS AND JACKS

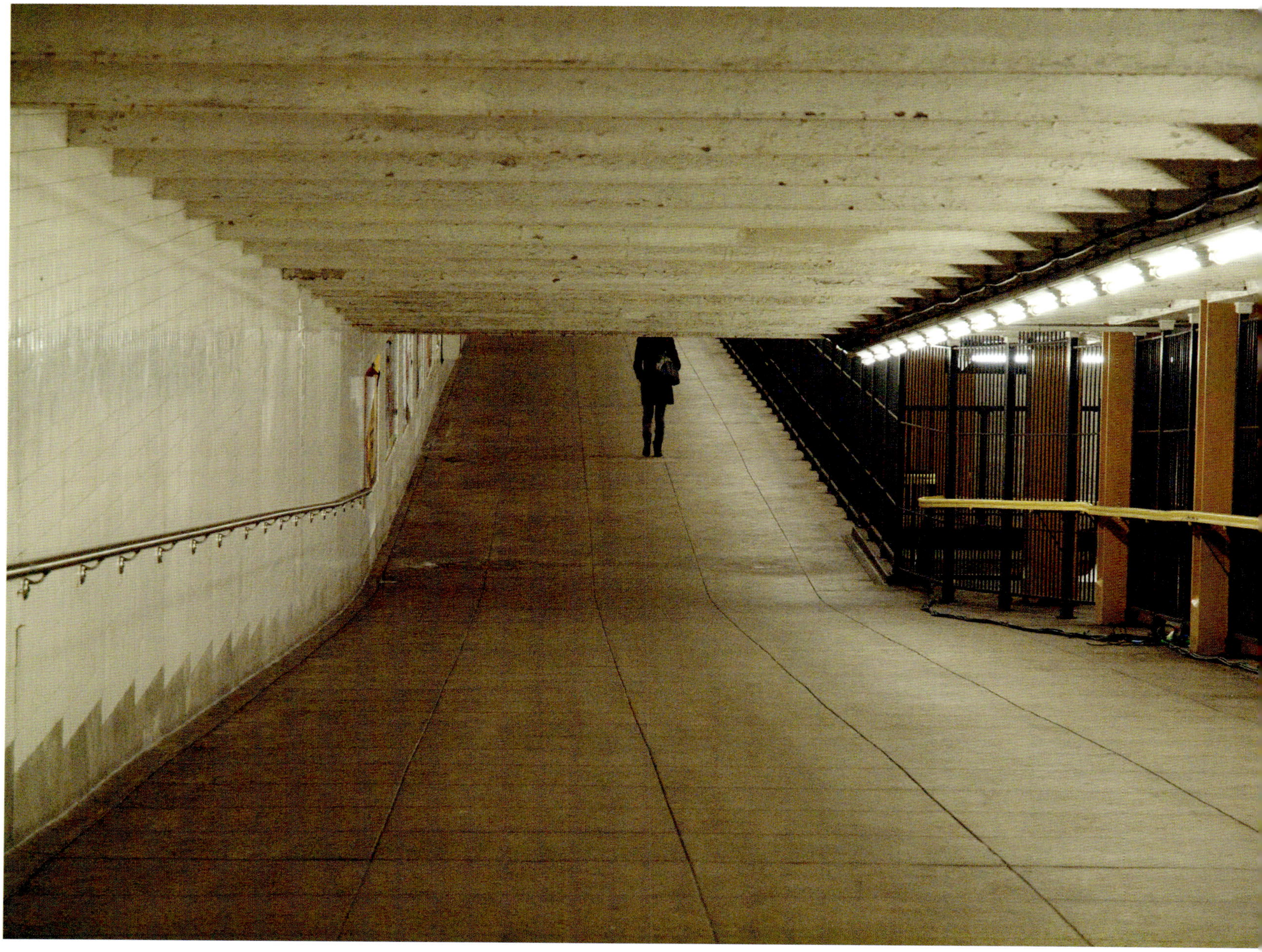

"THE SORCERER'S APPRENTICE", DISNEY ENTERPRISES, 2009

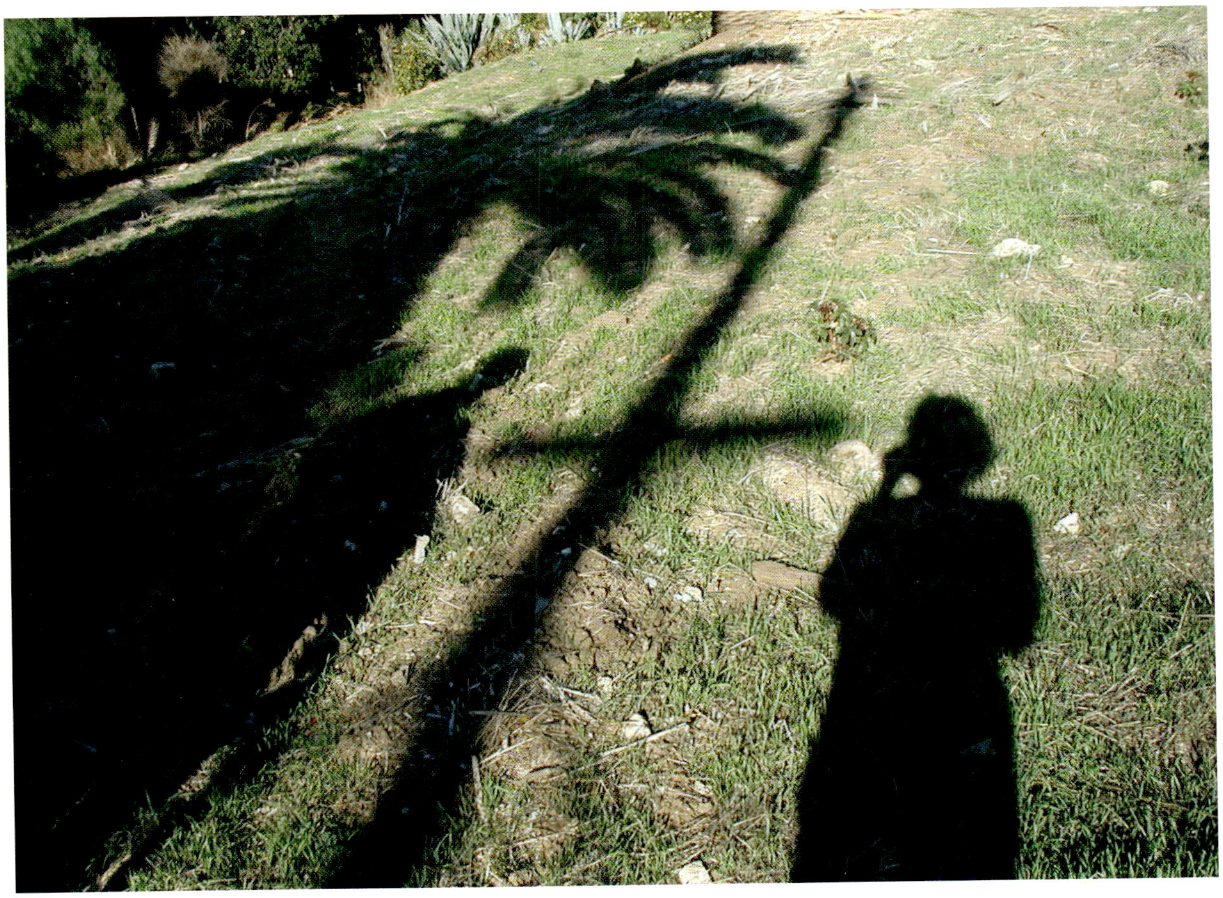

LOCATION REFERENCE, LOS ANGELES

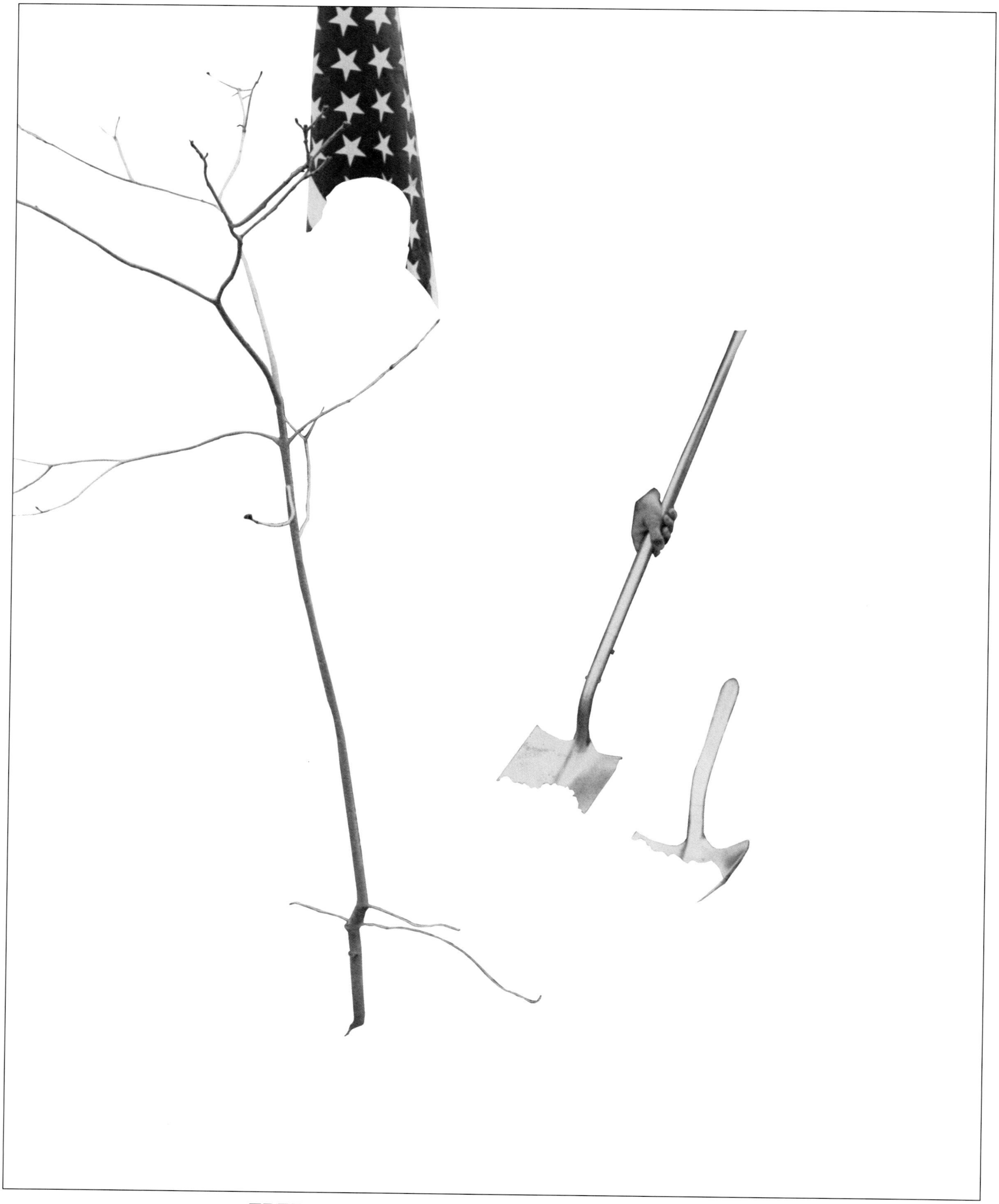

TREE, PORTION OF FLAG, SHOVELS AND HAND

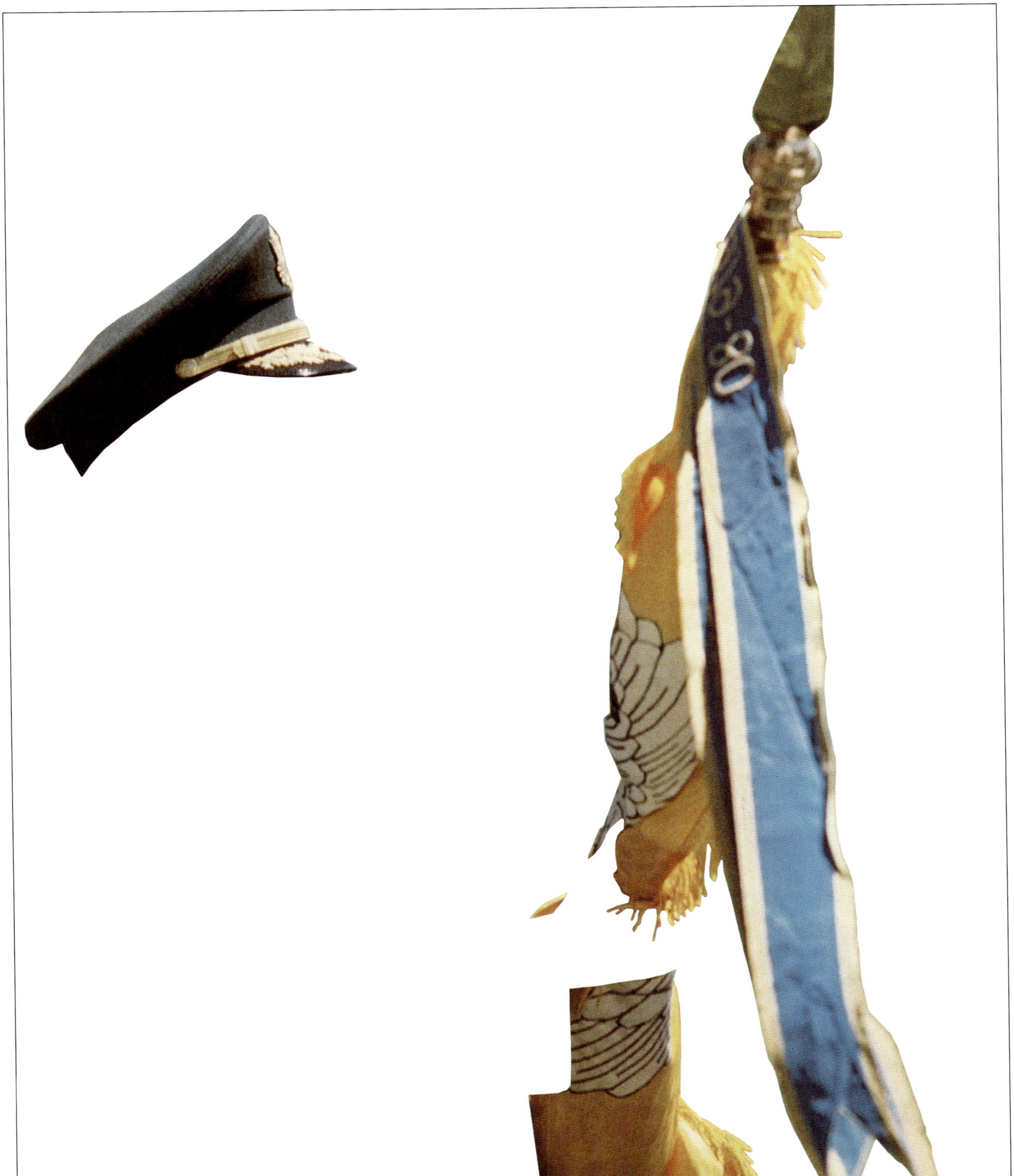

HAT AND FLAG

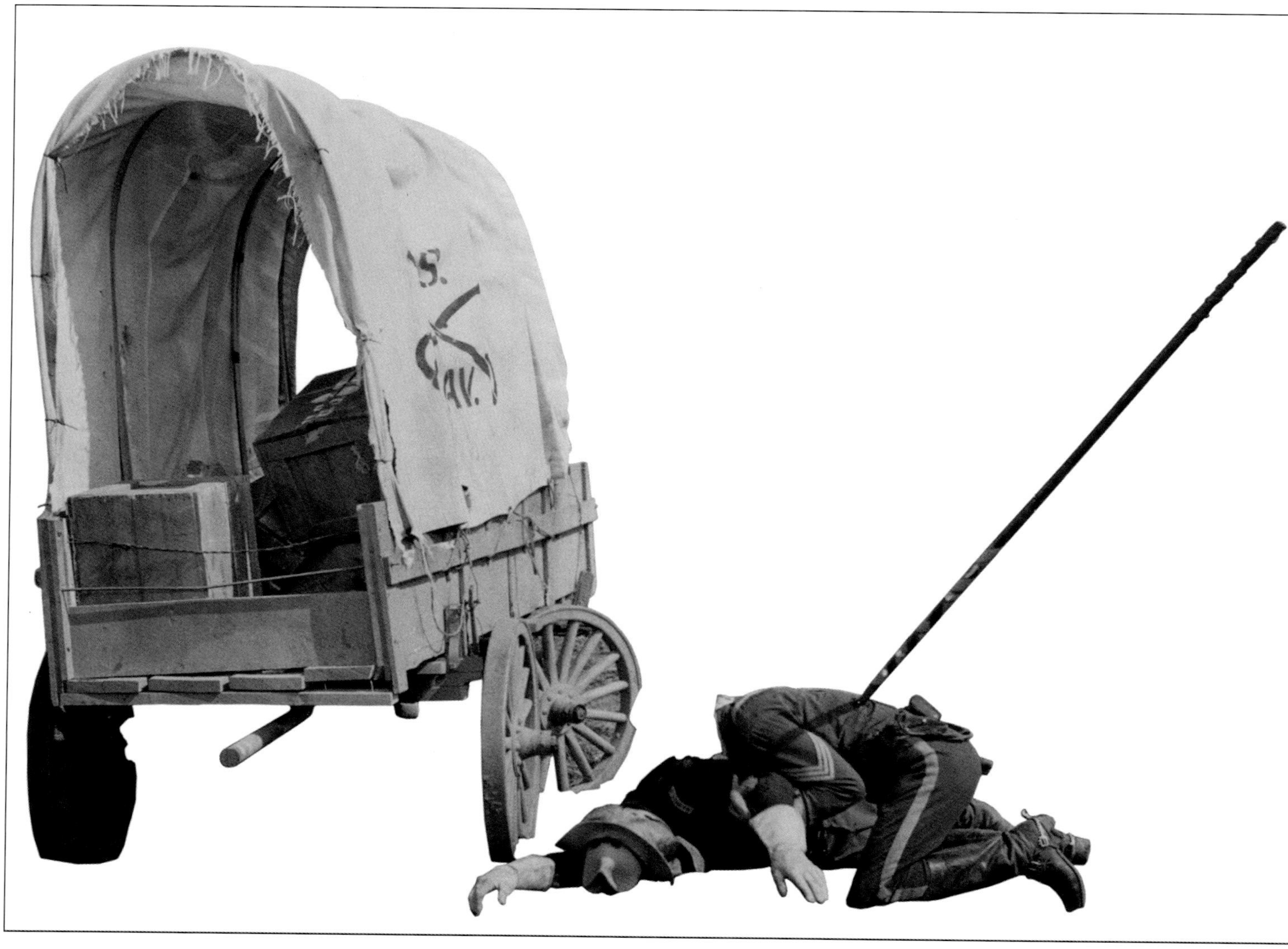

COVERED WAGON, PEOPLE AND SPEAR

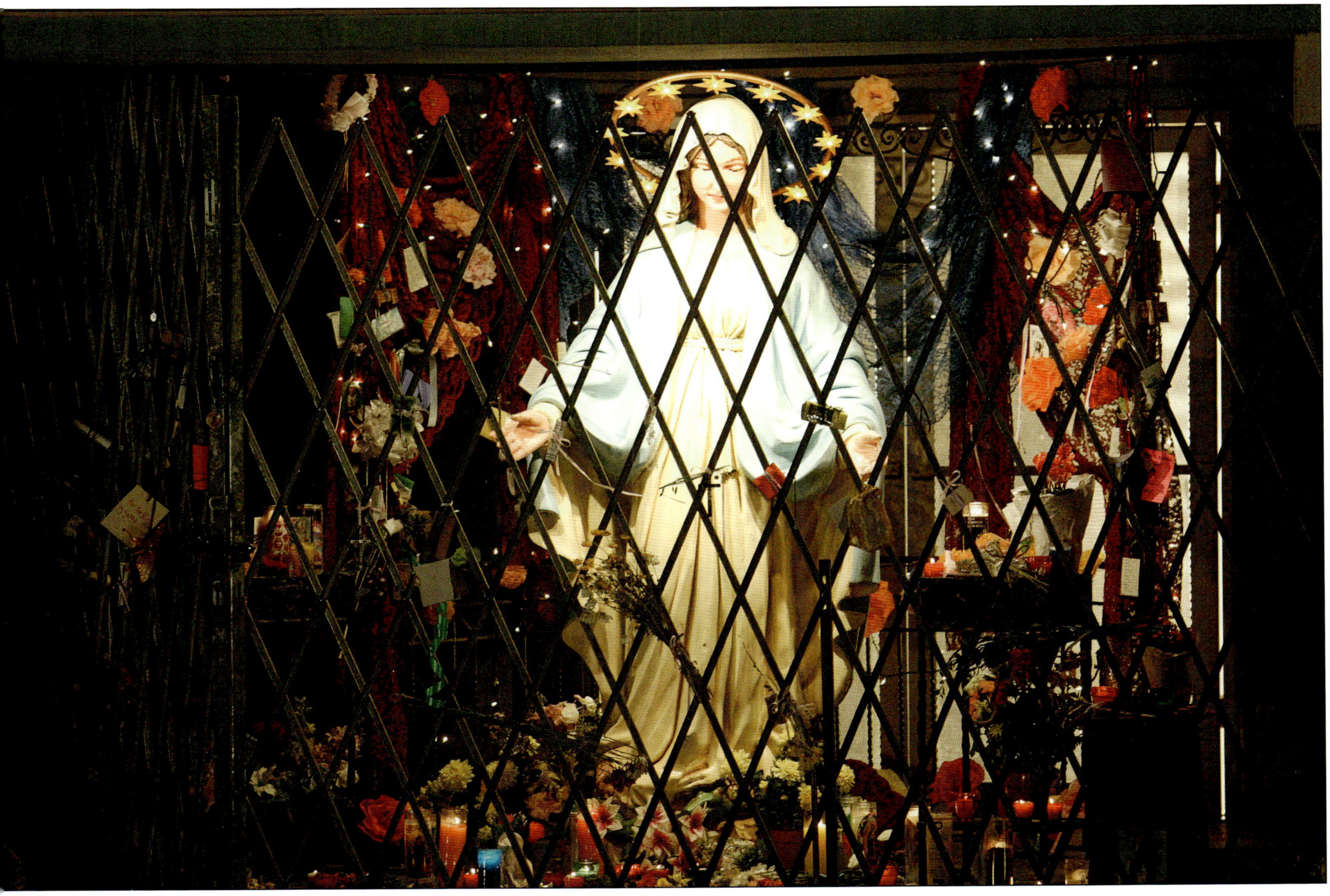

“CONSTANTINE”, WARNER BROTHERS, 2005

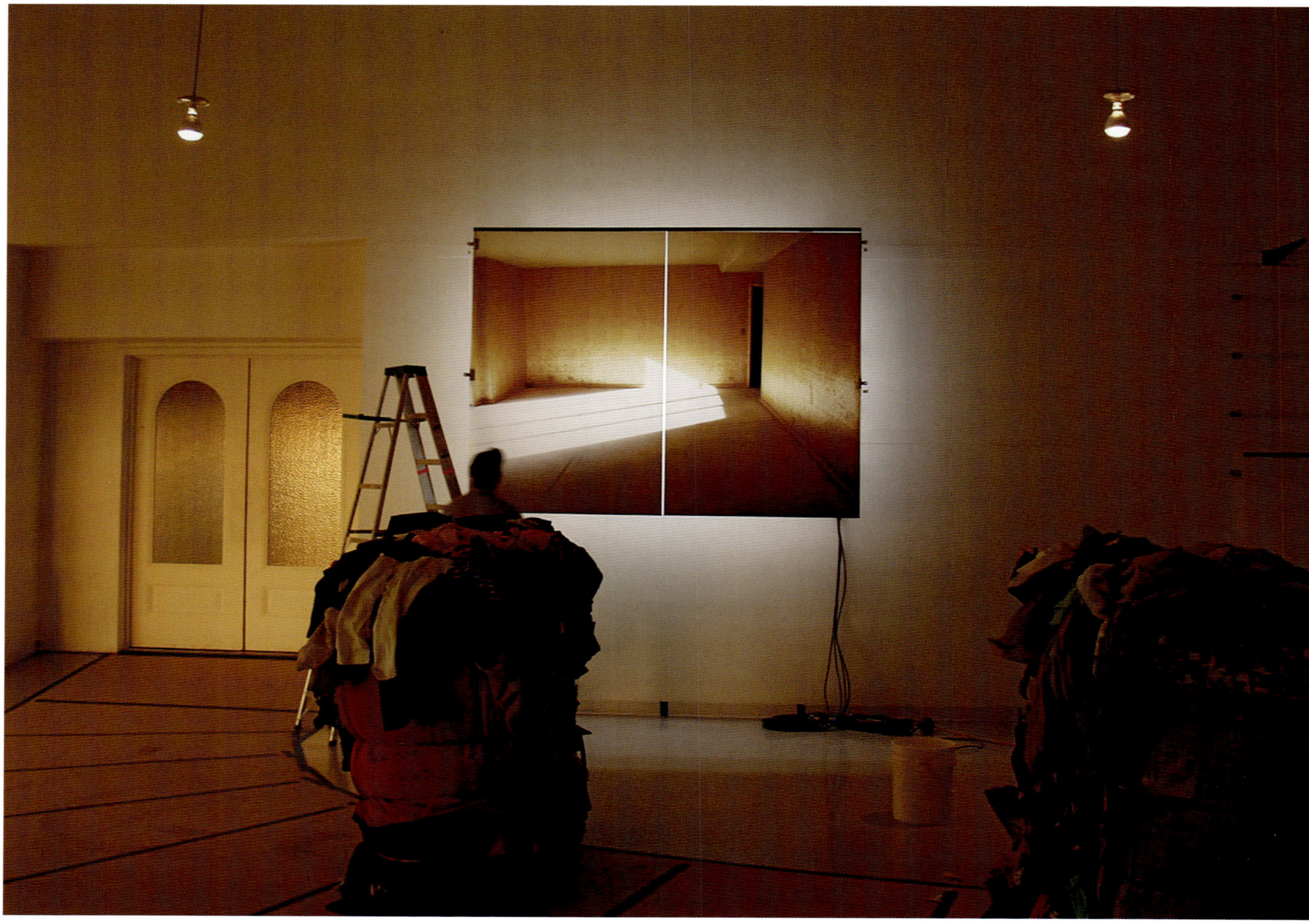

"MUST LOVE DOGS", WARNER BROTHERS, 2005

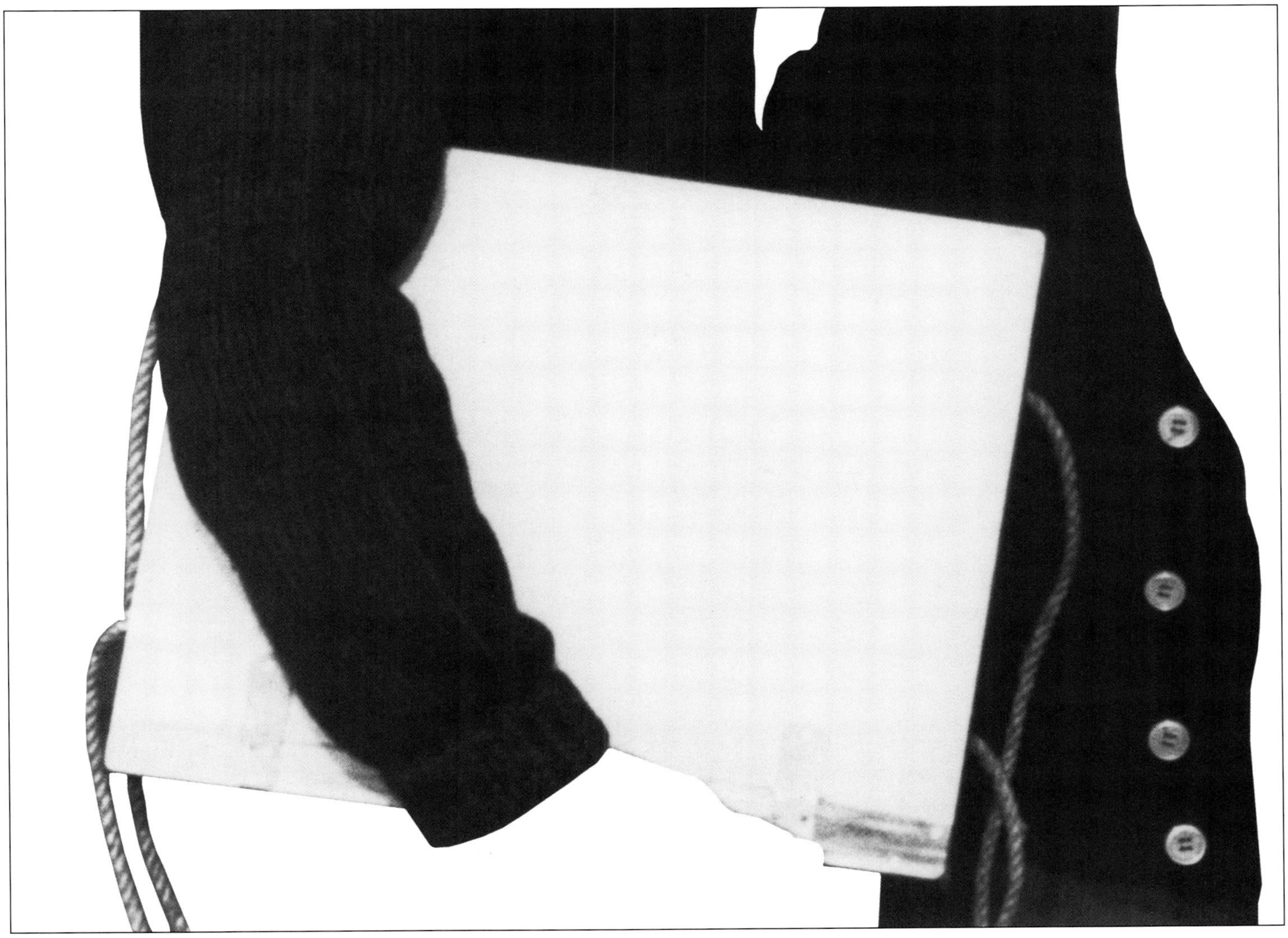

BRIEFCASE, SWEATER AND JACKET

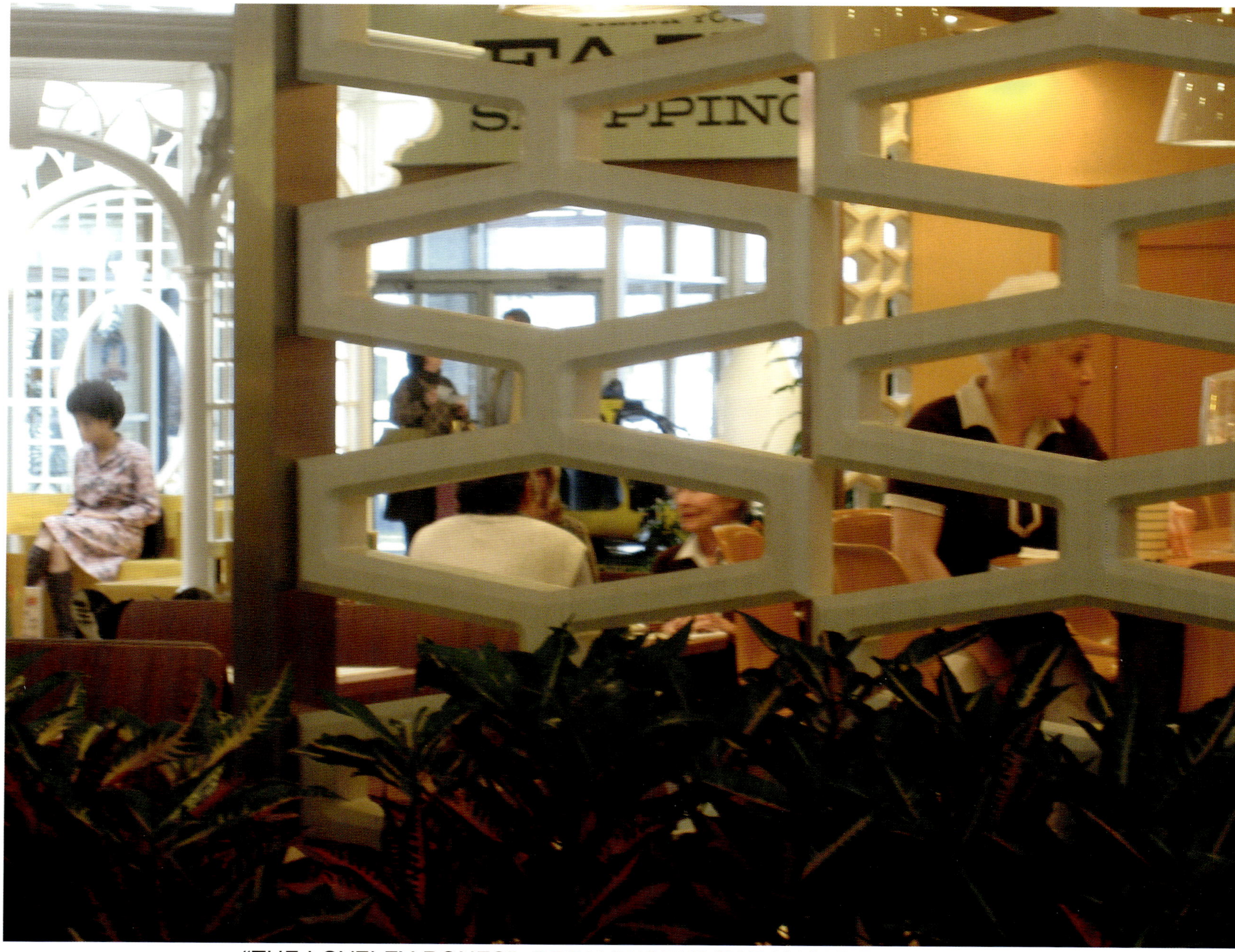

“THE LOVELEY BONES”, DREAMWORKS/PARAMOUNT, 2009

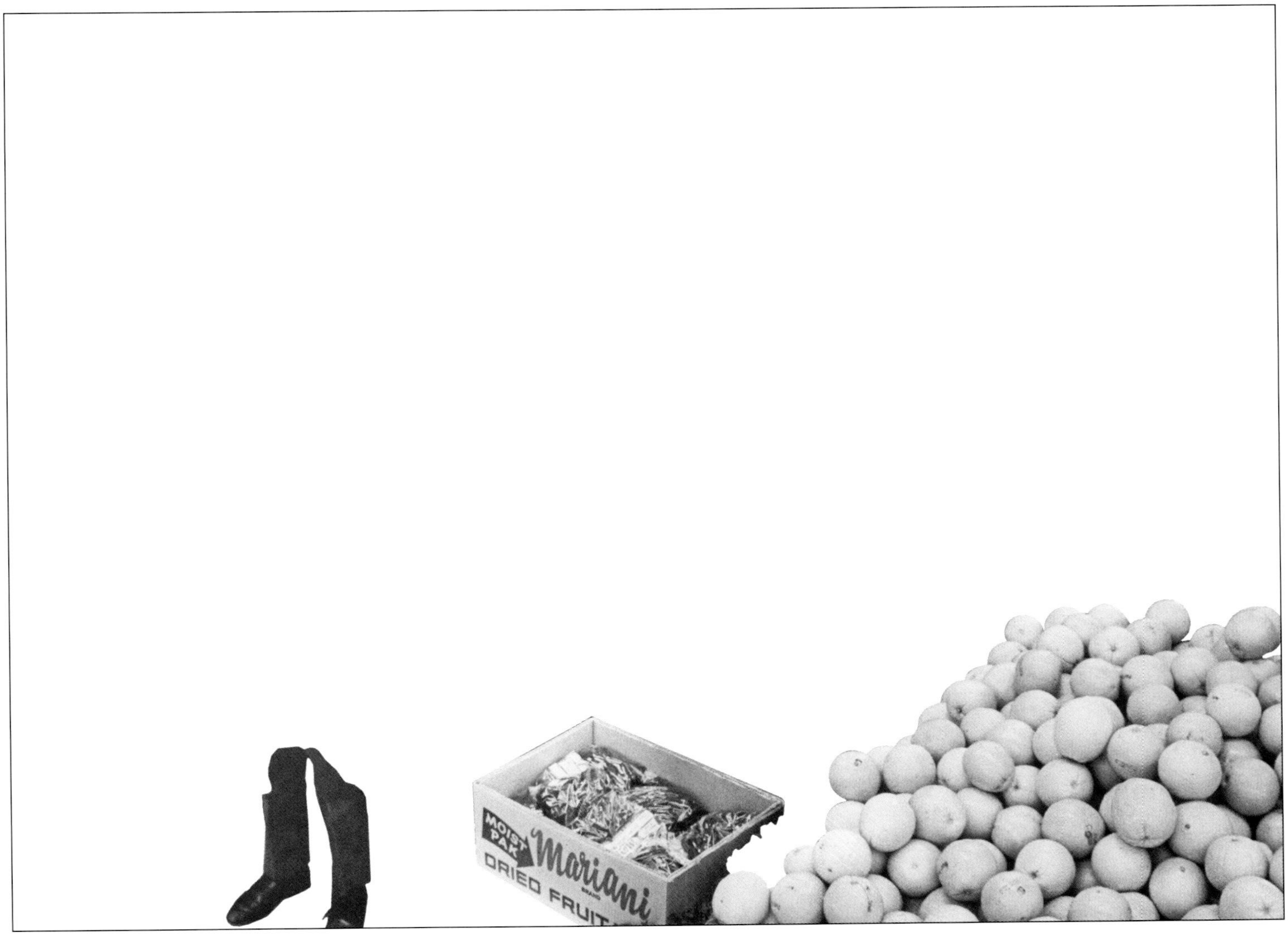


LEGS, BOX (WITH FRUIT) AND ORANGES

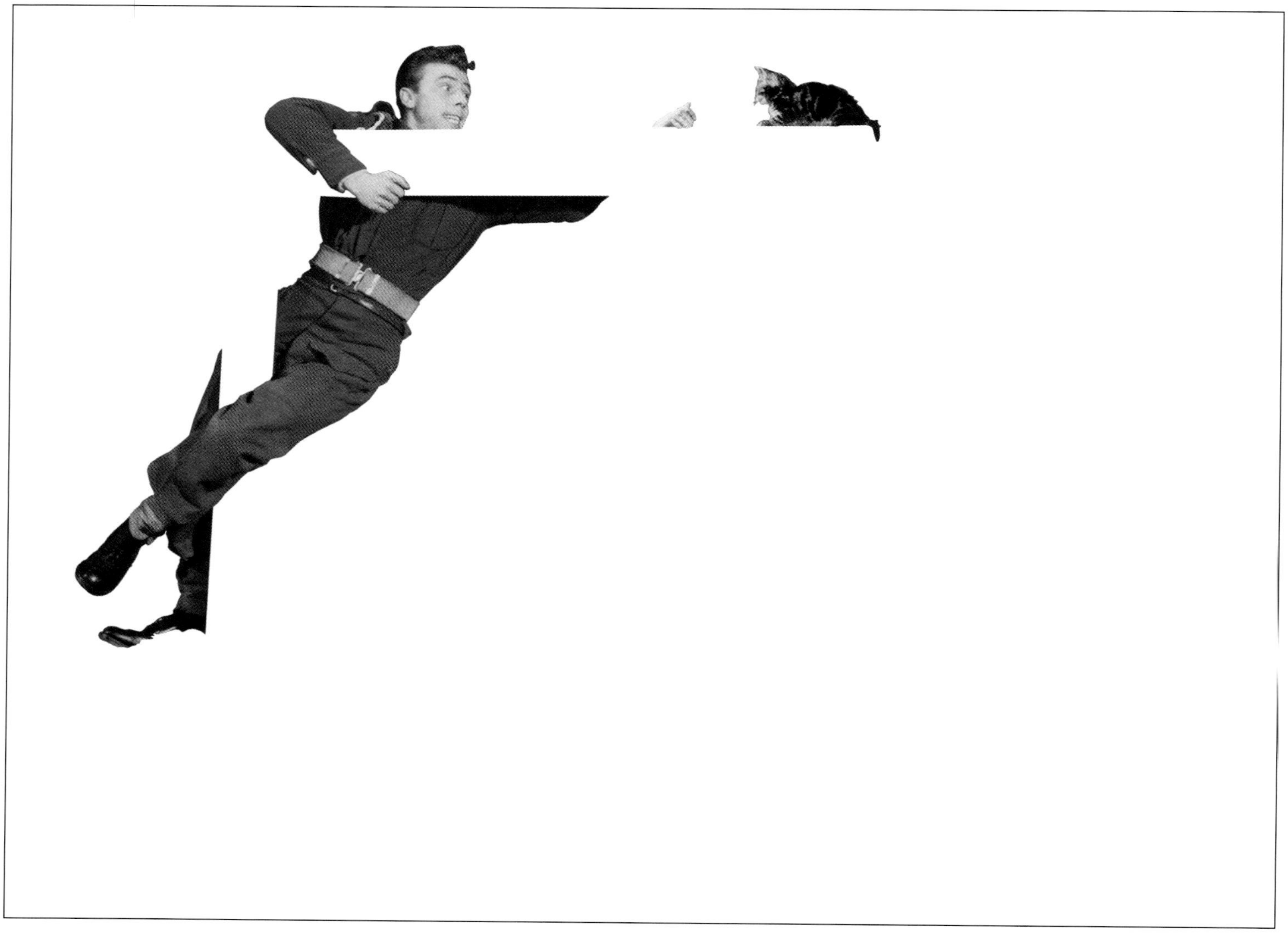

PERSON AND CAT

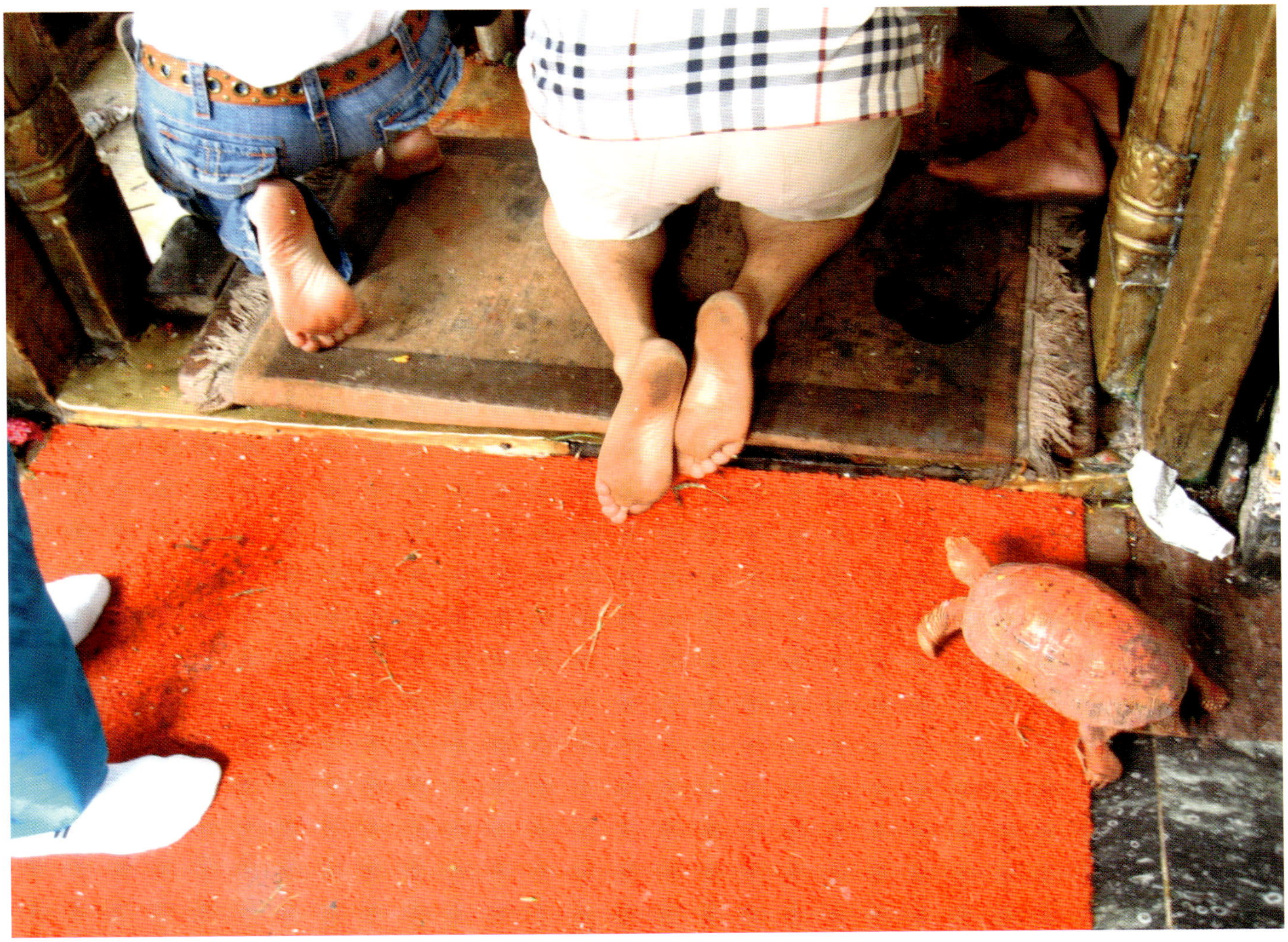

LOCATION REFERENCE, KATHMANDU

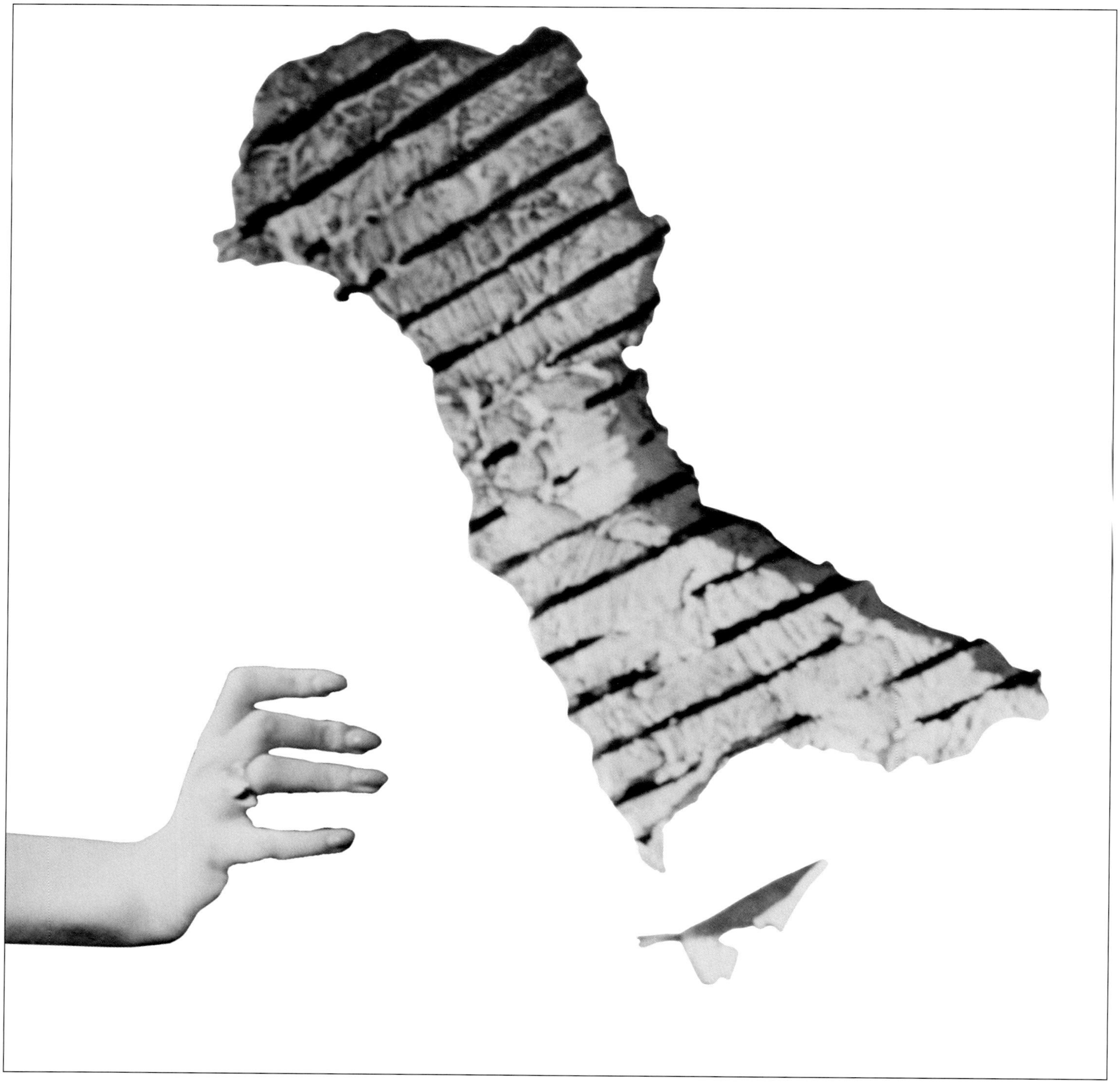

HAND AND DAMAGED PLASTER CEILING

SET IMAGE “THE SORCERER’S APPRENTICE,” DISNEY ENTERPRISES, 2009

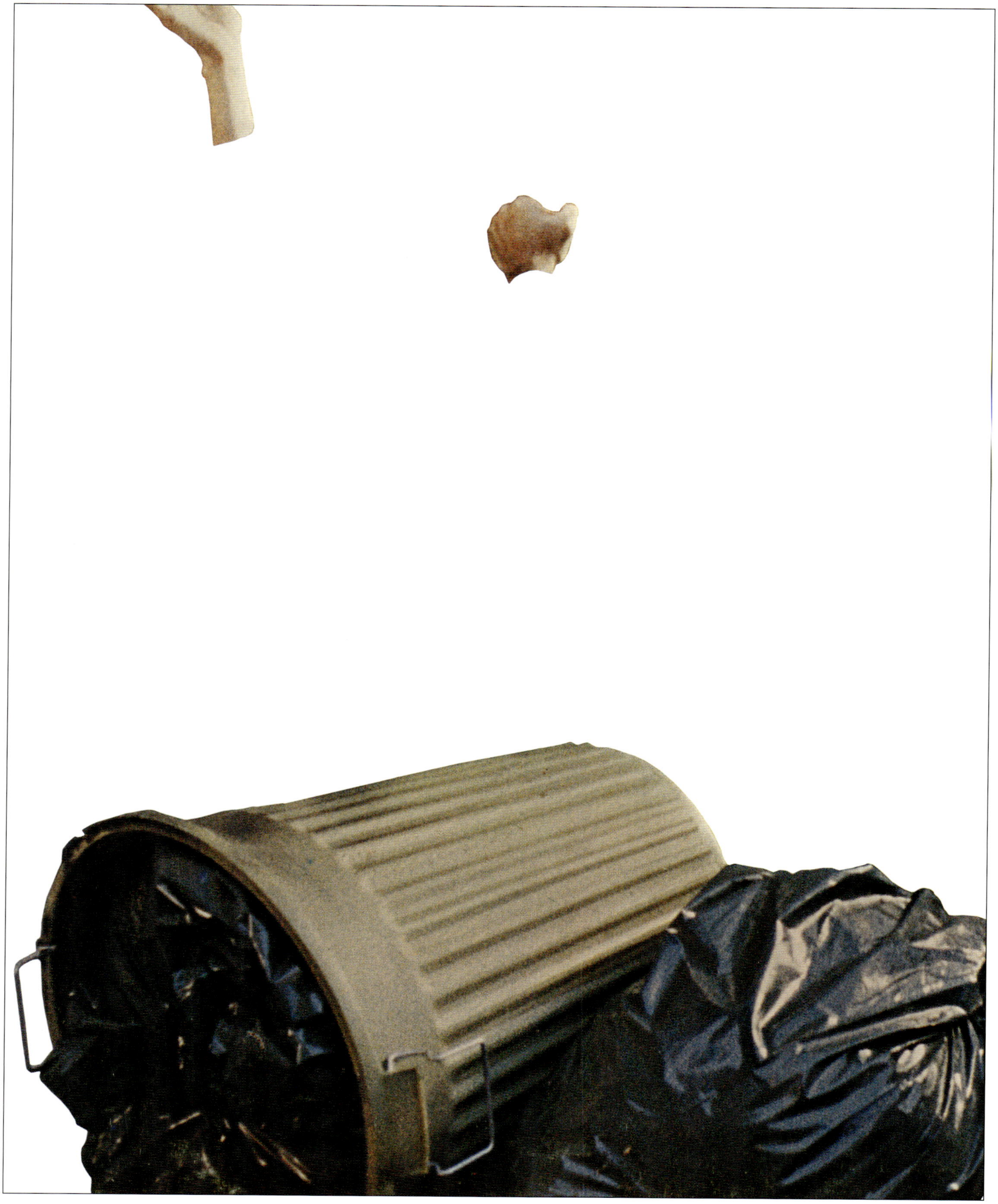

TRASH CAN, HANDS AND BAG

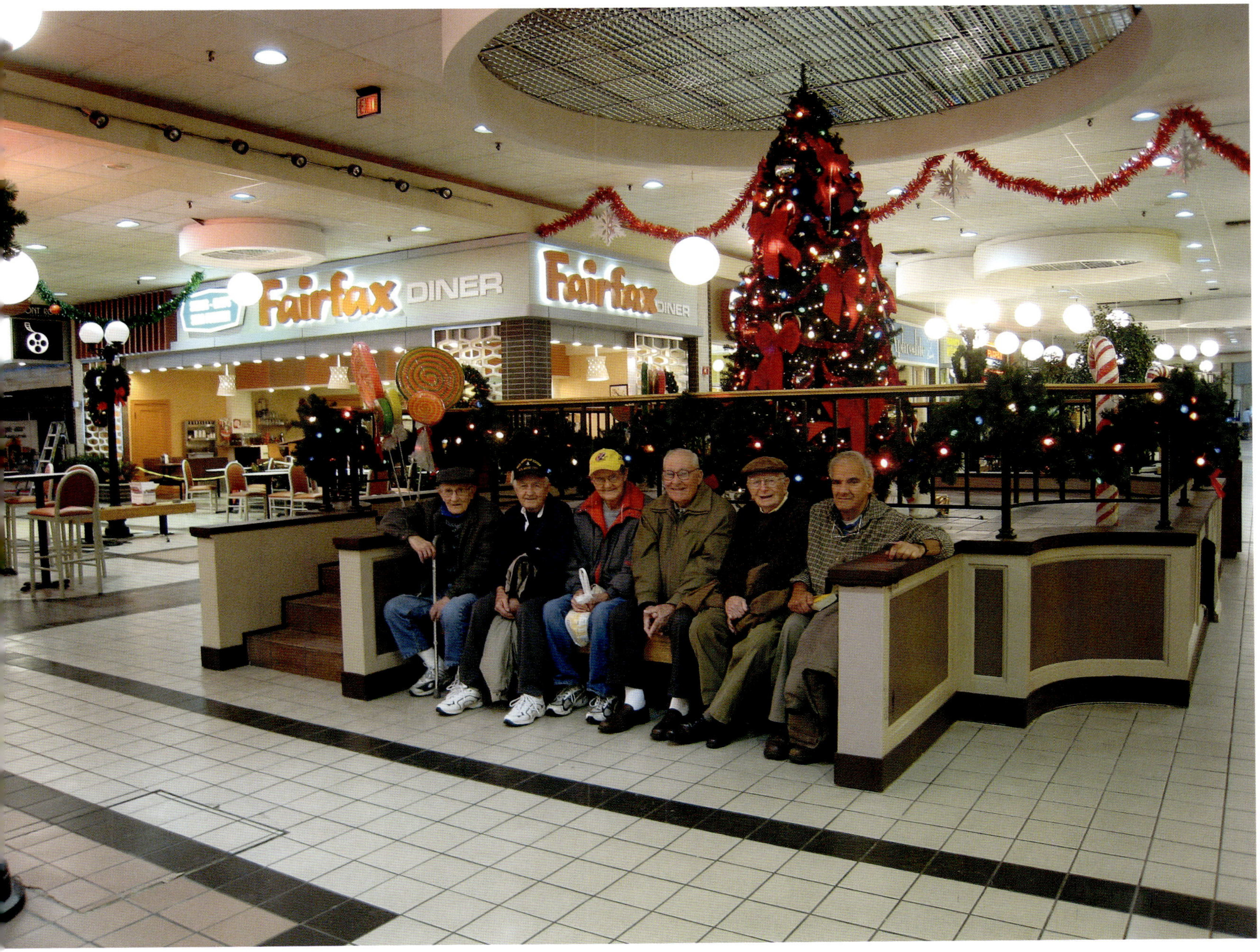


MALL MEN ON LOVELEY BONES SET

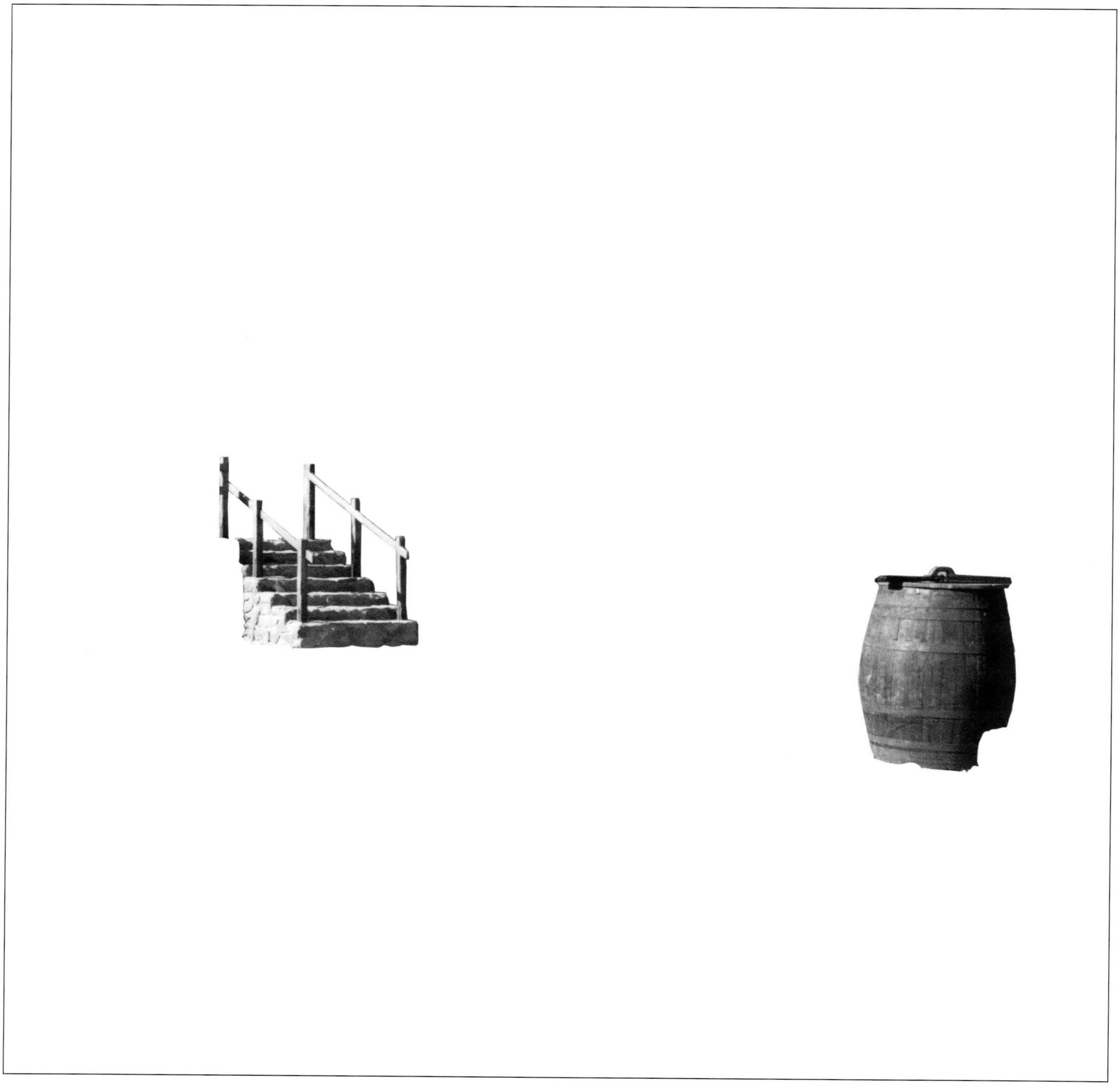

STAIRCASE AND BARREL

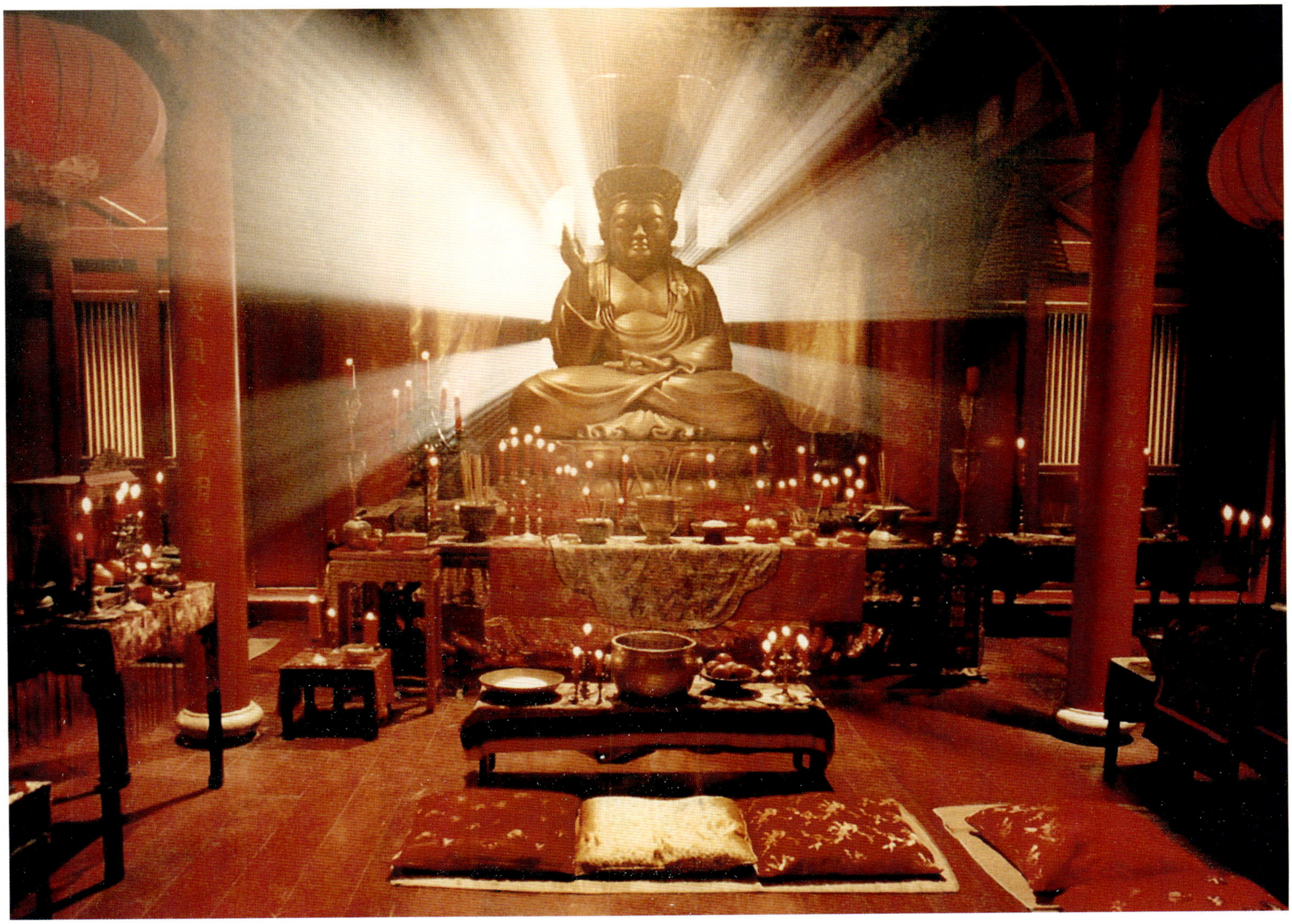

“THE REPLACEMENT KILLERS”, SONY/TRISTAR, 1998

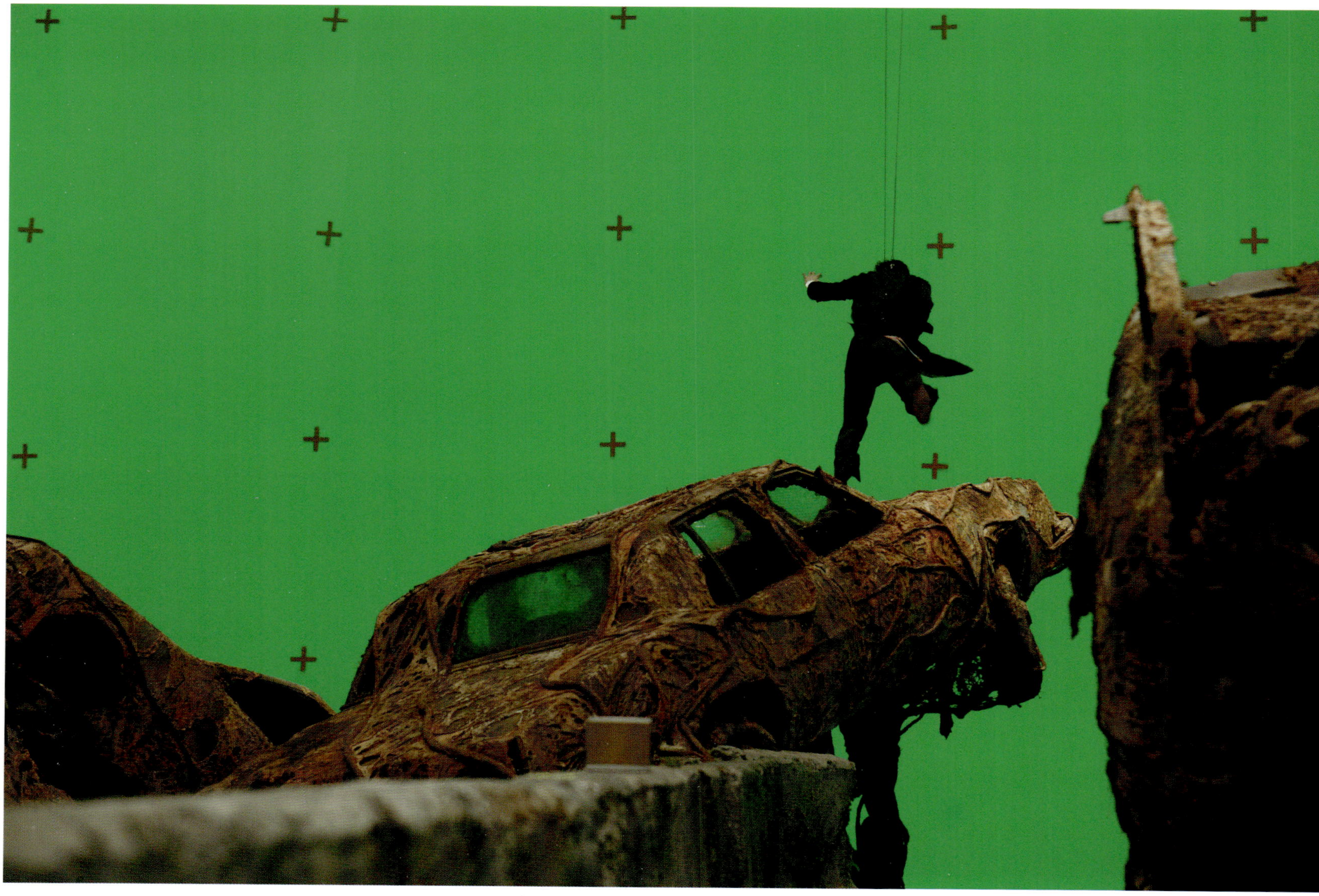

“CONSTANTINE”, WARNER BROTHERS, 2005

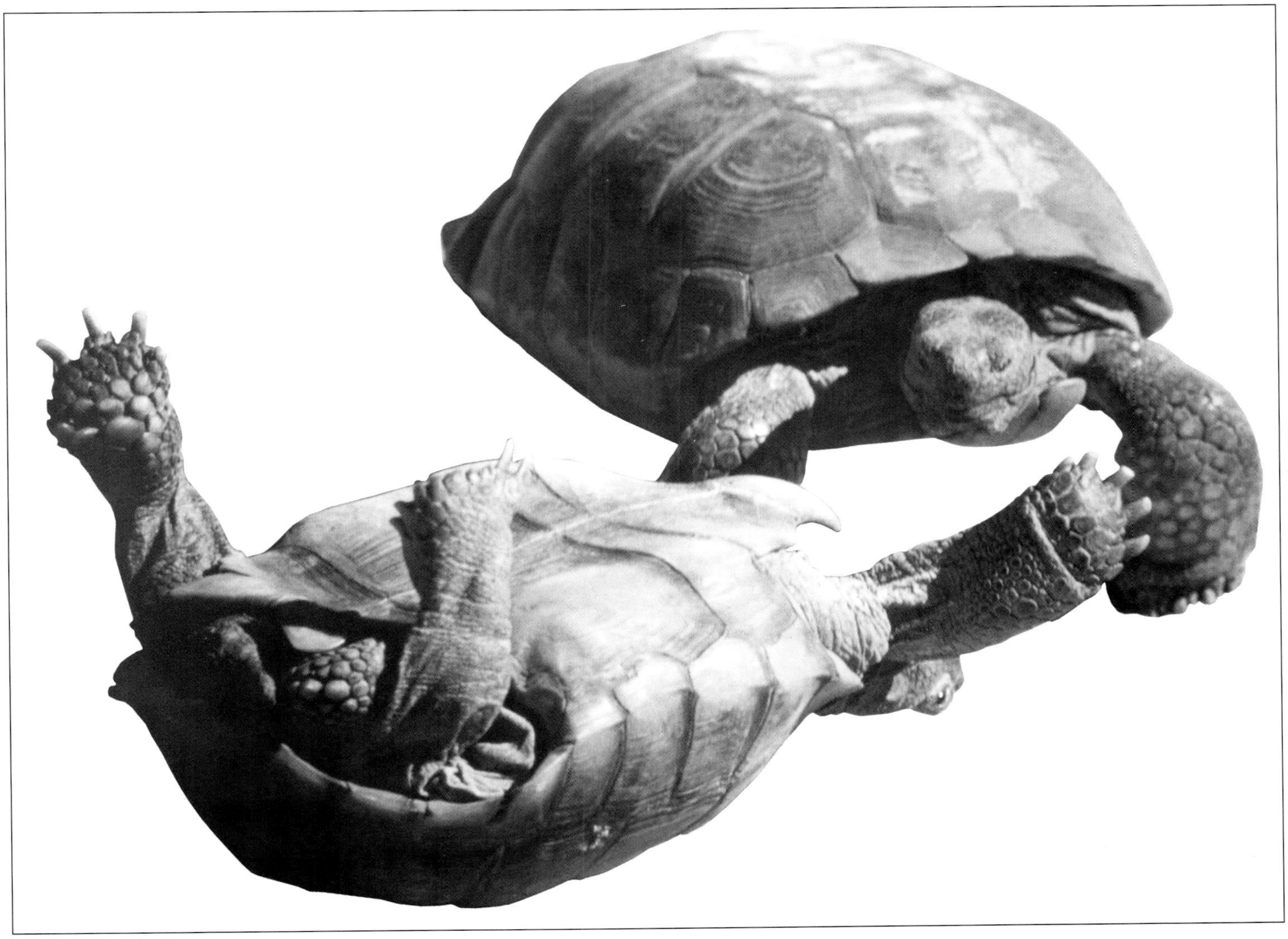

TURTLES

## List of Images

59 *Ashtray, Cup, Money, Poker Chips, Necktie and Bottle*

60 *Sweater and Rabbit*

61 Wes Bentley and Thora Birch in *American Beauty,* DreamWorks/ Paramount 1999


62 *Trophy, Head, Arm, Garland and Bottle*

63 *Helmet, Swords and Hair*

64 *The Sorcerer's Apprentice*, Nicolas Cage, photo: Robert Zuckermann


65 *Persons, Cigarette and Stairway*

66 Dead Body, *Tears of the Sun*, Sony/ Tristar 2003

67 *Snood, Phone and Arm*

68 *Plant and Arm*

69 Dead Body, *Tears of the Sun*, Sony/ Tristar 2003

70 *The Replacement Killers*, Sony/Tristar 1998

71 *Person and Serpent*

72 *The Sorcerer's Apprentice*, Film Frame (L-R) Teresa Palmer, Jay Baruchel


73 *Person, Globe and Hand*

74 *Piano and Person*

75 *Tires and Person*

76 *The Sorcerer's Apprentice*, Disney 2010

77 *Boots, Noose and Belt*

78 *Jacket, Dress and Hand*

79 *The Sorcerer's Apprentice*, Gregory Woo, photo: Robert Zuckermann


80 *The Loveley Bones*, DreamWorks/Paramount 2009


81 *Basket, Bread and Shepherd's Staff*

82 *The Sorcerer's Apprentice*, Miscellaneous Set Model,


83 *Person, Foot and Elbow*

84 *Constantine*, Warner Brothers 2005

85 *Pillows, Lamp Shade and Shelving*

86 Jesse Ramirez in *Constantine* Warner Brothers, 2005

87 *Hands, Glove and Pole*

88 *Stairway, Coat and Person*

89 Rachel Weisz and Keanu Reeves in *Constantine*, Warner Brothers 2005

90 *Jacket and Arrow*

91 *Water, Paddle, Kayak and Person*

92 *Tears of the Sun*, Sony/Tristar 2003

93 *Hand, Books and Jacks*

94 *The Sorcerer's Apprentice*


95 Location reference, Los Angeles, Naomi Shohan, all rights reserved

96 *Tree, Portion of Flag, Shovels and Hand*

97 *Hat and Flag*

98 *Covered Wagon, People and Spear*

99 *Constantine,* Warner Brothers, 2005

100 *Must Love Dogs*, Warner Brothers 2005

101 *Briefcase, Sweater and Jacket*

102 *The Loveley Bones*, DreamWorks/Paramount 2009


103 *Legs, Box (with Fruit) and Oranges*

104 *Person and Cat*

105 Location Reference, Kathmandu, Anthony Drazan, all rights reserved

106 *Hand and Damaged Plaster Ceiling*

107 *The Sorcerer's Apprentice*, Disney 2010

108 *Trash Can, Hands and Bag*

109 Location Reference

110 *Staircase and Barrel*

111 *The Replacement Killers*, Sony/Tristar 1998

112 *Constantine*, Warner Brothers 2005

113 Turtles

# Seeing is Believing

Jessica Morgan

Brought together for the first time: John Baldessari's signature images of suggestively occluded found film stills *and* the unadulterated stills produced by one of Hollywood's top production designers, Naomi Shohan. It seems somehow wrong, a little perverse even. Like Jeff Koons exhibiting the *Celebration* series in 'Toys R Us,' or Richard Prince making a billboard for Marlboro. The connection is there for all to see but isn't the physical separation—and with that the slippage and elision from source material to artwork—supposed to remain sacrosanct? Surely proximity could prove overwhelming, undermining even, of the process of distancing through copy, alteration or in Baldessari's case elimination?

Well, it's quite the opposite in fact. Once again our conveniently held beliefs and taboos about the distinctions between art and commerce, high and low, the raw and the cooked are found to be just that: unexamined convictions. Revelations come from picking apart such easy distinctions testing the boundaries of categorisation and generally muddying the waters of these neatly packaged formulas. Baldessari after all clearly loves films. His use of film stills does not stem from a critical desire to dismantle the structures of Hollywood. What he identifies and isolates in his process of dissecting stills are the tropes and themes, attitudes and poses that have characterised representation throughout the history of art. It's just that with film he has so much more material to work from. One of the significant differences to other forms of image making—be it painting or sculpture—is that the film still is indicative, indexical even, of the drastic proliferation of images in the twentieth century, in fact the complete submersion of our surroundings and everyday life in the tidal wave of representation that has only increased and accelerated with every new technological invention. To present Baldessari's forensically dissected imagery alongside film stills in their complete state—as is the case here—only adds to our appreciation of both the artist's keen eye for eliciting evocatively associative meaning through subtraction and the production designer's capacity to encapsulate a moment that will then remain printed on our mind, quite possibly altering forever our association with a whole set of references contained therein. What Baldessari identifies in the film still has, after all, been put there by directors and production designers such as Shohan. As he is only too well aware, the potential of film to inform our vision of the world is almost limitless, hence the importance in reading the images it produces attentively, seeking out 'hidden meaning' not in the sense of a 1970s style subliminal message but rather looking at what is being presented and how it might potentially be read. By reducing the film still to its elemental parts Baldessari sets out to reclaim the image for public inquiry rather than unreflective consumption.

Many differences, after all, exist between the work of Baldessari and Shohan. Most immediately noticeable perhaps, is the fact that the films stills selected by Baldessari are not immediately identifiable—B films, unknown actors and general views whether interior or exterior—rather than what we might normally expect—famous faces, iconic scenes, and easily recognisable locations. Next to Shohan's images which, by contrast, are all from major recent productions where the actors as well as many of the scenes themselves are largely familiar, Baldessari's selection almost appears to capture the origin or nascence of each quintessentially filmic moment: the first gangster shoot out (as opposed to the recent special effects of *Matrix*'s mid-air battle), dramatic telephone call (no email or Instant Messaging) or romantically charged embrace. Some of Shohan's work, however, despite its relative youth has already entered the mind's mainstream whereby film scenes—whether in fact witnessed or not—have become embedded and confused with our 'vision' of a particular type of person/scenario/reaction. We now use filmic moments as short hand for personal communication, the celluloid (or is it digital?) encounter proving more evocative than the 'real' one—images from *American Beauty* one of Shohan's productions, have already achieved this kind of collective status. Like a form of visual Google our capacity to see is affected by these creations that are embedded in our subconscious such that how we see ourselves, our interaction with others as well as our capacity to 'read' situations is informed and infiltrated by this simulacra of life. Or is it indeed anymore a simple simulacra? At this point we are experiencing a mille feuille of layering—from life to representation to film back to experience and so forth—such that who can say exactly where the 'original' lies? Baldessari's work focuses acutely on this associative aspect of the film still and its capacity to 'summarise' our life. In his titles, the artist typically lists the component parts of an image that has undergone his process of pruning down to its essential elements such that we are left with the ur-visuals of objects, types and signifiers of our time each summarised tersely in his words as: *Bear and Hand*, *Boots, Noose and Belt* or *Jacket, Dress and Hand*. Our lives are boiled down to a few nouns and suggested, overlapping themes: man versus nature; violence; romance; humour; occupation and uniform. While the film industry did not create these aspects of our life it has thoroughly permeated our understanding of how they should look and feel and Baldessari's scrutiny of this mediatised representation establishes the visual alphabet.

Baldessari's work typically features animals—both wild and domestic—and the selection of images here is no exception. From the classic fear of untamed nature—a hand reaching out to an oversize spider, a shark encounter—to the more endearing or absurd—a girl holding a goose or a fairly repulsive looking condor passing food to its young—animal encounters feature large, almost suggesting an entire sub-genre of *National Geographic*-style film making. Unlike the familiar outlines of posed actors and the man made surroundings or interiors of film sets, Baldessari's animals have an unfamiliar form, their instinctive movement and behaviour captured in their starkly graphic, extracted image, which acts as a foil to the learned and controlled actions of the human world. The latter is frequently absurdly reduced to the accoutrements of position, for example the farcical tiered arc of *Hats and Briefcases* (the sum total of a businessman?) or the equally ridiculous signifiers of 'accepted' creativity in *Canvas, Hand, Bow Tie and Palette*. While danger as survival instinct exists unabashed in Baldessari"s images of animals, violence perpetrated by humans is summarised by the uniforms of military profession or represented by arms and armour—from helmets and swords to spears and boots. War it seems, like other jobs, is largely about looking the part.

The partial images presented by Baldessari establish a game of sorts as we attempt to complete the picture and typically Baldessari will identify a note of tension or humour that is brought about or exaggerated by the mystifying lack of context. While in Shohan's images we are presented with the full story so to speak and what is missing are the frames that preceded and followed that might complete the action. The film still's purpose is typically to attract our attention: either so that we go to see the production or to encapsulate a memorable scene. What Shohan has selected here includes both the classic film still (selected specifically and shot by a photographer on location) as well as her own photography taken on set. As a student of Baldessari she has a keen eye for her teacher's favourite subjects and it is almost impossible with many of the images selected by her here not to 'do a Baldessari' on them eliminating what one imagines he would take out and picturing the resulting hilarious confusion. An image taken on the set of *Constantine* that shows Rachel Weisz and Keanu Reeves sitting at a typical diner counter, for example, is a Baldessari waiting to happen (minus the figures you can easily picture the floating cups, fork and the tie). But one can equally see the potential for erasure of all but the most evocative aspects of a still such as that from *Constantine* where Weisz is seen lifting the sheet from a corpse's face.

Shohan has spoken of the very different process involved in getting the picture that she wants on film to the individual artist's approach. As she says she has been 'hired to serve' and the making of the image in a movie is a collaborative project directed towards a given goal rather than the singular vision of an artist. That said, there are still similarities to be found and Shohan's work, just like Baldessari's, is conscious of genre, the history of film, and presumably the development of her own oeuvre, she develops a composition and has to consider light, colour and other formal effects. Of course the major difference between the two is that while Baldessari is essentially removing context, reducing the elements of the found image to the most enigmatic point, Shohan's job is precisely to create context, adding rather than subtracting. An image in which we see Weisz and Reeves handling some mysterious looking objects in a workshop filled with suspended glass jars reveals quite how elaborate the image Shohan creates must at times become. Interestingly though, even with such complex and dense production one can still imagine the 'Baldessari effect' eliminating in one's mind, for example, all but objects and hands.

Revealingly, Shohan has also included an image from *Constantine* that shows the film industry's own use of Baldessari-esque subtraction. Dominating the background of an image of Weisz and reeves making their way through an facility area overrun with pipes and ducts that she has selected from *Constantine* was clearly once a 'blue screen' that isolates and flattens the figures as we see them 'morphed' into this context. This image hints at the reality of the filmic process that in fact requires the ability to think in parts rather than a whole, the final image only appearing at the end of a complex process of editing. In the case of contemporary film making then the creation of complex scenes is almost a reversal of Baldessari's own approach: piecing back together the separate parts to create a whole. Seeing these two processes side-by-side one wonders what other collaborations might in fact be possible. In fact we already know one outcome from Baldessari and Shohan's collaborative tableaux vivant *Ear Sofa; Nose Sconces with Flowers (In Stage Setting)* (2009) which was installed in the window of the ex-shop front gallery of Sprüth Magers in London. The installation centers on an ear-shaped sofa, on which a model sits, posed and poised, flanked on either side by a pair of nose-shaped, wall-mounted sconces. A large decorative semi-circular arch frames the ear-shaped sofa and a sheet of sheer stretched silk shrouds the gallery's glass frontage. Redolent of an Art Deco aesthetic, the scene mimicked both a 1920s Hollywood glamour as well as, perplexingly, a Magritte-like surrealist fantasy. The artificiality of Hollywood was decoded so to speak by the contemporaneous constructions of the psychologically penetrating work of Magritte. So we can say there is much to be gained from this meeting of film and art, Baldessari and Shohan's combined perceptual perspicacity is just what we need to both re-evaluate our past as well as prepare us for the future.

# Editing Edited

David Campany

I've got nothing to express! I simply search for images and I invent, I invent... only the image counts, the inexplicable and mysterious image, because all is mystery in our life.
René Magritte, artist, 1951

The picture editor is the voyeurs' voyeur, the person who sees what the photographers themselves have seen but in the bloodless realm of the contact sheet... and now pixels on the screen. Picture editors find the representative picture, the image that will be seen by others perhaps around the world. They are unwitting (or witting, as the case may be) tastemakers, the unappointed guardians of morality, the talent brokers, the accomplices to celebrity. Most important – or disturbing – they are the fixers of 'reality' and of 'history.'
John G. Morris, editor, 2002

I don't like editing so I always try to fob it off on to someone else, whether it's a picture editor or someone in my office. You'll be surprised what other people can bring to your pictures.
Rankin, photographer, 2007

The essence is done very quickly with a flash of the mind, and with a machine. I think too that photography is editing, editing after the taking. After knowing what to take you have to do the editing.
Walker Evans, photographer, 1971

A successful photo is only a preliminary step toward the intelligent use of photography... Photography is like a mosaic that becomes a synthesis only when it is presented en masse.
August Sander, writer, 1951

August Sander's is more than a book of "type studies"; a case of the camera looking in the right direction among people [...] It is a photographic editing of society, a clinical process.
Walker Evans, photographer, 1931

Sander's work is more than a picture book. It is a training manual.
Walter Benjamin, writer, 1931

The series is no longer a "picture", and none of the canons of pictorial aesthetics can be applied to it. Here the picture loses its identity as such and becomes a detail of assembly, as essential structural element of the whole which is the thing itself. In this concatenation of its separate but inseparable parts a photographic series inspired by a definite purpose can become at once the most potent weapon and the tenderest lyric.
László Moholy-Nagy, artist, 1932

The mingling of real life and imaginary life, of present and past, of probability and improbability, could only be expressed hitherto in surrealist poetry and by the technique of cinema. To-day it is one of the most powerful devices of the art of layout.
Alfred Tolmer, designer, 1932

The photographic essay was born of the promise of another kind of truth from that given by the individual photograph or image on its own, a truth available only in the interstices between pictures, in the movement from one picture to the next.
Blake Stimson, writer, 2006

... the quick nervousness of pictures is a new language.
Daniel Longwell, editor, 1936

I am kino-eye. I am a builder. I have placed you, whom I have created today, in an extraordinary room, which did not exist until just now when I also created it. In this room there are twelve walls shot by me in various parts of the world. In bringing together shots of walls and details, I have managed to arrange them in an order that is pleasing and to construct with intervals, correctly, a film-phrase which is the room.
Dziga Vertov, filmmaker, 1923

Take photo after photo! Record man not with a solitary synthesized portrait but with a mass of snapshots taken at different times and in different conditions.
Alexander Rodchenko, artist, 1928

Rodchenko's entire floor was covered with piles of illustrated German and French periodicals: .[...]. With scissors in hand he was jumping about the room like a circus gymnast, cutting out various figures, pages and headings, then placing them in piles according to themes such as animals, fashion, technology.
Zakhar Bykov, photographer, 1995

Lying on the floor trying to find likenesses from the hundreds of photos spread out in front of me...whenever I see an interesting photo of a personality, an animal, or whatever it

may be, I put it in a box. Once a month when the printer is becoming urgent about material for the next issue I go into seclusion. I shut myself in a room and go over the pictures in the box. The pictures I like best I throw on the floor, then I go through the other boxes. I have got four of them. One is full of personalities, another of animals. The third is filled with women and children, and the fourth with landscapes and funny photographs. One by one I go through them - if I find a photo that would match one of the pictures on the floor, I put the pair aside [...] I think there is always somewhere a photo which fits... believe me, the whole business is much easier than one thinks. ... One only needs an eye to see the possibilities in a photograph, and one must have a good optical memory.
Stefan Lorant, editor, 1940

The dream of a universal archive is the belief that a photographic translation of the unruly contingency of the world can result in a rational-organised-industrialised system (equivalent to money currency), which may function as a perfect means of exchange and commodification within capitalist social relations. Thus it facilitates processes of rationalisation, industrialisation and exploitation; as well as fostering the legitimation of the modern romantic-colonial nation-state system.
Jorge Ribalta, curator, 2009

... diffusion is furthered by an ever subtler and more comprehensive outlook, whose effect is often to substitute for the masterpiece the significant work, and for the mere pleasure of the eye the surer one of knowledge.
André Malraux, writer, 1949

... we should ask ourselves who would be truly richer- the one who possessed photographs of every surviving building of the classical age, or Sir John Soane, who had measured every stone of the orders of the Colosseum and could quote its intercolumination even in his old age.
Reyner Banham, writer, 1953

In Godard's (1963), two sluggish lumpen-peasants are lured into joining the King's Army by the promise that they will be able to loot, rape, kill, or do whatever else they please to the enemy, and get rich. But the suitcase of booty that Michel-Ange and Ulysse triumphantly bring home, years later, to their wives turns out to contain only picture postcards, hundreds of them, of Monuments, Department Stores, Mammals, Wonders of Nature, Methods of Transport, Works of Art, and other classified treasures from around the globe. Godard's gag vividly parodies the equivocal magic of the photographic image. Photographs are perhaps the most mysterious of all the objects that make up, and thicken, the environment we recognize as modern. Photographs really are experience captured, and the camera is the ideal arm of consciousness in its acquisitive mood.
Susan Sontag, writer, 1977

Every edit is a lie.
Jean-Luc Godard, filmmaker, 1971

Thirty are Better than One.
Andy Warhol, artist, 1963

Repetition is the simplest path to looking like you know what you're doing.
David Campany, writer, 2008

To look at a photograph beyond a certain period of time is to become frustrated: the image which on first looking gave pleasure by degrees becomes a veil behind which we now desire to see. To remain too long with a single photograph is to lose the imaginary command of the look, to relinquish it to that absent other to whom it belongs by right: the camera. The image now no longer receives our look, reassuring us of our founding centrality, it rather, as it were, avoids our gaze. In photography one image does not succeed another in the manner of cinema. As alienation intrudes into our captation by the still image, we can only regain the imaginary, and reinvest our looking with authority, by averting our gaze, redirecting it to another image elsewhere. It is therefore not an arbitrary fact that photographs are deployed so that, almost invariably, another photograph is always already in position to receive the displaced look.
Victor Burgin, artist, 1980

... presenting groups or series of pictures.[..]. is a very well established way of imagining photography, a practice of photography — so established it is almost unnoticed. I notice it because I really cannot do it that way. I want each picture to stand on its own, with no sequential or thematic relationship to any other. At least, not any specific or organized thematic relationship.
Jeff Wall, artist, 2008

What is the one picture I can take that will say 'Vermont'?
Jack Delano, photographer, 1936

A good photo can be used big or small. A bad photo can only be used big.
Willy Fleckhaus, designer, 1970

Design is absolutely no substitute for content.
Harold Evans, editor, 2008

Perhaps true, total photography, he thought, is a pile of fragments of private images, against the creased background of massacres and coronations.
Italo Calvino, writer, 1958

... in a world in which we are entertained from cradle to grave whether we like it or not, the ability to rework image and dialogue ... may be the key to both psychic and political health.
Colin McCabe, writer, 2004

Artists are better at finding a way to kill their time.
John Baldessari, artist, 1980

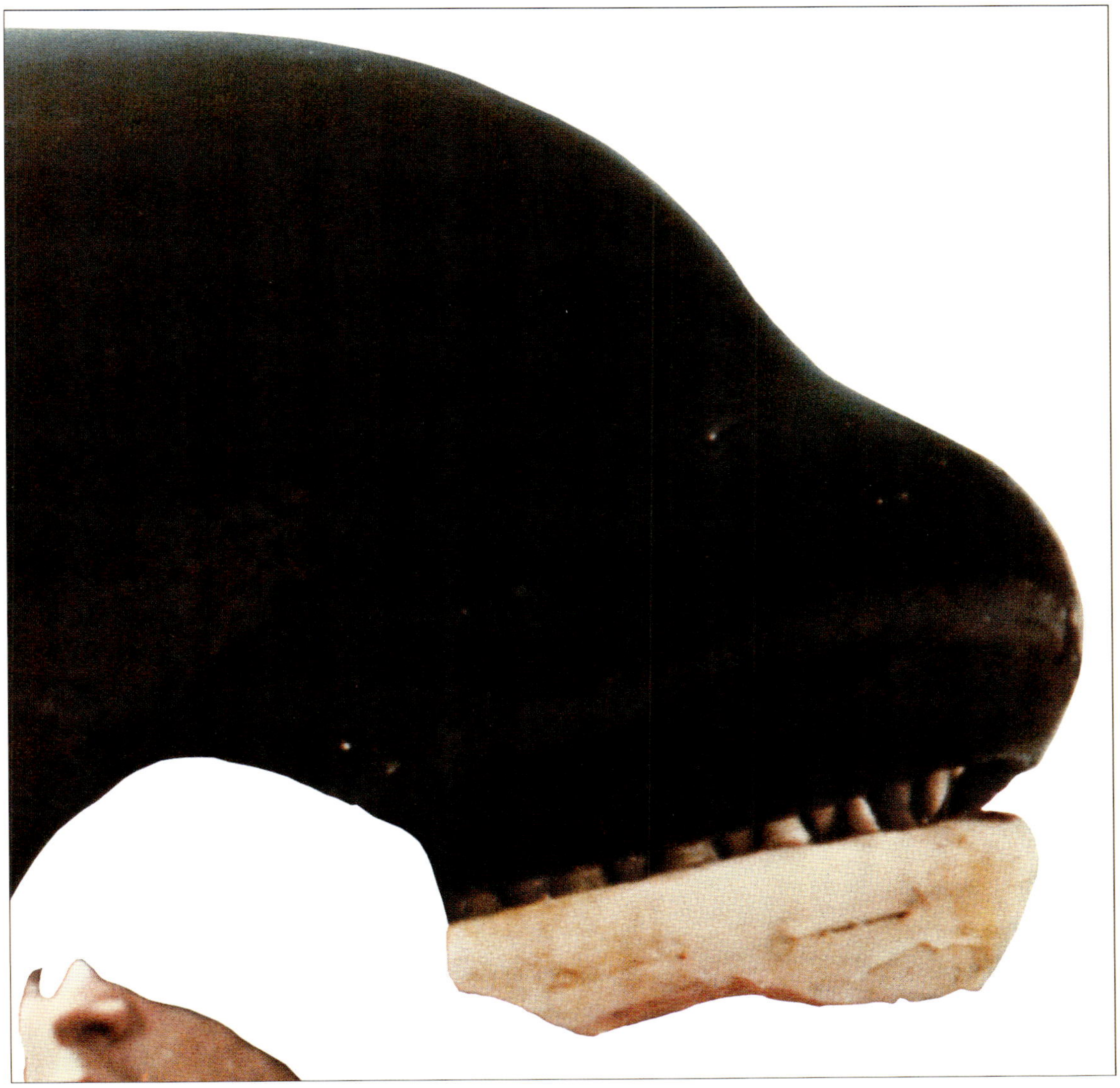

**Artist's Special Edition for PA**
**John Baldessari**
**FACE AND WHALE, 2011**

5 colour lithograph on matte paper, 45 × 45 cm
edition of 24 + 6 AP
numbered and signed by the artist
Price: 2000 Euro

The Artists' Special Editions are original works created exclusively for PA Magazine.

Each edition is numbered and signed by the artist.
If you wish to order the edition, please complete the form below and send to Inktree Editions.
We will then send you an invoice for the edition (including postage and packing).
Upon receipt of payment you will then receive the Artists' Special Edition.
(Please note that supply is subject to availability).

I would like to order John Baldessari, Face and Whale

Surname: ______________________________

Name: ______________________________

Address: ______________________________

Zip / City: ______________________________

Country: ______________________________

Email: ______________________________

Phone: ______________________________

Send this form to: INK•TREE, Quellenstrasse 27, CH-8005 Zürich
T +41 43 960 31 55, F +41 44 272 43 01, E info@inktree.ch, www.inktree.ch

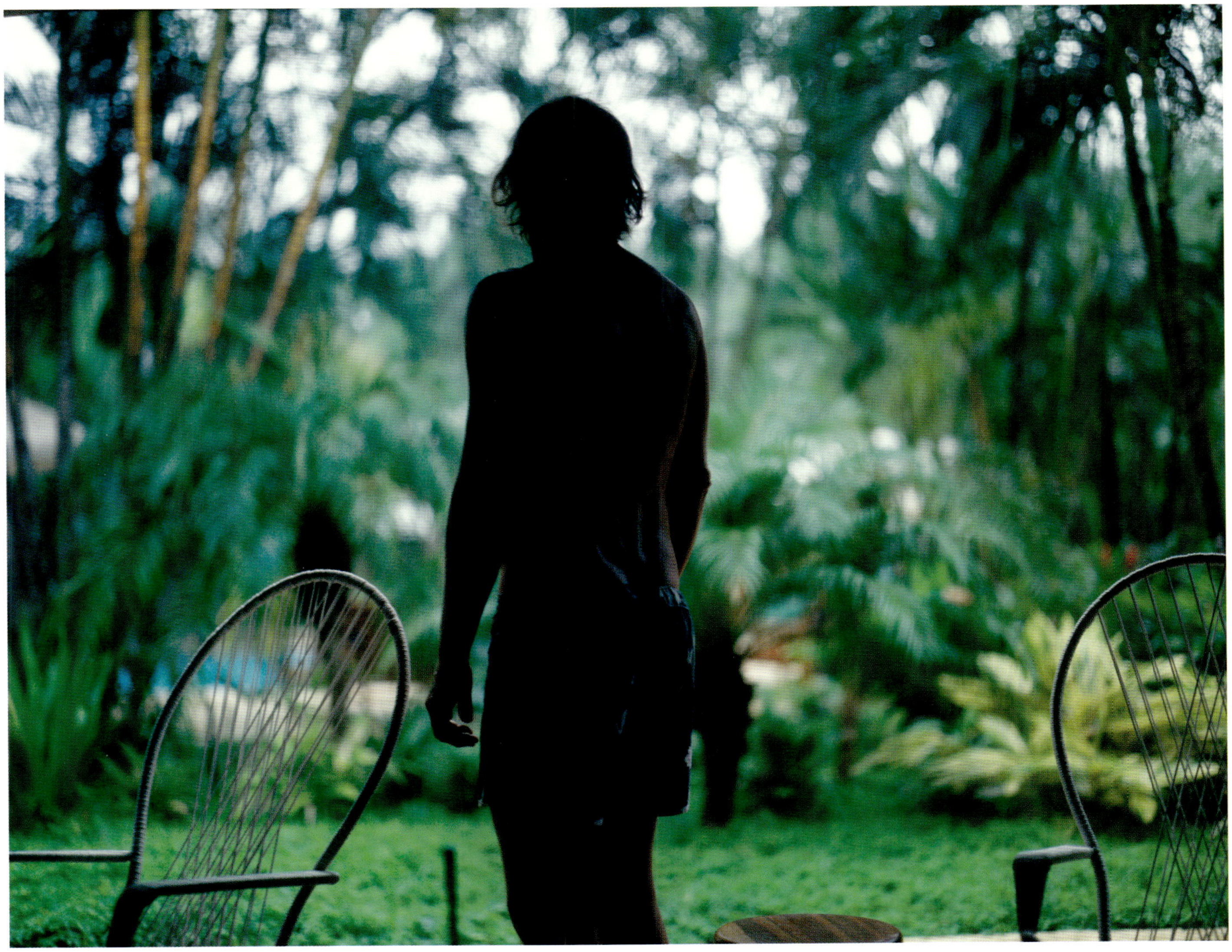

**Artist's Special Edition for PA**
**Doug Aitken**
**ISLAND (II), 2009**

C-Print, 45.7 x 58.4 cm
edition of 12 + 4 AP
numbered and signed by the artist
Price: 6350 Euro

The Artists' Special Editions are original works created exclusively for PA Magazine.

Each edition is numbered and signed by the artist.
If you wish to order the edition, please complete the form below and send to Inktree Editions.
We will then send you an invoice for the edition (including postage and packing).
Upon receipt of payment you will then receive the Artists' Special Edition.
(Please note that supply is subject to availability).

I would like to order Doug Aitken, Island (II), 2009

Surname: ______________________

Name: ______________________

Address: ______________________

Zip / City: ______________________

Country: ______________________

Email: ______________________

Phone: ______________________

Send this form to: INK•TREE, Quellenstrasse 27, CH-8005 Zürich
T +41 43 960 31 55, F +41 44 272 43 01, E info@inktree.ch, www.inktree.ch

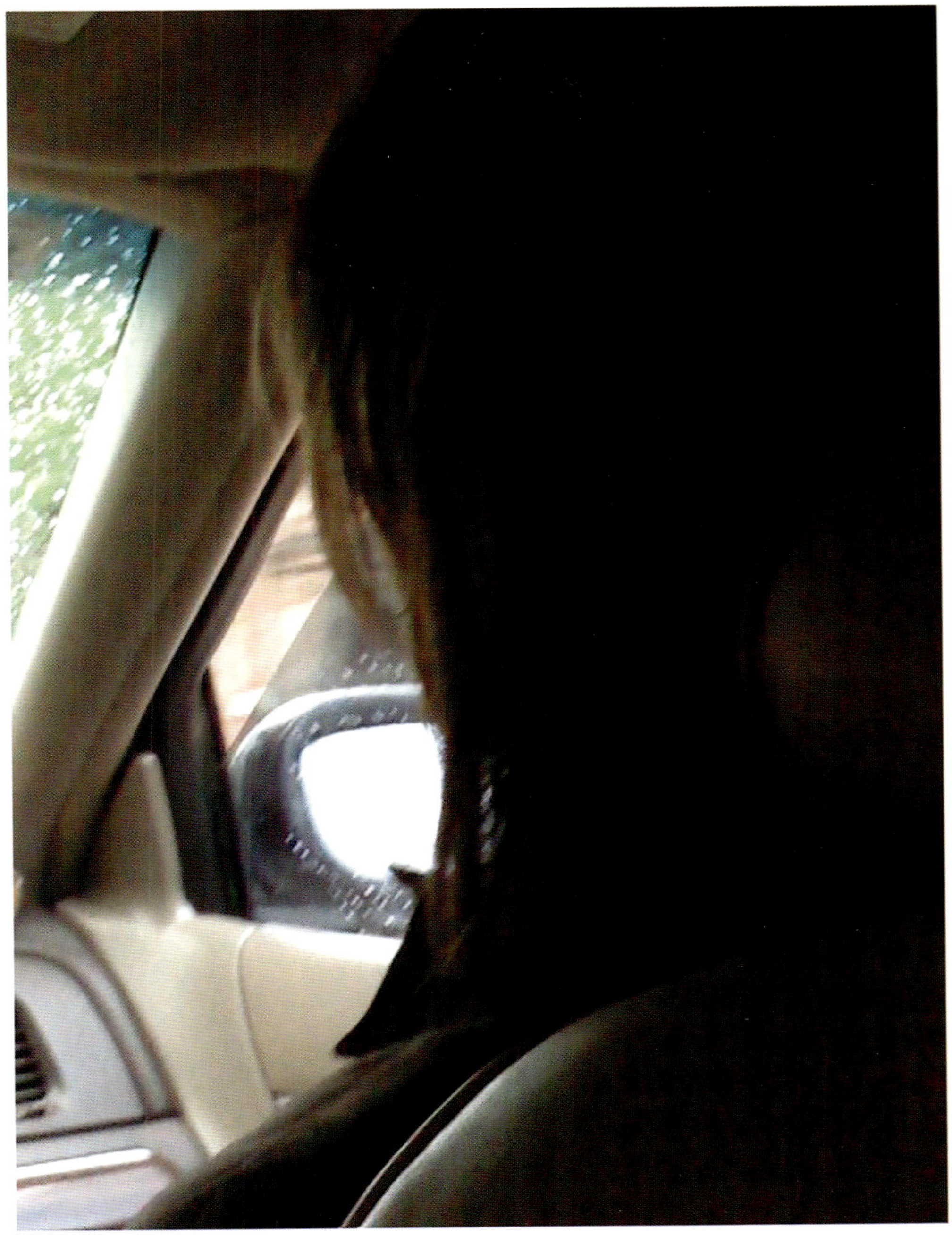

**Artist's Special Edition for PA**
**Jeff Wall**
**PASSENGER, 2006**

Inkjet-Print on paper, 20 x 27 cm (image),
33 x 48 cm (page)
edition of 50 + 12 AP
numbered and signed by the artist
Price: 3550 Euro

The Artists' Special Editions are original works created exclusively for PA Magazine.

Each edition is numbered and signed by the artist.
If you wish to order the edition, please complete the form below and send to Inktree Editions.
We will then send you an invoice for the edition (including postage and packing).
Upon receipt of payment you will then receive the Artists' Special Edition.
(Please note that supply is subject to availability).

I would like to order Jeff Wall, Passenger.

Surname: ______________________

Name: ______________________

Address: ______________________

Zip / City: ______________________

Country: ______________________

Email: ______________________

Phone: ______________________

Send this form to: INK•TREE, Quellenstrasse 27, CH-8005 Zürich
T +41 43 960 31 55, F +41 44 272 43 01, E info@inktree.ch, www.inktree.ch

PA MAGAZINE

**Publisher**
Cristina Bechtler in collaboration with Christie's



**Editors**
Cristina Bechtler
David Campany

**Graphic Design** (Cover and Layout)
Landolt / Pfister, Zürich

**Production and Printing**
Christie's, London

**Information**
Inktree
Quellenstrasse 27
8005 Zürich
Switzerland
Phone +41 43 960 31 55
Fax +41 44 272 43 01
Email info@inktree.ch
www.inktree.ch


Printed in England
ISSN 1662-7660